Author Biogra

Andy Brassell was born and raised in London. He went to his first football match in 1987 at the age of 10, when his dad took him to see Wimbledon play Everton at Plough Lane. A freelance writer and DJ, he has contributed to *Champions and tribalfootball.com* amongst other magazines and websites. He lives in Battersea with his girlfriend and his St Etienne toy panther, Pierre.

All Or Nothing

A year in the life of the Champions League

Andy Brassell

Note for Librarians: A cataloguing record for this book is available from Library and Archives Canada at www.collectionscanada.ca/amicus/index-e.html
ISBN 1-4120-8073-8

Printed in Victoria, BC, Canada. Printed on paper with minimum 30% recycled fibre. Trafford's print shop runs on "green energy" from solar, wind and other environmentally-friendly power sources.

Offices in Canada, USA, Ireland and UK
This book was published *on-demand* in cooperation with Trafford Publishing. On-demand publishing is a unique process and service of making a book available for retail sale to the public taking advantage of on-demand manufacturing and Internet marketing. On-demand publishing includes promotions, retail sales, manufacturing, order fulfilment, accounting and collecting royalties on behalf of the author.

Book sales for North America and international:
Trafford Publishing, 6E–2333 Government St.,
Victoria, BC V8T 4P4 CANADA
phone 250 383 6864 (toll-free 1 888 232 4444)
fax 250 383 6804; email to orders@trafford.com
Book sales in Europe:
Trafford Publishing (UK) Limited, 9 Park End Street, 2nd Floor
Oxford, UK OX1 1HH UNITED KINGDOM
phone 44 (0)1865 722 113 (local rate 0845 230 9601)
facsimile 44 (0)1865 722 868; info.uk@trafford.com
Order online at:
trafford.com/05-3071

10 9 8 7 6 5 4 3

Thanks

Big thanks to everyone who helped me out while writing this book to make it so vivid with their time, knowledge and kindness – Guillem Balague, Frédéric Breffeilh, Nicolas Bulostin, Emilio Butragueño, Rafa Carpacho, Matt Coates, John Collins, Jim Craig, Tim Danaher, Carina Dell, Uli Hesse-Lictenberger, Paul Lambert, Sid Lowe, Leanne Morgan, Tony Moylan, Maider Ortiz de Elguea, Tyrone Schorrer and all at Fotonet, Enrica Tarchi, Alexander Udaltsov, Acácio Valentim, Sander Westerveld, Paolo and Monica from Rio (wherever you are), and particularly Phil Ball and Xavier Rivoire. Also to everyone who gave their thoughts, criticism and tips - Tim Rogers for a great closing line and especially Matt Brown for being the best lecturer I never had. Love to all my friends for patiently asking how it was going every Saturday night for nearly two years (even when I didn't want you to) and for keeping me sane, especially Hannah, Dave and Sarah, Julian, Steve, Jamie, Bernie, Mark, Jake and Jo, Pete 'Funk' O'Brien, Dan and Olivia, Ian and Jannine, Andrew Fleming, Chris, Pete and Joelene, to Karen and her aggressive marketing plan, to Nikko, Stef and family for putting me up and making me love France, and to anyone else I may have forgotten. And big, big love to Michelle for everything x

For Caroline and Gerry

Contents

Author's note

The terms European Cup/ Champions League/ Champions Cup have been used fairly interchangeably. Generally, the term European Cup refers to the trophy up to the end of the 1991/1992 season, the term Champions League refers to the trophy after that point, and the term Champions Cup is a catch-all term to cover the two – after all, this is still the inscription that the trophy itself bears.

Introduction

What does the Champions League mean? I asked myself this when I started to write this book, but I'd started to think about it before - at the point when I noticed that I'd stopped calling it 'The European Cup'. In mid-1992, I had barely noticed the metamorphosis of the world's greatest club championship into the UEFA Champions League. I'm sure I wasn't the only English football fan whose attention it escaped. The English are notoriously parochial at the best of times but the five-year ban preventing English clubs taking part in European competition post-Heysel meant that European club football had more or less ceased to be relevant over here. This also meant that when the ban ended (also in 1992), the days of their leaving the rest of Europe trailing in their wake in the late '70s/early '80s period, via the exploits of Liverpool, Aston Villa and Nottingham Forest were long gone, and English teams were now the village idiots of Europe. In the first year English clubs returned to the European scene the champions Leeds United suffered an inglorious second round exit from the Champions League at the hands of - of all teams - Glasgow Rangers of the often-mocked Scottish Premier League.

The wider significance of the change in the European Cup passed me by, unlike the local and therefore more 'real' replacement of the First Division by the Premier League at the same time. What was happening across Europe represented the beginnings of a streamlining of the game's elite. In the late '80s there had been frequent suggestions in the media, pre-Premier League, of a breakaway European Super League, where the top few clubs of each country would leave their national championships to form the new continental elite. Clearly this horrified most fans (at least those of clubs outside the 'Big Five' of the time), who imagined the top flight of their league being degraded into a tin pot regional scuffle of minimal worth. I can remember scoffing at the idea, partly out of incredulity but partly out of fear too.

The Champions League was, in retrospect, a reasonably stealthy move in that direction. Initially it appeared a mere change of format, a freshening, simply substituting a straight knock-out cup with a round robin - something which would be not much different to the changes that had taken place in the format of the World Cup over the years. But after a few years passed, the league started to expand. First the clubs from the strongest leagues (Italy and Spain) started to receive extra places. Then the English and Germans. The definition of the competition was being stretched - basically, the 'Champions' bit of its title – which, some said, robbed the competition of its meaning as the cost of satisfying Europe's biggest clubs' lust for increased wealth and control.

It had before, they said, always been about the best of the best. This was the initial aim when the European Cup was introduced in 1956, the brainchild of L'Equipe writer Gabriel Hanot and endorsed by a few of European football's top movers and shakers including the legendary Real Madrid president Santiago Bernabéu (although not initially by UEFA). The final push that led to Hanot's idea becoming flesh actually came from England. In December 1954, when the then-mighty Wolverhampton Wanderers hosted and beat the Hungarians of Honved in a friendly, Hanot was the man who pointed out on behalf of the rest of Europe how premature British claims that Wolves were the continent's greatest were. His cup became the competition in which the Bernabéu club established themselves as the world's premier club side, winning each one of the first five tournaments. It made legends of the Ajax team of Cruyff, Keizer and Neeskens, who sealed their immortality by winning three in a row in the '70s. It bore witness to the great AC Milan side of 1989, with the Dutch trio of Gullit, Van Basten and Rijkaard at its heart. In other words, no way was this a competition for teams who scraped third place in their domestic league.

What it had become wasn't the in the spirit of the competition, or indeed the game as I understood it, for sure. The quality of the football involved didn't especially seem to suffer initially, but by involving more clubs to a greater extent, the breathing space in the football calendar was being squeezed out. Every time Sven-Goran Eriksson asks for a winter break in the season, more time together for the England squad or less club games, we are reminded that quality versus quantity is still a relevant concern. And you had to ask that if the maintenance of higher standards on the field wasn't the point, what was?

On top of this, the tendency of the broadcast media and accordingly some less informed members of the public to whitewash history, installing 1992 as a footballing Year Zero, with the 'birth' of the Champions League (and the Premier League), is an insult to football's rich history. It's especially grating to hear, as we do, about the setting of 'a Premier League record', as if everything that has gone before is worthless. Hell, I've used the phrase 'Champions League record' in this book once or twice myself. Who says people aren't a product of their environment? Truth is, 12 years on, I'm over the fact that The People's Game has become television's bitch - it's not an ideal situation, but it is reality and this progress has obviously improved the standards of what we watch every Saturday (or Sunday, Monday, Tuesday, Wednesday or even Thursday night) tenfold. What is sometimes harder to stomach for people who spend their hard-earned cash following their team to every corner of the country (and even Europe) is that saturation coverage and its thoroughly unendearing over-analytical bent have made every pub bore an authority on a game being dragged further away from the faithful.

I always found the only way of dealing with what the Premier League meant in terms of the direction of the game's ideals was ignoring the hype and concentrating on the real - the football and the fans. The same was true of the Champions League. Considering this issue only truly became a live issue for our part of the world in 1999, when Manchester United became the first British club to lift the Champions

League in its present incarnation. Before this I don't think anyone here really believed that an English team could win it. The Italian teams especially seemed to be footballing deities from another planet who would reign supreme in the Champions League until the end of time. In that year, when I cheered along with a pub full of Newcastle fans as we watched United beat Bayern in Barcelona, the façade of Italian invincibility had already died in that incredible semi-final second leg where United came back from two down to defeat the mighty Juventus on their own patch. The Champions League had started to become part of our football world.

Beyond the competition's cosmetic sheen, it just takes an occasion for the fans to reclaim the game. The first Champions League game I ever went to was in March 2002, when I saw Newcastle play Inter Milan at the San Siro. I wouldn't hesitate to put this in the best five games that I'd ever seen. The football was great (a 2-2 draw) but what I remember better is the 10,000 Geordies erupting when Shearer scored his first. I remember Christian Vieri tearing his shirt off, running shouting towards the *Negrazzuri* after heading in an equaliser. And I remember the sour-faced Italian youth muttering 'your Queen is a whore' from behind us after he heard our English voices. This is what the Champions League is undeniably good at – creating the sense of theatre on which the game's supporters thrive.

The idea of writing this book started to take shape after a trip to Marseille in August 2003 to write something on their Champions League qualifier. It may seem funny that it was in France, a country not widely renowned for its football passion prior to their 1998 World Cup victory, that I started to feel a genuine affection for the Champions League. But this was the whole point. It was becoming clear to me that whatever the Champions League was intended to be, it was more than just Manchester United, AC Milan and Real Madrid, for all that they – and the latter in particular - have done to make the competition the pinnacle that it is.

Whether being demonised as 'killing football' or hyped on the back of the game's biggest names, it's too often overlooked that the competition is a truly European event, a universal currency to stir excitement and awe from Trondheim to Rome, Athens to Moscow and everywhere in between. Since that first final at the Parc des Princes back in 1956, the trophy has been lifted by clubs representing ten different countries. If ever there was a moment that screamed the blindingly obvious to me - that the occasions thrown up by the competition could mean so much more than the sum of its well-oiled commercial parts – then that night in Provence was it. I knew I'd be visiting other grounds in Europe to write, and to practise my French and Spanish. This was a chance to communicate with the fans and players, the people and the environments that make the competition what it is. The Champions League is a complex beast and to get to the heart of what it's about I needed not just to watch some games and check the history but to really *live* it. That's what I did.

The Champions League has changed considerably even during this book's gestation period, with Liverpool's unbelievable win over mighty Milan showing the competition in its most flattering light again. When people have asked me about the book over the last few months, a question about what I had put in about that night in Istanbul has never been far behind. But to be honest, I'm glad that Liverpool's triumph wasn't the season I'd decided to cover. Yes, it was one of the great finals, but based in England, I would have had no chance of judging it with any objectivity, even as someone who doesn't support Liverpool, such was the maelstrom of coverage before, during and after the game. In the term I covered, I was able to keep preconceptions to a minimum, to go places, see things and let the mood – and the football – take me. I was able to fully absorb the Champions League's European flavour.

Has it all given me an answer to my original question? I couldn't say. It would be arrogant and just plain wrong to present a definitive answer. This isn't meant to be a history of the competition or a statistic handbook - others can do that far better than me and that was never the aim. It's just a snapshot of what's happening at the peak of

European football right about now. This is part sports reportage, part travelogue and part voyage of self-discovery, drawn together by chance, judgement and a fair bit of busking. I hope it brings you closer to what the Champions League tastes like.

Andy Brassell
summer 2005

Marseille

3.45am, Thursday 28th August. Gare St Charles, central Marseille. Pavements are partially covered with bodies in white and blue shirts and scarves. People sleep. People doze. People murmur to each other in various states of semi-consciousness. People idly check their phones for messages they know aren't there with the glazed look of the desperately bored. People chase each other round the car park throwing Coke bottles and shouting obscenities. People here are doing just about anything to pass the time until the station opens at half five for the first trains back to the provinces. But it's been worth it.

There could be no better place to start my journey than here. As far as a lot of people are concerned, Olympique de Marseille *are* French club football, due to the fact they've been without doubt the most successful French team in the European Champions Cup/Champions League. Because of this, there's something just indefinably special that people in Marseille feel about the European Cup.

When my flight touches down early on a scorching hot Provence afternoon, there's not really anything to suggest this feeling to you. I can't spot any OM fans on the aeroplane, or on the bus into town. Arriving at Gare St Charles, the central station, there's no mad buzz about the place. It's just like so many other central European train stations, with only hot, bored punters sitting around, seemingly not waiting for anything but to get more hot and bored.

You'd never know that you're about half a kilometre from La Canebière, the main artery running through the heart of downtown

Marseille. So it's a relief to leave the world of constant transit and stumble upon what any guidebook worth its salt will no doubt imaginatively refer to as the most 'real' of French cities. I remember how Dylan Thomas once referred to Swansea as a 'lovely, ugly town'. Though the two places are ostensibly worlds apart, it's a description made for Marseille. The place is completely filthy – think London with incontinent dogs during a road sweepers' strike – and consequently it smells pretty bad in places. Similarly, the word 'bustle' was clearly coined with here in mind. Yet from the chaos emerges a madly endearing, unique city.

Key to this is the Vieux Port. Although no longer the centre for commercial activity it was in previous centuries, it's still the second busiest port in Europe (behind Rotterdam), now containing mainly yachts and some fishing boats which bring in the seafood for which the city is famous, dished up at its freshest on the restaurants on the Port's north side. The Vieux Port is what's made the city a hub of immigration over hundreds of years and it's this mix of different nationalities and origins which gives the city its character. When you stroll round the markets at Noailles, fresh fish competes with halal meat and oriental vegetables for your attention.

But first things first. Though I've said to myself and others that sampling the city's atmosphere for a Champions League qualifier will be enough, and I'll watch the game on TV if I have to, I've really no intention of coming all this way to watch it in a bar. As soon as I hit La Canebière, I'm looking for a ticket. The club's official website stopped selling tickets a couple of weeks ago and I know that there's never really such a thing as an under-subscribed home game here. I get to the Vieux Port and spot the OM café. A sign marked 'billeterie' sits above the left-hand entrance. Bingo.

The helpful bloke behind the counter has none himself – as I suspected – but he calls over a man in his mid-30s wearing a very central European rocker's bandana and points him in my direction. This is handy - a guy who's bought tickets for some pals and one of them has to work late and can't come. I've lucked out and he's not going to be lumbered with his spare. It's mutually advantageous. Is it fuck. The guy pulls out a wedge of 10 or so tickets and sells me a 35 euro ticket for 60. I'm quietly proud of myself for conducting a black market transaction in perfect French, but can't help thinking my damn English accent's added a good 10 euros to the price (even if I did knock him down from 70). Still, like I said, I really haven't come all this way to watch it in the pub.

Having done the difficult bit I can now relax and check out the city. At least that's what I thought at the bottom of the hill on the way up to the Basilique Notre Dame de la Garde. Having laughed to myself at the wimpish idea of catching the bus up there, I'm now trying to power walk up a 45 degree slope in 34 degree mid afternoon heat, drowning in sweat and rapidly running out of sparkling Italian drinking water. Every time I think I've reached the bottom of the entrance to the Basilique, I've just reached the bottom of another set of steps which leads to the next bloody slope up. That said, it is worth it when you get there. An ornate mid-19th century basilica with a golden dome attracts not only tourists (an extraordinary number of whom are French and sport OM shirts, giving you an idea of how many of the club's fans come from outside the city) but a number of worshippers to its chapel. A queue of middle-aged Hispanic women waits to run their hands over the face of a statue of the stricken Christ and pray for his blessing. Despite being a bona fide tourist trap the atmosphere is respectful, reverent even. My main reason for coming up here though was the view – at over 160m it's the highest point in the city and provides a good chance for anyone unfamiliar with Marseille to get their bearings. It's an incredible sight to catch my breath to, and seeing the random urban sprawl set against the coastline with its sparkling sea gives as succinct an expression of this old city's history as any could muster.

Back down in the centre groups of people are already gathering for the match later, though it won't start for another three hours yet. Packs of young men loiter outside the OM shop on La Canebière wearing home shirts, while more mixed groups – including a surprising amount of women – meet in and outside the bars lining both sides of the Vieux Port. All the bars on the south side - bars populating the south side and restaurants the north, as a rule of thumb - will be packed with fans watching the game later. They advertise the showing of tonight's game and every other for the next few weeks on blackboards outside. I stop at one of the bars on the north side, a small, funky, laid-back looking place, to get a Coke and even that comes in a glass emblazoned with the club badge and motto, 'Droit au but'. This really is a proper football town. The nearest comparison that springs to mind in England is Newcastle, a place where football is the city's defining characteristic, something that's there everywhere you go. Every second bloke you pass on the street between 4 and 45 is wearing an OM shirt, and you would be hard pushed to catch anyone wearing any other team's colours. But that's where the similarity with their English counterparts ends. It's not just white guys wearing them, it's black kids, groups of young North African men, women, all sorts. Incidentally, while touts on the Vieux Port will continue to knock out tickets for tonight's game at ever more extortionate prices as the afternoon progresses, St James' Park will be less than two-thirds full for Newcastle's own Champions League qualifier against Partizan Belgrade tonight.

Yet OM aren't only representing one football mad city. They're still unquestionably the biggest and most keenly followed club in France, despite Lyon's back to back title wins. Today's *L'Equipe* documents that the club had applications for tickets for tonight's home leg from an astonishing 88 different *départements*, a figure that is nevertheless quite normal for any regular league game at the Vélodrome. The former Everton striker Ibrahima Bakayoko, who led the attack when OM were last in the Champions' League four years ago, recently said, 'You play also for France' when playing for OM in Europe. Of course a lot of this goes back to the glorious exploits of the early '90s OM team of Papin, Boli, Pélé etc that wowed audiences home and abroad, culminating in the Champions League win of 1993. The merest sniff of Champions League action brings all those heady memories flooding back. *France*

Football rarely needs an excuse to put OM on the cover and true to form the edition of August 12 - just before the first leg of the Vienna tie - included a lengthy retrospective of OM in the European Cup and Champions League.

The memories of 1993 are however not, or should not be, untarnished. French journalist Xavier Rivoire, now based in England, refers to it as 'this so-called victory'. Marseille actually lifted two trophies in that season. Three days after the historic win over the mighty AC Milan in that Munich final, they beat the visiting Paris Saint-Germain 3-1 at the Vélodrome to clinch what would have been a French record fifth league title in a row. If, however, you look at the list of past French champions in record books nowadays, you will find the words 'none' or 'not awarded' next to 1993. That's because OM were stripped of the 1993 title in the aftermath of the scandal that was the biggest ever to hit the French game. Less than a week before their date with destiny in Munich, OM had played a league match at Valenciennes, which they won 1-0. But after the game one of the Valenciennes players, Jacques Glassman, claimed that he and two of his team-mates (one being the Argentine World Cup winner Jorge Burrachaga) had been offered FF 200,000 (around £20,000) 'if I didn't try too hard.'

Rarely have so few words shook a sport as much as Glassman's did that night. By the time the repercussions of the affair had reached a conclusion, Marseille managing director Jean-Pierre Bernès, player Jean-Jacques Eydelie (who had acted as the go-between for his board and their targets) and the Valenciennes pair Burrachaga and Christophe Robert (plus Robert's wife) received an assortment of suspended custodial sentences and fines. It was, however, OM's charismatic president Bernard Tapie who ended up carrying the can, being sentenced to two years' imprisonment, with one year suspended, and being banned from holding public office for three years. The fans suffered too, as the team were relegated (effectively for two years as they were refused the promotion the team earned in 1995) and banned from defending their Champions League title in 1994. The European ban cost the club between FF 350 and 450 million, according to journalist and all-round OM authority Avi Assouly.

OM's fans and the club itself have understandably tried to draw a line under the whole affair, and still tend to eulogise the 1993 European triumph – after all, it's still on the club's honours list, unlike the domestic title won in the same year, which they were stripped of. Xavier Rivoire appreciates this, but isn't convinced by the romanticism of it. 'There is nostalgia,' he concedes, 'but I have many reservations about the whole campaign. Not only this one against Milan.' The lack of a UEFA investigation into the Champions League win can't dull the thought that if there was shady moves behind the league win, there may have been similar skulduggery afoot in the European campaign. 'The methods used to win the league could have been the same in Europe,' he says. 'Before reaching the final, Marseille had to play Eastern European teams for instance. At the time offering a new tracksuit to a Russian player, or a Walkman to an official from Hungary (could be) enough to win the game. Tapie said in '91 when the team was beaten by Red Star Belgrade in the (European Cup) final he understood now how games should be won. He didn't say should be *played*, he said should be *won*.'

It's deeply sad in a way that the boardroom machinations are forever destined to taint the biggest success in French club football history. 'I'm not saying the Marseille players were not great,' stresses Xavier, 'and I'm not saying the team assembled by Tapie wasn't brilliant, because I think it was. But if you had to compare Marseille to a club today, it would have to be Real Madrid. Madrid aren't going to win the Champions League this season.' Then he adds with a wry grin; 'But Madrid with Tapie as chairman might.' Another thing that OM have in common with the Spanish giants is pulling power. Whatever the why and wherefores of the past, the media continues to need OM.

Not that this relationship is a one-way street. The effects of football's global recession make Champions League qualification today all the more vital, of course. The stock estimate of the cost of failing to qualify tends to be around £10-15 million – *L'Equipe* estimated earlier this month that non-qualification would lead to OM making an overall loss this season of €11 million - that can make or break the seasons of most clubs. Certainly, having largely recovered from their mid-'90s meltdown when the collapse of the Tapie era brought the club to its knees, Marseille are better financially placed than most in France. Yet it is only thanks to the personal investment of adidas CEO Robert Louis-Dreyfus that they were able to spend even prudently this summer, addressing the team's long standing scoring problem by buying strikers Didier Drogba, Mido and attacking midfielder Stepan Vachousek for a combined total of €13 million (around £9.3 million). Defenders Sylvain N'Diaye and the French international Phillipe Christanval were also signed on Bosman frees. However, the biggest signing made this summer by president Christophe Bouchet was the kit deal signed with adidas, guaranteeing the club an estimated €75 million (around £53.5 million) over the next six years, giving the club a degree of financial security and scope to able to compete both at home and abroad.

I was hoping for a leisurely seafood dinner but most places don't start serving until gone 7 and I want to get to the ground in good time to soak up the big match vibes. With my stomach whingeing like a small child en route to a family holiday, I get on the Metro and it's only about 10 minutes (including a change) to Centre Pont du Prado, where the ground is. The lack of pissed-up punters pre-match is noticeable (even bearing in mind this is a midweek game), as there's a bit of banter on the trains, but little in the way of actual singing. The station is more or less next to the ground and I'm chuffed I found my way from town so easily, no thanks to my guide book I might add. Lonely Planet books have their uses but finding football grounds is not one of them. In fact, it didn't even acknowledge the existence of one in Marseille (or, I figure from a quick flick through the rest of the book, in most other French cities). This country won the World Cup five years ago for God's sake! It's not like forgetting to include the local crown green bowling club! Although really I've never forgiven Lonely Planet for the time I went to this tiger 'farm' in Thailand which turned out not so much to be a great opportunity to see one of the world's largest collections of Bengal tigers as an opportunity to see them whipped by some Thai men and made to jump through fire hoops. We'll leave the story about being ambushed by a gang of Cuban *jiniteras* in a bar they recommended in Havana for another time.

The Stade Vélodrome is pretty awesome at first glance. And, for that matter, second glance too. It doesn't have the colossal, imposing height of the San Siro or the vast expanse of the Camp Nou, but unlike either of these two, it is just like a beautiful woman. The contours of its structure are curved in all the right places, rather than the rectangular drudgery of many a football ground, particularly some of the newer Meccano-style British efforts (hello Middlesbrough and Sunderland). By its corners it flashes you teasing glimpses of what awaits inside, offering you a peek of either *virage* (the areas behind the goals). It has a certain air of unattainability for the non-ticket holder, surrounded by a secure perimeter area like the entrance to a music festival, where you have separate gates for frisking punters and checking tickets. Actually it's the position of the Vélodrome, set back from the road, almost as if on a pedestal, that makes it such a great sight. I sit against a tree munching a sandwich and taking it all in as the *marseillais* stream past in their droves, while a few young people even stop and ask me for spare tickets.

It may look great from the outside, but it doesn't come close to doing the inside justice. Wow. With three sides of the ground uncovered, there's a very natural, open feel to the Vélodrome, which is juxtaposed to the way the stands hem in the pitch like at an English ground – you tend (often correctly) to imagine many continental grounds as having huge running tracks between the fans and the action. But it's less the ground that strikes you than the fans. 'The best fans in the country/world' (copyright Newcastle, Celtic, Portsmouth etc) is that most overused of subjective football clichés, but the OM fans really are something special. The first massed chant of 'Allez l'OM' begins around three quarters of an hour before kick-off, and regardless of what's happening on the pitch, the only time they stop is to shower the visiting Austria Vienna with as piercing a hail of catcalls as you are ever likely to hear as they warm up in front of the *Virage Sud*.

The mix of the crowd is totally striking too. Going to football regularly in London, a city with an extensively mixed ethnic palette, you see the same crowds as you see at football most places, i.e. exclusively white males. But here the variation of the city is actually reflected in the make-up of the crowd at the Vélodrome. Groups of young Algerians, groups of mid-20s women, mothers bringing groups of children – they're all here. I've got to admit that while I'd appreciate more of an ethnic mix at the grounds at home, whenever I hear some clueless chief exec promoting football as a 'family sport' I wince. 'Family football' means kids counting the clock down on the electronic scoreboard in pipsqueak voices, it means the embarrassing parent blethering mindless inanities throughout, and it means kids screaming for Gascoigne-era Spurs in the early '90s. Not here. Everyone seems knowledgeable, is vocal and above all *'fier d'etre Marseillais'* (proud to be Marseillais). The presence of families takes none of the edge away from what's an incredible atmosphere.

Famous though the Vélodrome is for its fanatical fans, tonight is especially charged, because they know that OM are on the brink of qualifying for the Champions League for the first time in four years. It can't be over-emphasised how much this means. Just in the run-up to what, after all, is just a qualifier for the Champions League proper, the press have been having kittens, and today's *L'Equipe* virtually quivers in your very hands in anticipation. For the OM fans though it's about their identity as a club, on a stage they feel that they belong, something that success in the league can't give them. They're grateful for the recovery of the club after the collapse of the Tapie era but they need these big nights to feel whole. With OM leading 1-0 from the first leg in Austria the mood is total celebration – they think they are here to witness a victory procession.

Their team try to make it exactly that, forcing the play early on in an effort to kill the tie off. The Brazilian Fernandão dictates early on, and he puts a chance on a plate for his strike partner Didier Drogba which he horribly miscues over an open net. It's the start of a bad day at the office for the young Ivory Coast striker, who goes on to spurn a few other presentable chances. As the breakthrough continues to elude them the team (although not, noticeably, the crowd) become tense, without ever looking like losing control. Drogba fails to lead the line with any great conviction, and Fernandão tires of probing and spends the rest of his game either reacting theatrically to tackles or lying on his arse. They miss the cutting edge of Mido, the young Egyptian signed in the summer. The coach Alain Perrin's line is that he injured a thigh in the warm up, though *L'Equipe* float a rumour the next day suggesting Mido rowed with his coach, stormed out, only to find – comically - his car boxed in at the car park. All conjecture of course but no less funny for it. At half-time though OM would seem to have it all in hand.

Then five minutes into the second half, they're in trouble. A neat passing move ends in a one-two between Helstad and Rushfeldt that leaves the former clear. Seven yards out. Just the 'keeper Runje to beat. Must score. Except he hammers it miles over the bar. The Vélodrome breathes a collective sigh of relief. Runje goes through the pantomime of half-heartedly scolding his defenders. He knows they've been let off.

And that's really the first and last proper scare they have. For all the claims of their coach Joachim Low in the morning papers that his side would strive to take the game to OM, and the fact that they rise fairly admirably to the occasion, the Viennese just don't have it in them to truly threaten. After the coach Perrin puts Fernandão (and us) out of his misery, replacing him with the impressive young left-footer Vachousek on the hour, they hold on fairly comfortably, whilst keeping the faithful hanging on to the end. Drogba sends a free header wide and the industrious Sytchev is flattened in the area with no reward. But four minutes into injury time, with the tetchy, sweating young lad next to me screaming '*Sifflez, putain!*'('blow up, for fuck's sake!') red-facedly and looking at his watch for the third time in a minute, the ref does exactly that and Marseille are through to the Champions League. The Vélodrome less erupts than lets out a collective gasp of relief. The players manage a tired wave at the stands. The management, sensing the mood of celebration, sneak out new loan signing Steve Marlet onto the pitch, raising the shirt of his new team over his head.

He gets a warm reception, as he's still fairly well regarded in France despite his shabby displays at Fulham, which have left me personally fairly underwhelmed by his appearance (particularly when you consider their title rivals Lyon and Monaco bag heavyweights Giovane Elber and Fernando Morientes respectively before the transfer deadline). The team's shortcomings – continued difficulty scoring goals, over-reliance on the immaculate defensive pair of van Buyten and Meïté – aren't important tonight though. Olympique de Marseille are back alongside the European elite.

The streets around the Vélodrome after the game are more content than ecstatic. The faithful have given everything and they're drained. Drivers blare on their horns Italian style, young men order celebratory shots from the bar kiosks on the street, but it's all for show, a bare covering to their relief. Still, they know now they'll have bigger nights to come this season. I just might have to treat myself to a trip back here.

Lyon

Paul Le Guen shifts in his seat, and then breaks into a resigned grin before eventually responding to the question. He answers in exactly that way that only football managers and players can. They try to act like politicians and play the party line, something blank, impenetrable and authoritative that neatly side steps the question. But football by nature is an emotive field and those employed in the game generally lack the oratorical guile to cloak their feelings, despite their attempts to stonewall questions with platitudes and clichés. The Olympique Lyonnais coach has just been asked about whether he feels it is time to repay the backing of his president, Jean-Michel Aulas. And if the public image of Aulas is to be believed, you would want to repay his backing as soon as was humanly possible.

Lyon is France's second biggest city, but it's easy to forget this as you're walking round its calm and spacious streets. Even in the city centre you never feel swamped or overrun by the bustle of urban life. As in most French cities, there is of course a café every ten or so steps where people take time to live rather than just exist, but what really lends Lyon its relaxed air is that eating is treated as a real event here, even by French standards. Lyon has been renowned for its gastronomy since the early modern period – the man who coined the actual word 'gastronomy', Joseph Berchoux, was moved to write in a nineteenth century poem that it '..is the place you will find yourself able, To gather and lay the best fod on your table' - and was often considered the world capital of cuisine in the early twentieth century. Much of Lyonnais social life centres around *bouchons* (literally corks), small traditional restaurants that specialise in traditional cuisine, most famously *andouillette*, a sausage made from pig's bladder (vegetarianism tends to be a bit of a struggle in France generally).

The city seems calmed by the two rivers that run through it, the Rhône and the Saône, which together with some of its old buildings (notably the university) make it about as picturesque as a city this big could be. It would, however, be totally misleading to talk about a city that's purely an expression of its history. Even on Friday nights, there are large groups of people, of all ages, who eschew trawling pubs and bars and instead glide around Place Bellecour (the main square) on roller blades. Throughout the week I see more people darting around on roller blades than you see on bicycles in most cities. This is as good an expression as any of the city's vibe – young, progressive, on the move.

It doubles as a decent analogy for the city's football club. Olympique Lyonnais is a relative stripling in football club terms, founded as recently as 1950, and for much of that time they have been considered provincial also-rans. At the time when Monsieur Aulas, a prominent local businessman, became president in 1987, OL had been languishing in Ligue 2 for four years. They have just won a second consecutive French title, the previous one in 2002 having been the first in the club's history. To say that he has revolutionised the club during his tenure is a bit like saying Zinedine Zidane's quite popular in this country. Always a trailblazer, his transformation of OL's playing fortunes by recruiting high-profile names (Jean Tigana, Sonny Anderson etc) has been matched only by his pursuit of power at the game's highest levels. He helped create the UCPF (the union of professional football club presidents) in 1992, became general treasurer of the French League (LNF) the following year and in 2000 was elevated to LNF vice-president.

Aulas' main coup however came in August 2002, when OL were invited to become members of G-14, the conglomerate of Europe's most powerful football clubs (to give you an idea of OL's relative power in Europe, Arsenal were invited to join at the same time). The G-14 was founded two years earlier in September 2000, as a pressure group to lobby for these clubs' interests as they sought to gain firm ground in the constant battle for power with the European and world football authorities[1]. Just recently the G-14 signalled the extent of their ambition by demanding that clubs in future be paid a percentage of profits from international matches and also by threatening to boycott the 2005 World Club Championship in protest at FIFA's indifference to extended and meaningful dialogue with the group.

This ambition tallies with that of Aulas. He has long spoken of, and acted towards, expanding the OL 'brand', and of course progress in the Champions League is imperative to achieve this. Whereas Marseille and their fans have a great historical attachment to the competition, Lyon don't. They have the problem of their lack of history when compared against other clubs, and if you're looking at their direct rivals within France, with Marseille in particular. They don't generate the passion around France that OM do having captured the hearts of the nation by beating the best on the continental stage. Sure, they've had their moments – hammering Bayern Munich at the Gerland in 2001, winning in the San Siro against eventual semi-finalists Inter in last year's competition– but no Munich 1993, no Glasgow 1976 even, no real *defining* moment. OL need to produce something special on the biggest stage of all, to bring them up to the next level and to scrub themselves of the whiff of *nouveau riche* that makes them so unloved within their own country.

Xavier Rivoire knows of the club's dilemma well, being a native of the city himself. 'They have been the dominant force (in France) for three or four years now,' he says. 'I'm including the league cup they won in 2001, which was really the first trophy they won in modern times.' Though this period of success has been quite emphatic, it is still relatively recent, while the club's image is more deeply rooted. 'Even if their game hasn't always been flamboyant, it has always been quality football, yet they're not well liked,' admits Xavier. 'They (the rest of

France) see Lyon as this very bourgeois city.'

Perhaps one factor that has undermined OL's chances of being received by the French public as a bona fide giant is Aulas' style of club management. From what I've listened to over the few days I've spent in Lyon, and in opinions I've read previously, fans have accused him of caring more about the money than the football. The president seems to believe that no player is indispensable, that they all have their price. A cursory glance at the Premiership quickly reveals a few high-profile Gerland refugees. Fréderic Kanouté joined West Ham in 2000 for £3.75 million, Steed Malbranque went to Fulham for £4.7 million in the same year, and the following year Fulham coach Tigana again raided his old charges for Steve Marlet (for a whopping £11.5 million). The Marlet transfer is an exception – it was a mind-boggling amount of money and Fulham are, in fact, still disputing the figure (at the time of writing they are going to the Court of Arbitration for Sport in Lausanne to overturn FIFA's order to pay Lyon the £3.2 million they still owe for Marlet. They were unhappy with the role agents played in the deal). However, the consistent sale of important players - and in the case of these three, young players with a future - doesn't bode well for the building of a football empire.

'It's a dangerous type of policy,' Xavier agrees, 'but Aulas has been able to be both (empire builder and money-maker) because he is a shrewd businessman.' They have always found a rich, and continuous, seam of talent in years past. 'They know the Ligue 1 market pretty well,' Xavier points out, 'and they have good connections in Brazil (which have yielded the defender Claudio Caçapa and free-kick deity Juninho).' Whether this policy is reconcilable with Aulas' plans to make the club (and team) all-conquering for years to come still remains to be seen. 'But the trophies speak for themselves.'

It's wrong, however, to paint Aulas as a one-dimensional, money mad megalomaniac. That would be denying the complexity of an intriguing character in European football's modern day elite. After making a couple of appointments to interview him only to be blown out at the last minute, I finally get to meet the man briefly after a league game at the Gerland, against Nice. Aulas is not physically an imposing man (only standing at about 5'7, perhaps), but his oratorical style is persuasive, insistent without being aggressive. If you didn't know who he was or what he did, you could probably guess he was a businessman anyway. What makes him interesting is that, unusually for a club president, he articulates informed, in-depth opinions on events on the playing field. Most chairmen or presidents give little impression of sharing the supporters' feelings, and seeing Aulas opine with passion and certainty puts him in a light juxtaposed to his public image as a breadhead. In fact, I'm even forced to stifle a laugh when he complains about the 'aggression of Nice' and attributes it to 'the close relationship between (Gernot) Rohr (Nice's German coach) and Bayern Munich' – the German champions who Lyon face in their following Champions League match. It's the type of conspiracy theory you would expect to hear from your dad in the bar after the game, rather than a high-powered board member.

With Lyon now established as French champions and Ligue 1's top team, Aulas really has something to build on. Making OL the most bankable name in French club football is just the precursor to making them big hitters in Europe. He has managed to make the first step towards being taken seriously on a wider stage by signing Giovane Elber from Bayern a few weeks ago. OL's attempts to replace their much-loved Brazilian striker Sonny Anderson, who left for Villarreal in the close season, had become French club football's running joke. They spent the summer being linked with virtually every striker under 35 who wasn't a first-teamer at either Real Madrid or Man United – Pauleta, Drogba, Heskey, Viduka, Morientes. They also had an offer of €15 million for Shabani Nonda accepted by hard-up rivals Monaco, before last season's French league top scorer had a change of heart and decided against the move. Most were expecting some sort of panic signing as the deadline for registering players for the Champions' League approached, with only the inexperienced youngsters Viale and Bergagnoux as back-up to the excellent Peguy Luyindula. What wasn't so expected was the arrival of someone of Elber's quality – last season's Bundesliga top scorer is in the top ten of all-time Champions League goalscorers (20 goals) and was only forced out of the Olympiastadion following the arrival of the Dutch *Pichichi* Roy Makaay from Deportivo La Coruña. In other words, he is someone who is experience and class combined, someone not just to give the team the edge in big games, but someone who is also respected on the European circuit. The name signing that Aulas has been looking for.

It's part of the way towards the respect that Aulas craves, a respect that he and l'OL are only really going to get that through some major European feat. In that respect, a huge shadow from across the Loire Valley is hanging over them (and maybe always will). Saint Etienne's glory years of the '60s and '70s are legendary, and people remember them as the first French team to be competitive in the European Cup (falsely in fact, as the now-tiny Stade de Reims were finalists in two of the first four tournaments in the '50s, losing to Di Stéfano-era Real Madrid on both occasions). In a reference to the supposed bourgeoisness of Lyon, former Saint Etienne president Roger Rocher famously said before his death in 1997 that 'in football, Saint Etienne will always be the city and Lyon the suburb.' As time goes by, the myth surrounding Saint Etienne arguably becomes more powerful. 'Even if they (Lyon) matched their ten league titles, I'm not sure it would make any difference,' reckons Xavier Rivoire.

So as Aulas continues his grand plan to build Olympique Lyonnais into a European superpower, it falls to Le Guen to do the easy bit. Pick the team and win the games. It's as simple as that. Except it hasn't been that simple so far this season. OL are notoriously slow starters – they have astonishingly failed to win an opening match of the season in the top league since August 1981 - but winning only two of the first six, losing another two and scoring only six goals is a start that piles pressure on the team expected to carry all before them. Reading Aulas' comments on the website after a defeat at Guingamp (if memory serves me correctly the words he used were 'unacceptable level of effort') I shuddered on behalf of the coach. There have been mitigating circumstances. With the departure of a few experienced players (notably Anderson and Violeau) and the bedding in of some new, younger ones (Essien, Malouda, Reveillere) the team has had a period of readjustment. Though talented, the side now has an average age of around 24, not something particularly unusual in Ligue 1 but of far greater significance when it comes to Europe. The quality of their football has touched startling peaks at times, notably in the win over Monaco at the Gerland in which Essien was outstanding, but slips at home against the likes of Toulouse can't be afforded too often. Particularly when the club has shelled out more on players pre-season than it has in any summer before in its history.

I like Le Guen, he seems like a really nice, genuine guy. And you have to admire his enthusiasm for a job where success is surely the only means of survival. When I first see him in the flesh, at a press conference held at the Gerland the day before the opening Champions' League game against Anderlecht, he is fielding a stream of monotonous questions from the assembled local and national media. Will Elber's experience be important to the team in Europe? Is he worried that the team haven't scored many goals so far this season? Which is more important, the domestic league or the Champions' League? And the questions continue in the same vein or variations thereof. Journalists in whichever country and their general ability to ask the same bloody questions again and again never ceases to amaze me. The French media are a slightly different breed from their British counterparts however, not as bloodthirsty for a start. They are less like wolves and more like teenage fans, probing for every minor insignificant detail like fanzine writers. Yet Le Guen manages not only to stay awake but also to remain polite and courteous, especially when you consider that these people are basically asking him what it will take for him to hold on to his job.

You can forgive him the grin when the boss is mentioned. It may seem nervous, but it's probably more incredulous at the obviousness of the question. *Of course* he's under pressure to deliver for Aulas. Le Guen has been here before. He was said to be on the brink of resigning just before Christmas last year in the wreckage of their narrow Champions League exit, in the midst of a situation compounded by some ropey league results and reports of warring egos in the dressing room. He managed to survive with his reputation as one of the new generation of bright young French coaches, as well as his job, intact and went on to win Le Championnat in his first season at the tender age of 39. Behind the benign smile lurks a steely resolve. He is a pragmatic enough character to know that managers at his level operate in a climate where success provides only temporary relief, and having operated with significantly less financial backing in his previous post at Rennes, is grateful of being able to call on the resources of a club with Ligue 1's largest budget.

Although Le Guen may bear the brunt of the pressure, it's fair to say the players have a job on their hands as well. The likes of Essien (only 20 years old) and Malouda (24) are expected to adjust quickly to big club life and deliver consistently major performances straight away, when they have limited experience of such demands, having played at Bastia and Guingamp respectively last season. Competition for places, particularly in midfield where OL have an embarrassment of riches, is so intense that even internationals of the pedigree of Carrière, Müller and Deflandre aren't guaranteed a start. Müller is in the team at the moment, and captaining the side in the absence of the injured Caçapa. The latter fact also affords Müller the dubious privilege of joining his coach at the press conference. If coaches feel that the press conference is part of their job, perhaps even a forum to get their ideas and opinions across, then it's clear that that's not always the case for players. Müller wouldn't normally have to do this. Although he's in no way discourteous, he seems even more exasperated than Le Guen by the gathered throng. Yes, it will be a difficult match. No, neither Le Championnat nor the Champions League is more important than the other. After the press have dispersed and the TV and radio people surround his coach, Müller fiddles with his 'phone in the background.

He's around the same age as me, which must make him at least 5-10 years younger than anyone else here. This is a real ball ache for him. The press officer has obviously got better things to do having seen this circus of clichés a thousand times before and has disappeared a while ago, leaving almost as soon as he's introduced Le Guen and Müller to the press.

Talking of clichés, one of the most often used in football tends to be the one about only being as good as your last match. Which describes exactly why Lyon are getting some stick at the moment. They put in a shabby performance against Auxerre at the weekend, lacking any sort of fluency or focus. Elber was the one real bright spot, also salvaging a point with his first goal for the club. He's going to be important if they're going to do well in Europe. And they need to hit the ground running. Anderlecht are widely expected to be the group whipping boys (the other two teams they will face are Bayern and Celtic) and if that's the case, this fixture at home is the closest to a banker that they're going to get. The pressure couldn't be more on these players to deliver. They can't afford to stuff it up – it's win or bust.

The Belgian fans start coming into Lyon in numbers from around midday on match day, and immediately start taking over the pubs, bars and cafes around Bellecour. They're jovial, in colours, some thumping huge drums and all singing songs (many of them, interestingly, in English). It's no surprise - after all, a trip abroad with your team is great, and more so in the Champions League. As the team widely thought to be the group's no-hopers, there's no pressure on the Anderlecht team and they also arrive in far better form than the home side, having won all five games in the league thus far, including a 6-0 away win on Saturday.

You can't help thinking that with this backing it could be tough for Lyon. The Anderlecht fans are noisy enough as we emerge from the Metro station to be faced with *gendarmes* in improbably casual attire, deck shoes and cords – imagine seeing a copper outside a ground in England wearing a 'Frankie says Relax' T-shirt – carrying batons and accompanied by slavering Alsatians. I, sadly, am forced to leave the hardcore as I have been invited by a friend as a 'client' to attend a corporate reception. Which is harder than you might expect, as whilst knocking back free champagne I'm also trying to avoid any staff who may have spotted me at yesterday's press conference seeing me brazenly take advantage of their club's hospitality. I've never seen a match from a corporate box before and if someone from the host company collars me to talk about expansion in the UK I might not make it that far tonight either. Making as little contact as possible with business sorts, I instead settle to what is a magnificent view in the open seats in front of the boxes, high in the Tribune Jean Jaures.

People never mention Lyon when they're talking about the great atmospheres in French club football. It's always Marseille or Lens. But the Gerland tonight is something to behold. I'd noticed similarities between the crowd here and in Marseille on Saturday – fairly mixed, racially and sexually, constantly noisy and lively in the areas behind the goal -'chaud' (hot), as the French put it. Tonight the Virage Nord, where the ultras congregate, is alight with noise – and flares – and so is the rest of the stadium. I had thought that the Belgians would out-sing their French counterparts, having been part of an away minority enough times to know that numbers have nothing to do with the amount of noise you make, but not a chance. Like the Marseillaise, the *Gones* know their night is a big night.

The team know it's a big night too – how could they fail to? – and accordingly start nervously, their lack of confidence betraying their recent ordinary form. Anderlecht meanwhile knock it around like a team with nothing to lose, not to mention a team which has won its last five games. OL, however, start to get it together and a good move puts Essien through on the 'keeper, but he drags his shot wide. A minute later though the 'keeper isn't so lucky as his 50-50 challenge with Sidney Govou leaves the young Frenchman on the floor and the referee pointing to the spot. Lyon know they've lucked out – indeed Florent Malouda is quoted in the next day's press as saying 'Was it a penalty? I don't know, but why look a gift horse in the mouth?' Juninho is unfazed and tucks away the penalty with the minimum of fuss, then runs to the Virage Nord before being submerged by his team-mates. The relief in everyone Lyonnais inside the stadium is palpable.

With the goal behind them OL play a much more fluent second half. You get the impression that if they could bag a second, they would go on to hammer Anderlecht flat. But despite the increasingly powerful prompting of Essien and particularly the influential Vikash Dhorasoo, it doesn't happen. Juninho goes close with a trademark free-kick, and Malouda pushes a shot narrowly wide after another storming run from Dhorasoo. As it stays at 1-0, so the tension starts to creep in. Elber and Govou are increasingly on the periphery of the game and look as if they are tiring, while Anderlecht have the speedy Dindane as their forward outlet. With a few minutes left the Belgians get their chance. After another run from Dindane the ball breaks to the playmaker Zetterberg just inside the box. He hits it hard and true to Coupet's left....only for the French number two to push it one-handed around the post. Such saves are what makes a truly great goalkeeper – Coupet has stood around scratching his arse with nothing to do for most of the game but has pulled off a class save when he had to. And in that moment, he earned the three points that Lyon desperately craved.

In the car on the way home my friend says he reckons that Lyon would have been stuffed had they been playing Bayern (the group favourites) tonight, and he may well be right. It was a fairly unspectacular performance, and no-one can know better than Paul Le Guen that the hard work starts now. Given the group they're in, it's going to be an opening stage of hard graft for them, while Marseille large it in a glamour group with Real Madrid. It's the Champions League now, not the European Cup, and not every game is not the dictionary definition of glorious. These days it represents an extra third added on to your season should you reach the latter stages. But they're in it for the long haul, and OL mean business.

Celtic

It never ceases to amaze me when I hear people from England who've never been to Scotland. There's no reason why anyone down here shouldn't have made it – it's not exactly the moon after all. Similarly, there's no real reason I haven't made it to Parkhead before now. I've wanted to go for ages but never quite made it. Like most English football fans, I have a passing interest in the Scottish game but it's just that, with its tribalism tending to hold more fascination than the football itself. I went to Ibrox once, about 11 or 12 years ago when I was travelling around Scotland with a mate, to see Rangers play a League Cup 1st round tie against some second division team. Up until then I guess, like a lot of English football fans, I would have classed them as 'my Scottish team', feeling some sort of affinity to the club due to their load of English players I suppose. But it was crap. Absolutely terrible. Given the stature of the game, I wasn't expecting an atmosphere like an Old Firm game, but I also wasn't expecting half of the crowd to bugger off home with half an hour left because their team were only winning 1-0. I've never seen anything like it before or since. Much as I could convince myself that I root for Celtic in Old Firm games because of the whole 'my Irish Catholic bloodline' blah, the truth is that I just can't bring myself to root for Rangers.

I always liked Glasgow. One of my best mates came to university here, and although I first came here at 15, I can't say that I really got to know it until I visited him. It is of course debatable whether you can have a proper feel for a place without going out drinking in it.

Glasgow always felt more Scottish to me than Edinburgh somehow, the real deal. Other people I've spoken to mainly agree, even the ones who prefer Edinburgh. Don't get me wrong, Edinburgh's a nice city – again, I had a friend at the university there – and I've great memories of its legendary New Year's Eve celebrations. But you get the impression that Edinburgh wants to be in England. Glasgow has no such pretensions. And it doesn't have the rather smug festival either.

This trip is definitely a good one to get out of the way early on. Sure, it was one I was looking forward to, but Newcastle winters are still fresh in my mind from when I lived there and I didn't really want to come up here in mid-December if I could possibly avoid it (note to self – get Moscow out the way too ASAP if you're going to do it). It's a touch fresh but still pleasant. I feel at home here straight away. This is possibly because I'm invited to a post-match party at my hostel as soon as I get there. The pubs are also pretty friendly – big shout out at this point to the Drum and Monkey, which is hospitable, does decent food and has the Arsenal game on. To be honest I didn't really expect any sort of welcome as a lone Englishman, knowing how the English (and especially Londoners) are often regarded by the Scottish, but it's a far warmer city than I remember it being. Even allowing for the sniggering bar girl who later takes great delight in giving me 50p change in 5p coins (it must have been a slow day). It's been a while since I've had a proper pre-match drink, unless you count the champagne reception in Lyon, which wasn't exactly routine. A few pints before the game hasn't been – and, generally speaking, isn't - the norm in Europe. Whereas I often feel I need stone cold sobriety abroad in order to take everything in abroad, to cope with the sensory overload of a different culture, this is all relatively familiar.

Unless you've been living in the outback for the last couple of years, you'll have noticed that there's been an escalating clamour of voices over that period excitedly trumpeting the idea of Celtic and Rangers joining the Premiership, not least those of the two clubs themselves. If you can put aside thinking about what a catastrophic effect this would have on the Scottish Premier League – sending it into financial meltdown, putting it on a par with the Welsh league - the argument for this seemingly drastic course of action isn't without its merits. Both the clubs, particularly Celtic in reaching last season's UEFA Cup final, have shown signs of being able to compete in Europe in recent times, thus raising the question of whether they should be fitted into a more suitable level of competition. Casting aside the frankly tiresome Premiership debate, it's clear that these two teams deserve to be recognised as representatives of Britain as a whole rather than ghettoised as part of a frequently derided league.

Celtic, of course, have already done their bit for Britain in Europe. When recounting English domination of the European Cup in the late '70s/ early '80s (English clubs won six consecutive finals between 1977 and 1982), it's often overlooked that Celtic were in fact the first British club to lift a European trophy. In fact, not just *a* European trophy, but *the* European trophy. On the 25th of May 1967, they pulled off a shock win over Inter Milan in Lisbon's Estádio Nacional to bring the European Champions Cup to Britain for the first time. It's a great feat anyway, particularly when you think that Inter were the dominant team in Europe of the day. Managed by the legendary Argentine Helenio Herrera, they had already won the trophy twice by the time they came to meet Celtic. Basically, for the Inter of then, think the stature of Real Madrid of now. Set into historical context, British football has few, if any, greater achievements. The Celtic class of '67 is now immortalised materially, by the naming of the Lisbon Lions' Stand behind the east end goal at Parkhead, in eternal gratitude to the players who took part in that triumph.

One of those players was Jim Craig, the team's right-back that night in Lisbon. Now working for the club in their new media department, Craig's shockingly modest about his and his peers' achievements. Well, certainly more modest than I'd be in the same circumstances. Their calm approach to the final itself was, however, more by luck than judgement: 'I remember it being an awkward bus journey to the ground. The bus driver didn't know where the national stadium was. All the cars seemed to be going the other way, so Jock Stein had to tell the driver to follow everyone else. Although we weren't able to soak up the pre-match atmosphere, it probably worked in our favour because we didn't have any time for nerves either.'

Although they weren't over-analytical in the build-up, the team became aware afterwards of the magnitude of what they had done. 'Obviously it was important. When you break that barrier it makes it easier for others to win it afterwards.' And they weren't the only ones in Glasgow who knew it. 'Obviously we didn't get an open top bus through Glasgow (with the trophy) because it's a split city, and we took the route back via the Clyde tunnel to avoid Ibrox. Having said that, the first person to meet us off the plane was the Rangers chairman at the time, John Lawrence, which was really magnanimous of him. Especially since it made him pretty unpopular with his own fans.'

What's also forgotten outside the east end of Glasgow is that Celtic made a huge impact on the European Cup throughout the legendary Jock Stein's reign as manager, not solely on that one night in Lisbon. Stein had been at the club for barely two years when he masterminded the victory in Portugal, having arrived from Dunfermline in 1965. He'd already ready worked his magic there, leading the Pars to a 1961 Scottish Cup final win over Celtic (who he'd previously played for), and made his mark on Europe too. Stein's Dunfermline team had hammered the highly accomplished holders Valencia (who would go on to retain the trophy) 6-2 in the 1962 Inter-Cities Fairs' Cup[1], despite having lost the first leg 4-0 in Spain. They narrowly lost the play-off in Lisbon – away goals didn't count back then – but it had still been a huge achievement.

Celtic had form in Europe before Stein's arrival, having improbably lost to MTK Bucharest in the Cup Winners' Cup semi-final in 1964 having won the first leg 3-0, but it was under his stewardship that they became a genuine, consistent force. They lost another Cup Winners' Cup semi, this time to Liverpool, in 1966. Then, three years on from

Lisbon, they reached the European Cup final again, this time against Feyenoord, of Rotterdam. Tommy Gemmell – one of seven survivors from Lisbon's winners – put them ahead, but the Dutch eventually ran out winners after extra-time, Ove Kindvall scoring the winner just three minutes from the end[2]. They missed out in agonising fashion again in 1972, losing in the semi-final to Inter on penalties after two goalless legs, and they lost the 1974 semi too, played this time against Atlético de Madrid.

With Celtic still of course the only Scottish club to win the European Cup - or indeed any European trophy excepting Aberdeen's 1984 Cup Winners' Cup triumph - the heroes of 1967 are set apart in history. With the introduction of the Champions League format in the last decade, it becomes less and less likely with the passing of time that Celtic's victory, achieved with 11 Scottish players in the side, will be replicated. Craig agrees. 'The Champions League isn't really a champions' competition anymore. With the group stages it's organised so the big teams don't go out. Teams can have an off game here or there and still be in the cup. Look at Arsenal (this season) – they had a really bad start but could still get through now. It was different after we won it in '67. There was no seeding then, and we drew Dynamo Kiev in the first round the next year – and that was a really tough draw too[3] - while having League Cup and World Club Championship matches at the same time.'

Celtic's efforts in the past few years to re-establish the club as a European force may seem like baby steps in the context of the '60s, but are highly significant in modern terms. And like the dynasty of Stein, this has been played out under the guidance of an inspirational coach. Martin O'Neill may not have endured the major financial upheavals of the first half of the '90s (which required Canadian-based businessman Fergus McCann to completely restructure the club's finances following his takeover), but even the most fervent of optimists could have seen the man from Northern Ireland had a job and a half on his hands on arrival. He took over a team in 2000 who had won just one title since the 1988 double season – in 1998 under coach Wim Jansen who, ironically, had played for Feyenoord against Celtic in the 1970 final - and had finished a colossal 21 points behind arch-rivals Rangers the previous season. Winning the domestic treble in his first season was astonishing, but to win the league by a 15-point margin was a nigh-on miracle.

This (and a qualifying round win over Ajax set up by a stunning 3-1 first leg win in Amsterdam) gave O'Neill, and Celtic, their first crack at the Champions League proper in 2001/2. Granted, O'Neill had had some cash to spend, but had used it wisely to bring in quality players like Chris Sutton, Joos Valgaeren and Alan Thompson, all of whom became mainstays in an organised, disciplined and capable team. They were narrowly eliminated at the group stage despite a 100% home record, turning over Porto, Rosenborg and Juventus at Parkhead. Last season saw a disappointing qualifying round exit to the underrated Swiss side Basle on away goals, but as it turned out, this was just a tune up for the main event.

The UEFA Cup may be sometimes denigrated as a mere support act to the Champions League, but let's face it, only a very elite set of Europe's clubs can afford to turn their noses up at it – the likes of Real Madrid, Manchester United, Juventus. For everybody else, it's a European trophy, and it's definitely worth having. Celtic's performance was great, not just in the final, where they pushed an excellent Porto side every step of the way for the whole 120 minutes, but during the whole run. They dispatched teams of the quality of Stuttgart, Boavista and Celta Vigo, ties in which they showed they could play effectively in European competition. They also put out the English sides Blackburn and Liverpool, with their accomplished and - you have to say - European-savvy away performances being a highlight. The wins in England (particularly the one at Anfield) were also one in the eye for a country whose public and media constantly belittles Celtic's domestic achievements, bearing in mind the perceived quality of their league, and therefore the extent of the Celts' own ability. Pertinently, this was something Blackburn (and former Rangers) boss Graeme Souness had made disparaging reference to after his team's first leg at Parkhead. The season made Europe sit up and take notice, besides giving the team confidence to take forward into the Champions League. As the current captain Paul Lambert says; 'Looking at the UEFA Cup, people would have seen that and thought 'Hope we can avoid Celtic'.'

While the Champions League is still emotionally resonant for Celtic, they're not immune to the financial pressures that make the competition such a necessity for a lot of clubs of their size. Craig's history in the competition doesn't blind him to its shifted priorities: 'Of course the Champions League and football in general have changed out of all recognition these days. It's not just about fans now - following football has become almost a cult thing, and definitely more about business. Nowadays you get big crowds for all games, not just the big ones. I mean, if you've paid £700 for a season ticket you're going to want to go to all the games.'

From the outside though, it doesn't seem just about the cash with Celtic. Seeing their progress to the UEFA Cup final last year, there was one element that was far more conspicuous than the team, despite their laudable performances. The fans. Celtic supporters have a reputation for travelling in numbers - something that continental clubs, lest we forget, generally don't have such a great tradition of - and raising the roof wherever they go. Despite only 20,000 tickets being available to Celts for the Sevilla final, tons more travelled to southern Spain. Estimated numbers (and they would have to be just that) ranged anywhere between 50,000 and 80,000. This is destined to go down as part of British football folklore in generations to come, but although the volume of people is extraordinary, this kind of zeal for Celtic has always been there according to Jim Craig. He admits his memories of his own final are 'a blur', but the sense of occasion has been preserved clearly in his mind. 'I remember taking the steps up from underground dressing rooms, and just being amazed at the number of Celtic fans who had made it. I don't know how the crowd was split or the actual numbers, but all you could hear was Celtic fans.'

Not that they could ever be accused of lacking any passion at home. At the start of the Champions League campaign, Lyon's captain Patrick Müller said that although he expected Bayern Munich to dominate the group, the away match at Celtic looked potentially the most difficult. Like with Marseille, the buzz at Parkhead on Champions League night is all historic pride. Parkhead's one of those grounds that looks like it was built for such occasions. On the ten minute walk there from Bridgeton station, you can see it looming in the distance for all but the first minute after you come out on to the main road. It looks big and pretty impressive. But rather than the San Siro, which is more imposing from the outside, it reminds you of the Camp Nou and its stunning interior. You may have thought that the loss of the Jungle, the legendary terrace that was closed in 1993 (and subsequently seated over), would flatten the atmosphere, but approaching kick-off as they prepare to take on Lyon you can see what Craig means by 'Fortress Celtic'. 'It's become an in-thing to talk about it, yes. Of course it helps when you're comfortable in your surroundings. And since the ground's been redeveloped, the fans are a lot closer to the pitch than they were in my day.'

This claustrophobia adds to the atmosphere, but that's the same at most British grounds, and it's something more than that here. The Vélodrome was thoroughly noisy but here it's absolutely deafening. I can't recall seeing anything quite like it. Champions League protocol dictates that the two teams walk out side by side and line up, standing to attention while the familiar Champions League anthem is played, but the PA here, despite being modern (i.e. audible to the point of discomfort in normal conditions), is pissing in the wind. You can't here a note of the anthem over the singing from the stands. This party exclusively belongs to Celtic, rather than UEFA or anyone else. It's fantastic.

Le Guen, the Lyon coach, has concurred with the opinion of his captain pre-match, and has said that he thinks the atmosphere is what will make it most difficult for his team. Lambert says of it that 'you can't hear yourselves shout to each other on the park. It's a wall of noise. If you look at the teams we've beaten there – Valencia, Porto, Juventus…' I doubt, then, that Le Guen will be that pleased with his striker Elber, who is quoted in the morning papers as saying Celtic are second-rate. I never knew *The Sun* had a Portuguese translator - you learn something new every day. Predictably though Elber is booed whenever he gets the ball. Maybe Lyon's confident start affects them, but the crowd seem to calm noticeably once the match starts. The opening crescendo is replaced by something akin to, maybe, St James' Park – noisy and rousing when the home team are in the ascendancy, but reduced to a uncomfortable, muffled, almost eerie murmur when they're not. The tubby guy next to me in the puffa jacket and tracksuit sighs, huffs and fidgets catatonically throughout the first half (damn these all-seater stadiums). It's almost like the crowd are waiting for the team to lift them rather than the other way around.

The Celts in the stands never fail to amaze though. When the excellent Alan Thompson misses a golden opportunity just before the interval - driving a poor penalty against 'keeper Coupet's legs after a questionable award - the faithful respond with a chant of 'There's Only One Alan Thompson'. Even in a tight match with a tension in the air so palpable you can almost feel it pressing into your head – they've relied on their home form in Champions League past, after all - there's no blame or recrimination, they just want to pick their player up. It's rare, and pretty touching too. The club are acutely aware of the supporters' part in the effort. There's a conscious, continental style cheerleading effort to keep the crowd on the boil here, with Celtic songs being played instead of current pop at half-time. It works too. I mean, I can't remember the last time I saw or heard a full-on singalong in the toilet.

It's no doubt also borne of the acknowledgement that though the fans here start the atmosphere, it's up to the players to help them keep it going. Which is exactly what they do in the second half. Having spent the first 45 huffing and puffing, mostly in vain, against the French team's superior finesse, Celtic finally get properly stuck in. Given so much time in midfield before, Lyon are unsettled by Celtic's aggression. However, to say that the French team's apparent disorientation is due to a mix of Celtic's renewed purpose and the discernible lift it gives the crowd would be an insult to the home side's ability. With their pace and harrying, they allow themselves to play to the best of their capabilities. The pressure becomes relentless, as it often is in European ties at Parkhead. 'The amount of goals that we score late on, because we keep going and going at the same tempo, is incredible,' says Lambert. 'A lot of that's the crowd.' Craig had agreed with my assertion that this is also the best – as well as the most driven - Celtic team in living memory and they prove it by playing Lyon off the park. Coupet makes a few good saves but it's noticeable that they break through despite withdrawing the fantastically brutal John Hartson, the man that you would think was the one most likely to unsettle the opposition.

Hartson's replacement, the young Liam Miller, has only been on for five minutes when he heads Henrik Larsson's cross goalwards from six yards. The ball bounces and it seems like an age - like the slo-mo bit where Pele shoots towards the end of *Escape To Victory* - before the ball hits the net and lets Parkhead do what it has been dying to do - erupt. My God it's loud. Packets of cigarettes and chocolate bars must be falling off the shelves at the petrol station a mile down the road. Relief, elation, the feeling that they've got what they deserve at last, they're all in there. You forget the league structure of the competition. This is more like proper cup football, and in keeping with this Le Guen sends on a striker (Luyindula) for a midfielder (Dhorasoo).

He's left it too late though. It's hard to imagine Parkhead relinquishing its grip now as the opening bars of 'Fields Of Athenry' start up in the stands again. Even from the stands, you can almost see the colour draining from Lyonnais faces and you just know Celtic have the game now. If any doubt remained, a second goal that's eerily similar to the first dispels it as Sutton this time nods in another terrific Larsson centre. It's hard to describe but it seems like it's been fated, as Lyon go through the motions of the closing minutes in a state approaching shell-shock. There is an unquantifiable power about Parkhead in the Champions League. The list of teams that have fallen here in their Champions League campaigns thus far is notable, particularly when judged against their away record - complete success at home matched to complete failure away. Maybe the hosts are as bewitched by Parkhead as their visitors. Then again maybe Celtic just put in their best Champions League performance tonight.

I leave the stadium buzzing. After ringing some friends to enthuse wildly about the game, I find a pub – there is of course only one way to bookend a famous victory when in Britain. And it is celebrated as you would expect, the pints flowing as people sing together, sing in their friends' faces and allow themselves to truly believe in their heroes' invincibility for a few weightless hours. It makes me think of something Jim Craig said while recalling the fighting and shenanigans during Celtic's World Club Championship match in Buenos Aires against River Plate following the European Cup win. It was the year after the infamous England - Argentina 1966 World Cup quarter final at Wembley, after which Alf Ramsay referred to the Argentinians as 'animals'. They had targeted Celtic for a revenge mission- '(they) didn't know there was any difference between the Scots and the English'. Yet even amongst the veneer of the familiar, tonight's been a real eye opener. I've found the signs of a real heart beating inside the Champions League, closer to home than I might have imagined.

Monaco

Champions League fever in the build-up to the game of the group? Not a bit of it. Having taken a leisurely stroll down the hill to the Stade Louis II, the sight greeting us at the ticket office is more your regular Tuesday morning at the Science Museum than full-on European football frenzy. After a whole 30 seconds of queuing, we bag our tickets to tonight's match with the sort of casual ease usually reserved for picking up a mid-morning coffee. Just as we knew we would.

Despite Monte Carlo being its own separate principality, its football club is wholly part of the French elite in Ligue 1. It's only 60km up the road from Marseille (to the east), but Monaco is in a different world. Marseille is the bustling, mixed, working city, whereas Monaco is the fabled millionaires' playground. Though the cliché has its ring of truth, being the tax haven where the likes of Michael Schumacher and Boris Becker come to protect their hoards of cash, I'm not sure I'd refer to it as a 'playground'. It's more of a playpen.

Monaco is no normal place but even from a perspective used to a big city, it's claustrophobic too. The wealth of many of its residents is certainly inescapable wherever you look. When you leave the railway station by the Jardin Botanique you're met with stunning views downwards to the coast (not for nothing is this place referred to as 'The Rock') and the inevitable fleet of pleasure yachts that line every stretch of water you see. Of course the overwhelming perception of the Principality as the preserve of the rich means that when you first see a bus going along the road, you nearly keel over with shock. And as for realising that they have a Carrefour too...

The Casino Monte Carlo is its extravagant centre piece. Early on a November evening, it's subtly lit up, looking beautiful and ornate, definitely fancying itself as one up from Vegas. There is, though, an aura of flashiness here too, with a row of top-of-the-range, 'do you know who I am?' sports cars parked out front as an in-your-face reminder of the clientele's status. While you can get onto craps or a card table for a modest €10 punt, the one-arm bandits at the back of the room demand a minimum €100 a spin. There is a less exclusive second tier gaming room across the square, attached to the Café de Paris, if you lack the pretensions - or cash - to be a high roller. When I say less exclusive, I mean that this collection of downmarket pokies is nothing you won't have seen if you've been to Brighton. Or indeed any pub in the gaming frenzy that is New South Wales, Australia. That said I do get the thrill of paying €6 for a half of Kronenbourg and taking a slash stood next to erstwhile motor racing legend Eddie Irvine.

If football clubs really are extensions of the wider community around them, then AS Monaco is perfectly suited to its surroundings. While it wouldn't be entirely accurate to describe the club as the *bête noire* of French football - and to its credit, the club has never truly sought to assume the victim's role by portraying itself in this way - ASM stands detached from the generally closely-knit feel of Ligue 1. Like the principality itself, there's something surreal about the club. Of course, it's largely due to the continued support of Prince Albert that the club has consistently found itself occupying the upper echelons of the country's game. The Marseille comparison is particularly pertinent - where l'OM are driven by the passion of their fans, Monaco continue at the top in the face of the exact opposite. The stadium itself is attractive, despite being a little on the small side – something dictated by demand, or lack of it - but there's no genuine feel of football here. They've had their share of snide remarks from French rivals affronted by the club's lack of history and vigour, and people who think they're living on royal favour. It's an understandable reaction. When I saw TV highlights of the currently league-leading team's home game against *lanterne rouge* Le Mans at the weekend - played in front of just 3,500 - I couldn't help but think of the scene in *The Simpsons* where we see the Play Room in Mr Burns' mansion. It's where an elite theatre company perform productions on rotation to an empty theatre, just in case dear old Monty feels like sticking his head round the door once every so often. While, in one way, this is an unfair comparison, as Prince Albert is a virtual ever present at home matches, it's hard to see how the club survives in this oasis from football's oxygen of glory and fervour.

I'm unshaven and a touch hungover when I meet John Collins at Heathrow Airport on a spring Sunday evening, throwing his tidy, suave appearance into particularly sharp relief. Collins officially retired from playing in summer 2003, but give or take the odd fleck of grey in his hair he doesn't look a day older than he did in his heyday for Celtic, Everton and Scotland. And, of course, Monaco. He arrived at the Louis II in 1996 having played 250 games in six seasons at Celtic, and was one of the first major free moves following the Bosman ruling, and 'the first British player to move under it', as he's quick to point out. When choosing to leave Celtic, it had been widely expected than Collins would follow the well-trodden route of so many of his compatriots, south to England, but he had been carefully weighing up his options. 'Monaco called,' he remembers, 'and I went over (to talk). I was impressed.' After just a few minutes in his company, it's clear that Collins has no truck with the notorious parochialism of most British footballers. 'It was a great opportunity to try something totally new.'

Collins ended up spending two seasons in Ligue 1. His Monaco team won Le Championnat in his first season there and though they didn't retain their title, they reached the Champions League semi-final in the following campaign. It's easy to forget the quality of the teams Collins played in at Monaco – the distinction between teams being important as the club immediately sold five of their title-winning side, including the top scorer Sonny Anderson and Emmanuel Petit. It makes his achievement in not only adapting remarkably well as a

British player abroad, but in becoming a mainstay while surrounded by such talent, highly impressive. This season's Monaco team have been drawing universal plaudits for their exciting football, but when I ask Collins what he thinks of the current side, he unflinchingly and unapologetically shoots back that they 'aren't as good individually as my team was.'

It's hard to argue. From Fabien Barthez between the sticks, through the almost metronomic Franck Dumas at the back and the incomparable Ali Bernabia feeding Anderson, they were top class all the way from front to back. The post-title exodus in 1997 then gave young players like Thierry Henry and David Trezeguet the opportunity to come to the fore and begin to assert their own quality. Despite the 1998 Champions League run, Collins seems to remember the title-winning team of the previous season most fondly. He revelled playing as part of a then-little-used midfield diamond, employed by coach Jean Tigana and spearheaded by the lavishly gifted Bernabia. 'He was the same sort of player as Zidane, just amazing,' he says with barely concealed awe.

It was in the 97/98 Champions League campaign, however, that Henry and Trezeguet began to cut their teeth on the big stage, with Henry netting seven goals in the competition and Trezeguet scoring four. Even as raw talents they were able to turn matches, as they did most notably when recovering from two down at half-time to defeat Sporting Lisbon at Stade Louis II in a crucial group match (Trezeguet scoring once and Henry scoring twice). To his credit, Collins doesn't attempt to spin the 'I always knew he was going to be world-class' line about either player. He instead remembers that Henry 'sometimes kept his head down a bit (much) when he was running. He always had good physical attributes though.'

Ligue 1 is, on the whole, a young league. French teams don't have the financial clout to compete with the biggest in Europe and take full advantage of the products of their largely excellent academy systems. The average age of a French Ligue 1 team is 24. Monaco made up for most of what they lacked in experience that season in skill and enthusiasm, but that lack of experience meant that like other young teams thrust into the top level of European competition, they were learning on the job. Looking back on their 2001 Champions League run, few remember Leeds United's four-goal humbling at the hands of Barcelona in the Camp Nou, at the very beginning of the group stage. Likewise, the team representing the French champions had a baptism of fire, going down 3-0 in Lisbon to Sporting first up. Collins almost shudders at the memory. 'The pitch was horrendous, which didn't help. They'd had a pop concert there the previous weekend.'

But learn they did. Though Collins clearly thinks highly of Tigana – having of course joined him at Fulham in the latter days of his career – he points out that it wasn't the coach who necessarily led from the front. 'He was very quiet, very laidback. The training and the preparation was unbelievable though, fantastic.' Instead, senior players like him would provide the motivation. 'There were quite a few leaders in the team.' This helped Monaco to pull off one of the biggest shocks of the tournament, beating Manchester United at the quarter-final stage. 'That was the ultimate, without a doubt,' Collins says. After the first leg, a goalless draw at the Louis II, the hosts were the clear favourites to go through at Old Trafford. The experienced Tigana, meanwhile, was characteristically unfazed by the situation. 'He was very calm. He told everyone that the tie was 60-40 in our favour.' Proving how canny their coach was, the Monégasques eventually went through on the away goal rule after Trezeguet had struck early on to stun the 50,000-plus crowd.

Collins' thoughts on the semi-final with Juventus are tinged with a little regret – he missed the first leg in Turin, where his team were heavily beaten (4-1), suspended for cautions accrued in previous rounds of the competition. 'When you're suspended, you tend not to travel (with the squad). I watched it on TV at home, which was terrible,' he explains through a grimace. So how good exactly were this Juventus team, stacked with stars like Alessandro Del Piero, Zinedine Zidane, Edgar Davids and current Monaco coach Didier Deschamps? 'Not *that* good, to be honest,' he remarks, matter-of-factly. The return wasn't as comfortable as the Italians might have hoped or expected. Despite taking an early lead, they found themselves behind to another Henry goal in the second half, an equaliser from Del Piero rendering the Croat Robert Spehar's goal that won it on the night ultimately irrelevant. 'We pummelled them, especially after the second (Henry's) goal,' insists Collins. 'Their 'keeper had to make loads of saves, and we really could have won it (the tie). The wry look of 'what if?' on the Scotsman's face is clear.

That home leg against Juventus was attended by just 15,000 spectators – the Louis II holds 18,500. Maybe Monaco would have pulled in a few more on that occasion in '98 had they managed a more encouraging first leg result in Turin, but the fact remains that for a semi-final tie against one of the biggest clubs in Europe (and indeed the world) in a competition based around glitz, glamour and the big occasion, 15,000 is hardly a clamour. 'Because the fans don't push you forward, the motivation has to come from within,' says Collins. French journalist Xavier Rivoire is sceptical. 'It's a very romantic idea that you find this energy, this drive from within. But these guys are pampered. They can go out at night without getting hassled. You can park your Ferrari in front of the casino, then you go to the training ground and you can see the sea. It's not like playing in Siberia in front of 200 people.' Collins does have a theory, however, that Monaco can use the lack of a big match atmosphere to their advantage. 'Monaco's not the usual atmosphere the big teams are used to. Big players like tension, they like that edge. Instead when they come to Monaco, they think 'this is nice,' and so are maybe a bit off their guard.'

Even bearing in mind the presence of royal assent, it's difficult to see how AS Monaco sustains itself in the light of such indifference. Last summer, it looked as if it might finally catch up with them. On Wednesday May 28, the LFP (Ligue de Football Professionnel) announced that despite finishing 2002/3 as Ligue 1 runners-up, just a point behind champions Lyon, Monaco were to be relegated on financial grounds, with reports saying club president Jean-Louis Campora had failed to provide the necessary guarantees to officials. The LFP has some of the strictest solvency criteria for its member clubs in European football, unlike in say England or Spain where high-profile clubs regularly maintain sizeable debts. Monaco's official debts were given as around the €53 million (£38 million) mark, but many media and financial pundits posted estimates of anything up to €87 million (over £62 million).

Campora had always insisted that the club's opulent image was a myth and it seemed he was being proved right. The wide range of guesses to the club's liabilities only hinted at the level of financial chaos enveloping the club. In October 2002 reports surfaced in French newspapers that Monaco had borrowed up to €170 million (over £120 million) to offset debts and losses incurred in two years' absence from European competition. Then in December, with the team top of the league, the club couldn't pay the players. As the team enjoyed a great season, eventually winning the League Cup and of course achieving automatic qualification to the Champions League, the money problems were almost forgotten about until this rude awakening from the LFP.

Characteristically, Prince Albert stepped into to save the day. He was only really able to act as a intermediary, organising a rescue package – again as part of its financial controls, the French league limits the extent to which a local authority, in this case the Principality, can subsidise its team – but his intervention allowed the club to present €25 million (£18 million) worth of guarantees, much of it from the Albert-endorsed Monaco Football Investment group. In the light of this, the FFF (Federation Francaise de Football) accepted the club's appeal against relegation in June, although emphasising that any player recruitment would be 'controlled.' Campora stepped down after 28 years at the helm to be replaced by Pierre Svara, who was from an administrative background and also thought to be closely linked to Prince Albert.

The role of the team itself in this escape was considerable. Their qualification for the Champions League and the revenue that goes with it meant that the size of the guarantees the club had to provide for the FFF were much lower than they would have been otherwise. Talking on the day after the LFP's original decision to relegate the club, Prince Albert couldn't have been any clearer about the credit he gave the team: 'I can't accept letting down the players who have proved their attachment to Monaco.' The team's spirit was becoming the stuff of legend. Players like Jerome Rothen, captain Ludovic Giuly and Shabani Nonda could have had their pick from a plethora of Europe's top clubs had they decided to leave the stricken ASM, but they pledged to stay and fight on. Their resolve and commitment was personified by Nonda, Ligue 1's 26-goal top scorer, and his decision to reject a move to Lyon after the champions had a €15 million (£10.7 million) bid for him accepted.

Yet, just like Take That, they're not invincible. Nonda was a victim of the fickle finger of fate when, having started the new season much as he finished the old (scoring 4 in the first 3 games), he suffered an injury to his cruciate knee ligament in the early on in the 4-2 win over Paris Saint-Germain at the Parc des Princes. Having effectively lost their main striker for the season in only its fourth game, the Monégasques were going to have to try and replace him. Bearing in mind the lack of money at the club and the 'controlled recruitment' clause placed on them when the FFF approved their appeal against demotion, together with the short time before the transfer deadline, it was difficult to see how they would be able to find, let alone afford, a satisfactory stand-in. Enter Fernando Morientes.

Morientes had a tough old season in 2002/3. Here was an international striker of some pedigree, having up to the beginning of that season scored 20 goals while collecting 30 Spanish caps. He had been a distinguished performer for Real Madrid too since joining them from Real Zaragoza in 1997, scoring 89 times in just over 200 league and Champions League games. He was highly popular with fans and team-mates (being down with the now-infamous Bernabéu dressing-room clique of Raúl, Gutí etc) alike for his whole-hearted style.

Then Real president Florentino Pérez, always with an eye open for a marketing opportunity, moved to sign Ronaldo from Inter Milan. The Brazilian who made it back from the injury wilderness to be top scorer in the 2002 World Cup expressed a need to start again after putting four years of struggle behind him, and El Real were in on the situation quicker than an alcoholic going through a pub's door at opening time. When Inter reluctantly sold, Morientes' first-team place disappeared overnight. The club's superstar-weighted politics meant Ronaldo would always play when fit and 'El Moro' was cast aside. His frustration grew such that when coach Vicente Del Bosque told him to get ready to come on as a substitute in a Champions League game against Borussia Dortmund at the Bernabéu in February 2003, the striker shouted at Del Bosque in front of a shocked first few rows behind the touchline exactly where he could stick his ten-minute run out.

Clearly the purchase of Morientes would have been well beyond Monaco's current limited means, but hours before the Champions League deadline for registering players (and the closing of the European transfer window), Didier Deschamps persuaded the Spaniard to come to the Louis II on a year's loan. Monaco's Ligue 1 rivals were not best pleased. It brought to a head an ongoing complaint by leading French clubs that Monaco enjoyed unfair advantages over their fellow clubs – while it's not necessary to pay tax in the separate state of the Principality, France's income taxes are some of the highest in Europe. Therefore, as Lyon's Jean-Michel Aulas (a rival, incidentally, for Morientes' signature) pointed out, Monaco could afford to pay players up to twice what others could. Marseille president Christophe Bouchet had already called for UEFA to grant the French league an extra Champions League place in the event of Monaco qualifying, as they 'take a Champions League place away from other French clubs', and Aulas has called for Monaco to be charged a fee to enter Ligue 1 at the start of every season. Certainly the idea of a club on the brink of bankruptcy being able to bring in an international star two months later is faintly ridiculous. As Xavier Rivoire says, 'They (i.e. the players who come to Monaco) are almost mercenaries. I'm not saying they're not great players or there's not a great footballing history there. Basically in my mind, you sign for Monaco for the money above everything else. Say you're a great name of European football, say Morientes. Milan and Monaco come to talk to you. Who would you go for? Milan, from a sporting point of view, anytime, every single time. But if you can make double the money at Monaco, you start thinking maybe Monaco is not that bad.' That Monaco's unique circumstance makes such deals possible hints at why they may have got themselves in such trouble in the past, living beyond their means.

In the event, Morientes is unfit to take his place in the team when we arrive just before kick-off for the game against his countrymen Deportivo La Coruña at the Louis II, still hampered by the groin injury which has troubled him this week. After taking escalators to our level of the stand (a first for me, anyway), it's clear how unfamiliar they are with crowds here. There's nearly 16,000 here tonight, and we almost miss the kick-off – we are kept queuing for our seats by a single steward in his late sixties or early seventies with the manner of a senile nightclub bouncer, allowing us through one at a time at funereal pace. The atmosphere tells you that this is a stadium full of non-regulars, being lively enough without displaying the passion that you get on European nights at grounds like Marseille, Lens or Lyon. (I'm later reminded of this by Xavier Rivoire's comment that 'many go to Monaco (games in the Champions League) 'for the spectacle, just because a French team's in it').

We haven't even sat down when, two minutes in, Manuel Pablo's poor back-header gives Rothen the chance to intelligently loft the ball high over the head of visiting goalkeeper José Molina and into the net. Surprisingly, it's only the winger's first goal of the campaign. The ticketing and stewarding arrangements are clearly a bit of a shambles and we've only found a step to perch on rather than a seat by the time Monaco score a second. Giuly speeds on to Lucas Bernardi's pass through one of the least convincing offside traps I've seen in a while, rounds Molina and gleefully rolls home. By the time Dado Prso has taken advantage of the freedom of the six-yard box to head in a third, we've sussed that the best view in the lower tier is to go and sit on the steps at the very back. We're twenty minutes in.

This is crazy. This young Monaco team are playing Deportivo La Coruña, one of Europe's most consistent sides. This is the fourth successive season that Depor have been in the Champions League, and last season was the first of those in which they didn't reach the quarter-finals (and then only missed out on head-to-head records after finishing on the same points as the second and third placed teams). This sort of thing doesn't happen to them. On the half-hour Monaco's Gäel Givet heads a horribly shanked clearance by Depor's Jorge Andrade across goal for Prso to nod his second. The huge Croat – celebrating his 29th birthday tonight – goes nuts, as well he might. He wouldn't have even started tonight had Morientes (or of course Nonda) been fit, but he's making the most of his chance. Though not in Deschamps' first-choice starting line-up, Prso is never less than whole-hearted and scored 12 important league goals during his sporadic appearances last season. He always seems an all-round top guy and is thoroughly deserving of his moment.

Depor's reaction is pure knee-jerk. Having pretty much lost the game in the first 30 minutes, their response betrays the quality they possess but haven't shown this evening. Diego Tristán's free-kick draws a fine save from the impressive home 'keeper Flavio Roma, then minutes later he spins his marker, Julien Rodriguez, and drills a shot through Roma's legs. No-one in the stands harbours the thought that this is any more than a consolation, but on the stroke of half-time Tristán again forces Roma to parry a left-foot shot and the Argentine Lionel Scaloni sweeps in the rebound to make it 4-2.

Suddenly the Galicians smell blood, and when Roma can only push out a left-wing cross it takes a linesman's flag to halt the panic in the Monaco box. Amazingly, there's still time for a great twist to the half as – surprise – Giuly's direct running again exposes Depor's high back line and he squares for Prso to tap in his hat-trick goal. Depor must be kicking themselves as the half-time whistle goes, while Morientes – watching in the stands with his buddy Raúl – probably is too, thinking about the havoc he could have wreaked had he made the game. On the touchline Deschamps looks more than a little uncomfortable, having endured 45 minutes of the sort that no coach should have to go through too often in his career.

This is Deschamps to type, a selfless worker as a player, and (like Tigana before him) young enough and close enough to his players to feel their every move. 'He understands his players totally,' says Xavier Rivoire. When you think of players becoming managers and head coaches, his is perhaps one of the least surprising successes. It wasn't easy at the beginning. 'He was lucky to stay after his first season, when they finished 15th,' remembers Rivoire. At that point all the talk was of dressing room mutiny and Deschamps being out of his depth trying to get the attention of a group of established stars of the same age group – he was only 32 years old, having just retired from playing, when he got the job. Maybe it's easier for him to mould a younger group of players, many of whom probably watched him lift the 1998 World Cup and 2000 European Championship as France captain on TV at home, and with his triumphs fresh in the memory making him the ultimate living legend. John Collins rightly points out that 'it's one thing getting the players' respect, it's quite another keeping it.' Deschamps does though have the distinction of being probably the most decorated French player ever, and aside from his exploits with France, his achievements in domestic and European football are beyond compare. As well as winning French and Italian titles (playing in England and Spain too), there are the two Champions Leagues with Marseille and Juventus to his name, besides another two Champions League final appearances with Juve. If any coach can thoroughly prepare his team for the rigours of the Champions League today, it must be him.

The coach's bright thinking was certainly there to see in the first half, as he worked Morientes' absence to his team's advantage.

'El Moro' is usually the man to link the forward play for Monaco, so Deschamps has gone direct and used Giuly more centrally, where his pace has given the hosts much of their success tonight. Gustavo Munúa replaces Molina at the break after the latter's first-half nightmare, but Depor's interval team talk looks as if it went in one ear and out the other. A minute in to the second-half and another Giuly run again exposes the static Spanish defence. Munúa runs out to head clear, only for the young Czech midfielder Jaroslav Plasil to lob the ball back over the head of the prone 'keeper and two covering defenders – a beautiful-looking goal from our new vantage point, by the bar on the upper tier. Depor barely have time to regroup before Rothen rampages down to the left and pulls back to Prso, who takes a touch before blasting in his fourth. Prso by now is even running out of goal celebrations on the night of his life and runs to the crowd to execute a lamentable machine gun-style effort. The normally-staid Stade Louis II is now exploding with joy, knowing they're watching a great performance metamorphose into something monumental.

Depor refuse to cave in completely, and before long Tristán slaloms a couple of challenges before cleverly lifting it over Roma, but this time there will be no comeback. Midfielder Edouard Cissé – who memorably told yesterday's edition of *L'Equipe* that 'a draw (would be) a good result' in this game – finishes the night off with 20 minutes left by running from the halfway line, leaving the experienced Mauro Silva on his backside before steering number eight past Munúa from 20 yards. Though a lap of honour at the end of a group win that doesn't even result in certain qualification is unheard of, it's entirely justified in this case.

It's impossible to react objectively – Rothen calls it 'historic', Prso says 'it's magic. It's not as if we beat Luxembourg', while poor Depor coach Javier Irureta says that he's 'never seen a match that was so difficult to explain.' We can only laugh all the way back to Nice, where we're staying, while the great Ronaldo, watching at home on TV, admits the following day that 'it was great to watch. I was laughing the whole time.

Though maybe I wouldn't have found it so funny if I had been playing (for Depor).' Yet even when I meet Deschamps for the first time, a few months later in Moscow, he struggles with an explanation. 'You can't judge other performances against that. It was once-in-a-lifetime. We played at an incredible level that night, one that we won't reach again.'

Never were all the paradoxes of AS Monaco clearer than in this one November night. I've never seen a match like it, and – one for the romantics – neither have I seen a team create such a passion in a stadium. With the reprieve from demotion and with this young team, Monaco are starting again. Although with it being Monaco, they're not starting again from the bottom, just from the group stage of the Champions League. Theirs is an exceptional case, and covers the full range of the Champions League's rewards and pitfalls. Their absence from the competition was a major contributory factor in their problems, but now it promises, with a little help from the work of their team, to be their saviour.

Borussia Dortmund

It was one of those thrillingly unpredictable moments, a microcosm of how great the Champions League can be. The lean legs of Andres Mendoza were eating up the San Siro turf, leaving the AC Milan defence trailing in their wake. Without breaking stride, the Peruvian rifled home a stinging left-footer to give his side a first-half lead. They held that lead, and recorded an amazing win at the home of the European champions. Borussia Dortmund's players must have barely been able to look.

It wasn't meant to be like this. For Club Brugge, getting into the Champions League group stages represented a sizeable coup. The opportunity to rub shoulders with the mighty Milan, along with Ajax and Celta Vigo, was great enough – the sort of contests that distil what the competition is all about - but victory in Italy was just unbelievable. There's nothing like defeat in a Champions League qualifier to flatten a team's season before it's really started, and Brugge's win in Milan last month would have brought it all flooding back for the Germans.

That Borussia Dortmund (or BVB – *Ballspiel Verein Borussia* – the name with which they were founded in 1909) were knocked out of the Champions League at the qualifying stage was bad enough. To be knocked out in front of their home crowd at the Westfalenstadion was even worse. But to be put out by an supposedly inferior opponent on penalties was absolutely soul-destroying. BVB would well have reason to regret this. It was a costly slip. Failing to qualify for the Champions League is always expensive, but when you've actually budgeted for the season on the proviso that the team will qualify for the competition, you're in trouble.

When I take the train into Dortmund city centre on the day of the home game against Bayer Leverkusen, the November air is distinctly lacking in the smell of crisis. It's only midday, but there are fans in BVB's distinctive yellow colours everywhere already. The *Hauptbahnhof* (main station) itself is packed, with people singing, honking claxons and waving flags. There's a whole lot of drinking going on too. There are one or two smallish bars, but mostly fans are just drinking in the street. I see people in pairs or groups of four, from teenagers upwards, carrying around full crates of beer, backing up the stereotypes about Germans' quite heroic levels of ale consumption.

While we're on the subject of stereotypes, there are no concessions to fashion amongst the fans either. There's a heavy penchant for sporting denim waistcoats, embroidered with club badges. Many of these waistcoats have amusing badges mocking other Bundesliga clubs sewn on. Unsurprisingly Bayern Munich are a frequent target – patches I spot are annotated with the likes of 'FC Bayern – *nein danke*', 'Piss off Bayern'. I struggle not to laugh out loud when I see one such patch depicting a pig, with a speech bubble saying '*Ich bin Lothar's bruder*', in tribute to the German World Cup-winning captain.

I try to imagine what a scene like this would be in England, and the answer, frankly, is carnage. I can't ever remember being in an atmosphere where there was such a large concentration of people drinking such large amounts and not feeling even vaguely threatened. Football fans attract not a bat of an eyelid from 'normal' people in the town, like shoppers, of which there are plenty - the centre is already beautifully decorated for Christmas and bustling with people in general. The football club is clearly a huge and indelible part of the local community.

The fans are a good place to start looking at Borussia Dortmund. They are, after all, pretty much all that's stopping the club completely falling to pieces at the moment. The club's ground, the Westfalenstadion, is always more or less sold out, come rain or shine. This is some achievement given that the last phase of the stadium's expansion - completed in May 2002 - brought its capacity up to an enormous 82,000. The focal point of this is undoubtedly the Südtribhüne, the end behind one of the goals that is Europe's largest terrace with a capacity of 25,000 (for international and European matches, terracing isn't allowed of course, so the overall capacity drops to 67,000 for those games). Quite apart from the idea of the faithful keeping the spirit alive with their passion, the fact is that if creditors weren't looking at a club that could bank on a full house every fortnight, Borussia Dortmund would probably be completely screwed already.

Uli Hesse-Lichtenberger, the author of *Tor!*, a history of the German game (named after the German word for 'goal'), has been one of these fans all his life. Though I only speak to him over the telephone, I feel like he's resignedly shaking his head throughout our conversation about his club's current predicament. 'The club just became a bit… meglomanic,' he sighs. 'They spent over €100 million over the last three years on players, which is a huge amount for a German club.' Pricier signings include Tomas Rosicky, Jan Koller and Marcio Amoroso (the latter costing €22 million alone). This spending is on top of the €35 million pledged to the third stage of expanding the Westfalenstadion.

It's the sort of spending which speaks volumes of a club that assumes success. And which, subsequently, cannot get by without it. The fact that the failure to qualify for the group stages of the Champions League cost the club at least €15 million is no secret. Yet how dire the club's finances actually were didn't start to become clear until managing director Michael Meier started talking about the possibility of 'variable' salaries for the players. By the end of September an announcement from the club said that the squad had agreed to a 20% pay cut. President Gerd Niebaum was clear that the players were 'not actually relinquishing their pay,' but freezing it pending a point where 'the players achieve the appropriate success.' Niebaum also praised his players for taking 'remarkable responsibility for their failures on the field.'

It sounds cosy, but it wasn't quite like that. 'Basically, the players were blackmailed into it,' Uli says bluntly. 'The negotiations were 'mysteriously' leaked to the press beforehand.' Hence Meier thinking out loud rather than making an official statement regarding the pay situation. The negotiations in fact hinted at a bigger split in the camp. German tabloids reported that the overseas players at the club initially refused the cut, before an agreement was finally reached. Either way, the episode showed us a desperate club up to its neck in trouble.

It all makes 1997 seem like such a long time ago. This is when Borussia Dortmund won the Champions League for the first and only time[1]. It was part of a golden era for the club. They went into the 96/97 European campaign having won two successive Bundesliga titles. In this context, Paul Lambert was a surprise signing. He had received his first cap for Scotland a year previously in a friendly against Japan but was pretty much unheard of outside his homeland. What began as a blind step into the unknown ended with Lambert becoming the first British player to win the trophy since 1984 (when Liverpool won it) and the first to even appear in the final since the year after (when the same team lost in the ill-fated Heysel final).

Lambert was instantly notable in Britain for playing abroad at all. It was (and still is) a rare choice for a British player to make. He must have had to turn down a plethora of offers from south of the border to make the big step off the island when his contract at Motherwell expired in the summer of 1996.

'No.' Paul Lambert is disarmingly honest. 'There was nothing happening really and Tom Van Daalen phoned me.' Van Daalen was an agent who had fixed a move for Rob Mackinnon, who Lambert played with at Motherwell, to the Dutch side Twente Enschede. Lambert wanted to see if Van Daalen might be able to get him something similar. The agent asked for ten days to sort something out, and came back to Lambert ten days later exactly, with two trials to offer the midfielder. 'I expected two small teams,' he remembers. 'They were PSV (Eindhoven) and Dortmund.'

After a fruitless trial in Eindhoven - '(PSV coach) Dick Advocaat told me he just didn't need another centre midfielder' – he drove up to Dortmund with Van Daalen, where they met Michael Meier. '(We) had an agreement (that) for five days I couldn't sign for anyone else, or train with anyone else. I had nothing else, so I didn't have anything to lose.' So Lambert drove up with Meier to Lübeck (in the north) to meet the team, who were coming from a pre-season training camp in Lucerne, Switzerland. It started to dawn on him that he was in at the deep end. 'It was off the back of (Germany's win at) Euro 96. (Their) plane was mobbed by Dortmund fans. I started to wonder 'What am I doing here?'' Not that the size of the club itself had been any particular shock to Lambert. 'I knew it was a massive club because Motherwell had played them in the UEFA Cup.' If he was under any doubts at the size of the task facing him over the next few days, it was put into sharp focus when he got on the team bus. 'There was Stefan Reuter, Stefan Klos, Lars Ricken, Jörg Heinrich, Andy Möller, Jurgen Köhler, (and) back in Dortmund Paolo Sousa (freshly-signed '96 Champions League winner) and Karl-Heinz Riedle.' They also had Matthias Sammer, rated by many as the best player at Euro 96, and who would go on to win the European Footballer of the Year trophy in 1997. Still, it could have been harder. 'Stefan Freund hurt his knee in Euro 96 so I got to play in the centre,' Lambert remembers of the start of the trial period.

However, Lambert thought his big chance was over before it had really begun. In the pre-season Fuji Cup (played between Germany's top four clubs) he played in the opener against local rivals Schalke before being injured after only 25 minutes in the following match against Borussia Mönchengladbach. 'I thought 'That's it, I've blown it.' Then on the Friday before they played Leverkusen in the first Bundesliga game of the season they said 'the contract's ready, just go and sign it.'' Lambert had just turned 27. The real work had only just begun.

'You had to (improve),' he agrees, 'otherwise you wouldn't have got a game, I don't think. You were playing with some guys who'd won the World Cup, as well as Serie A, the Bundesliga, they'd won everything in sight.' He raises his eyebrows in still-intact incredulity.

'And I'm coming from Motherwell, so you just think 'hold your own'.' Nevertheless, he wasn't expected to fill a greater role than that of squad player. 'To be fair, I played in the Leverkusen game, the first game, and we got beat 4-2. Ottmar (Hitzfeld, BVB coach) said to me – and I scored in the game funnily enough – 'listen, you've done well, but we've bought Paolo Sousa from Juventus for about £7 million. If he's fit, if his knee's ok, then he's going to play,' which was fine. I never expected to play in the first place. We played Düsseldorf on the Tuesday and Paolo's knee didn't stand up to the fitness test. I played in that, won 4-0, and it just snowballed.' The transition from supporting actor to leading role was necessarily swift. 'You were constantly in the side, and then you were looked upon as one of them.' Lambert's performances dismissed any ideas he would be out his depth, but he had never been required to pass any 'test' by the established stars in the first place. 'Even when (I was) on trial, every one of them came and said 'good luck, hope you get your contract.' Never any jealousy or anything like that.'

Being thrust into the thick of it also meant being catapulted virtually straight away into the Champions League as well, with the campaign starting in the second week of September. BVB had no real history to speak of in the competition - their best achievements in Europe had been winning the 1966 Cup Winners' Cup, beating Liverpool in the final, and more recently a UEFA Cup final defeat to Juventus in 1993. Expectation had been raised considerably, however, by successive Bundesliga titles and reaching the Champions League quarter-finals the previous year, to be defeated by holders and eventual runners-up Ajax. The team negotiated the group stage without too many scares, in a group overwhelmingly dominated by the Germans and Atlético Madrid. After that they made surprisingly short work of reaching the final in defeating first Auxerre and then Manchester United, beating both teams in both the home and away legs. For a British player, beating United usually feels like a cast-iron promise of success to come, but Lambert was already quietly confident. Having had to adapt to such a high level, he knew the calibre of what was around him. 'I had the feeling we would win either the league (they eventually finished third) or the Champions League, looking round the dressing room at the other players,' he nods. 'I thought it's going to take something to beat us. As soon as we beat Auxerre away, I just felt in myself, we've got a really good chance of winning this.' The semi-final dispatch of Manchester United was so (relatively) comfortable after Lars Ricken's early goal in the second leg at Old Trafford gave BVB an overall two-goal lead, that it's almost just a footnote in the struggle for the trophy.

The final was, however, a different kettle of fish entirely. Juventus weren't just the holders, and the team that had snuffed out BVB's best previous effort to capture a European trophy, but they were one of the most successful clubs in Europe having just won the Italian title for the 25th time in the club's history. Then there was the team itself. Lambert raises the eyebrows and exhales again. 'Look at their team. Jesus. Peruzzi, Montero, Deschamps, Jugovic, Boksic, Vieri, Del Piero comes off the bench, Di Livio. It was an incredible team.' Nor were they particularly shy about the fact. 'When were walking out the tunnel, Di Livio had the score on his hand – 3-1. Big black writing on his hand, and I looked over for some reason.' Given the irony of this in retrospect, it's no wonder that this is one of the moments that sticks in Lambert's mind.

You could focus on the incident as something that would channel the mind in a moment of high tension, but although Lambert admits to a few nerves – 'Stefan Klos is sitting one side and I'm sitting on the other side. I can just see his knee going up and down.' – the mood amongst the squad was as normal as could be expected. The Scot seems to have drawn his own confidence from the poise and the professionalism of those around him. 'On the bus, nobody speaks. To be fair, it was always like that on a match day, no one really speaking. It was a big, big game and they were big, big players who'd been through it all before.'

Even though playing in their own country (in Munich's Olympiastadion) the Germans were still highly unfancied. There is, however, nothing to make a final go with a swing like the underdogs getting the first goal. Lambert set it up -'a diagonal ball to the back post, like the coach had been talking about before the game', which Riedle controlled and finished in style. 'Getting the first goal was vital for us,' Lambert agrees. This was just before the half-hour, and five minutes later the lead was doubled when Riedle sent a trademark bullet header into the top corner from Möller's corner.

Juve seemed affronted by BVB's cheek in defying them, something never more apparent than in their extended protests at the Hungarian referee Puhl's (correct) decision to rule out a Vieri effort late in the first half for handball. I mention to Lambert that I saw a re-run of the game on Eurosport a few months back. The co-commentator, ex-Northern Ireland manager Bryan Hamilton, seemed to share their offence, constantly complaining that 'Juventus shouldn't be losing' throughout. Lambert is unsurprised. 'That to me sums up the British Isles mentality. They don't know the Germans, their footballers, they don't what it's like working with them.' You can sense his irritation at the way German teams are derided for their efficiency, their achievements belittled as the work of mere spoilers. For the record, BVB scored exactly the same amount of goals on the road to the final (20) as the Juventus of Vieri, Zidane, Boksic and company.

The Italians did eventually pull a goal back twenty minutes into the second half. It was a goal justifying the pre-final hype, Boksic's low left-wing cross being imperiously guided home by the substitute Del Piero's back-heel. Paul Lambert's football life flashed before his eyes. 'When Del Piero scores – you think 'fuck'. You look at the clock and just say 'please', because you know this is the biggest tournament you're ever gonna be involved in.' He need not have worried. Just six minutes later Dortmund's own sub, the 20-year-old Ricken, ran onto a through pass before sending an outrageous chip over Peruzzi from 25 yards. It's amazing to watch a replay of the goal. The ball seems to hang in the air for an eternity before dropping in. God knows what it must have felt like watching it on the same pitch.

It was the most emphatic of denouements. 'When we went back to the centre (after the goal) I just knew in their faces they weren't going to come back. That's when I knew that we'd got it.' It's still the moment Lambert recalls most vividly from the game itself. Less than half an hour later Jurgen Köhler was lifting the trophy to proclaim Borussia Dortmund as champions of Europe.

Lambert had had the season of a lifetime, but the midfielder didn't stay around to bask in the glory of the Champions League win for too long. His young son had been ill and the family made the decision to move back to Scotland in November 1997. 'My last game there (at the Westfalen) was emotional,' he admits, unashamedly. Fittingly, it was a Champions League game. 'We played Parma, and the fans all gave me a standing ovation. There were banners saying 'Thanks for everything' and 'Good luck'. I was nearly crying – (I did a) lap of honour and the stadium was still full. At midnight, when I signed the release forms, I thought 'what am I doing?' My wife was back (in Scotland) and she'd seen the game, she was crying.' It was overwhelming. 'For the first two months I was back, I couldn't do anything right. I had a nightmare, because my head was still done in, because of the send-off.' He shakes his head as he remembers 'getting back to my car, hundreds of people crying and draping it with goodbye messages.'

The club struggled to maintain the upward curve after the triumph. Hitzfeld immediately moved upstairs to become sporting director (he became coach of Bayern Munich the following year) and was replaced by the experienced Italian Nevio Scala. Scala turned out to be the first of five coaches the club would have used by the year 2000 - he only lasted a year himself, the team reaching the Champions League semi-finals but finishing a disastrous 10th in the league. In the 1999/00 season BVB actually went dangerously close to relegation, eventually being steered to the safety of 14th place by the management team of Udo Lattek and Matthias Sammer. Sammer the playing legend quickly became Sammer the coaching legend, taking sole charge the following season. He took the club first back into the Champions League, and then to a third Bundesliga title in 2002, the same year the team bravely slipped to UEFA Cup final defeat against Feyenoord – played in their own De Kuip stadium - having played most of the game with 10 men.

The period following the Champions League win is when the club started to overstretch itself, thinks Uli Hesse-Lichtenberger. 'Maybe they shouldn't have really gone for it in 1999,' he ruminates, with a degree of understatement. There really is no competition that makes clubs spend money they don't have like the Champions League, but in Germany the devil on your shoulder is looking south. 'One of the problems in Germany is that there is Bayern,' sighs Uli. Bayern's rule over German football has been virtually absolute since the late '60s/ early '70s. Even though the Bundesliga is one of the most open in Europe, Bayern are always there or thereabouts. 'They might not win it for a season or maybe two, but they always come back.'

With an eye on Bayern's domination, BVB made perhaps its worst mistake in October 2000. This is when the club became the first in Germany to go public. 'Dortmund overreached in hindsight,' Uli says. 'Bayern Munich have always said they would never float the company. It's considered the last resort, desperation. Bayern just can't be emulated. They have been at the top for more than 30 years.'

Having made that futile attempt to match Bayern, BVB have now been reduced to pinning their hopes on the UEFA Cup. Even that's not looking too smooth. At the beginning of the month, they found themselves two goals down to French side Sochaux at the Westfalen before rescuing a draw. They travel to Montbéliard for the second round tie's return leg next week badly needing a result. If they fail, tabloid estimates claim the entire season's losses could stretch to anything up to a colossal €50 million.

The current tale of woe has its root before the Bruges defeat. It goes back to the last day of last season, which Dortmund started off in second place in the Bundesliga – which guarantees automatic Champions League qualification – and ended it in third after conceding a late equaliser to relegated wooden-spooners Energie Cottbus at the

Westfalen, and allowing Stuttgart to pip them. Dortmund's win at Eintracht Frankfurt at the start of last month was their first Bundesliga away win in eight months, and just to prove it wasn't about to become a habit, the team took a 3-0 pasting at nearby Bochum (hardly considered a serious local rival like Schalke) in the next trip. In the most recent game before last week's international break, BVB were hammered 4-1 at – you guessed it – Bayern Munich. Just as an excruciating Champions League qualifier defeat has turned Newcastle's Premiership season into a damp squib, Dortmund have struggled with the ennui of league chores, and Champions League qualification looks an optimistic hope even in November – they're already eight points off the pace, in fifth place.

This afternoon's task isn't much easier. The resurgent Bayer Leverkusen are the visitors to the Westfalen, having recovered from their own last day escape from relegation in May. Leverkusen are known for their own Champions League heroics of course, being unlucky losers to Real Madrid in 2002's Hampden Park final. They lack Michael Ballack and Zé Roberto from that team of course, both now at Bayern, though the familiar spine of Hans-Jörg Butt, Jens Nowotny (when fit), Lucio, Carsten Ramelow and company is still intact. They are now coached by 1990 World Cup winner Klaus Augenthaler, the man who successfully helped them scrape through the harrowing end to last season, and are now looking towards the Champions League once more.

True to form, the Westfalen is both full and fully behind the team when I arrive. Outside the ground, people congregate in large groups, singing heartily, drinking beer. Even coming from Scotland, Paul Lambert had been taken aback by the gusto with which the Germans embrace match day. 'They look at football as a massive day. You go to the Westfalen an hour before and it's full already.' The stadium is set in a nondescript industrial park but looks mightily impressive from the outside. Inside is even more spectacular, with the steep stands packed with people (the official attendance for today is 81,500). The Südtribhüne is amazing. It dwarfs the Kop, which was one of the

English game's greatest sights before Anfield became all seated. Viewed from the other end of the ground, it's hard to believe the vast expanse of collected heads under its roof only amounts to 25,000.

It's all very good natured as well. Friends sit side by side in Dortmund and Leverkusen shirts supping beers – naturally – with no hint of trouble or animosity (the official Dortmund website has some tremendous matchday stats detailing that 57,000 cups of beer and 12,000 grilled sausages are seen off in every game at the Westfalen). This is bearing in mind that this is an important game between two big teams in front of a huge crowd. These people know how to have a good time. When you go to the bars inside the stadium, local beers are served to you in sturdy plastic steins. The people sitting next to you make conversation, even if the language barrier limits it in my case – I begin to feel ashamed of my extremely basic German.

The game starts much as one might have predicted. The home side look scratchy and nervous, and struggle to get going, while Leverkusen move the ball about with confidence and authority. Yet just before the half-hour, Dortmund score against the run of play. The young striker Salvatore Gambino, only playing because of the extensive injury list (13 was last week's count), scores with a neat finish after side-stepping a defender. Gambino won't turn 20 until Thursday but swiftly helps himself to another early birthday present, controlling with his chest before cleverly lifting the ball over Butt from close range after man-mountain Koller muscles him some space in the six-yard box. It's hard to believe that BVB are two up after such a tepid showing in the opening half-hour. Maybe their luck is due a change.

Fat chance. Just a few minutes further on and the ball breaks to the hitherto quiet Oliver Neuville on the edge of the Dortmund penalty area, and he strikes home definitively. The loud cheers coming from sporadic patches all over the stadium show just how non-segregated the crowd is, and also that there are plenty of Leverkusen fans in today. It's also the cue for much resigned sighing from the Dortmund fans sat around me.

The pattern of play developing after half-time does nothing to soothe any nerves on either side. It's terrific, end-to-end stuff. Koller almost gives BVB breathing space again midway through the second half, but his superb chip hits the crossbar and bounces out with Butt reduced to the role of spectator. Rosicky wastes another chance to put them clear, shooting wide from ten yards when it looks easier to score. Further advantage does fall Dortmund's way in the 74th minute, when Leverkusen's Argentine defender Diego Placente receives a second yellow card for an off-the-ball incident. The visitors though take this blow in their stride, and four minutes later substitute Marko Babic sweeps the ball past Weidenfeller from 10 yards to level matters. It's too familiar, and demoralising for the home support. Nevertheless, when the final whistle goes they still stack up their plastic steins and return them to the bar – losing a two-goal lead is no excuse for littering, you know – before filing out in an orderly fashion.

Dortmund are now ten points behind leaders Stuttgart already. Coach Sammer is grateful for his team's efforts despite the injury list – unlike Augenthaler who chides his own side for being caught out by 'stupid breakaways' – but he knows that even in November, they are running out of chances already. Thursday's game at Sochaux just got bigger.

It's difficult to absorb the truth, that a club with these kind of crowds and fans this loyal can be in this much trouble. Their problems are thrown into sharp relief by events down the road in Gelsenkirchen, where Schalke have just received €75 million-worth of investment from the British investment bank Schechter. If they start splashing the cash in the transfer window, BVB's fall will be made to feel even more dramatic. This is a club tailor-made for the Champions League. But what are they without it?

Real Sociedad

'I'm fucked. Totally fucked.'

Sander Westerveld is not on top form. It's a marked contrast from when I met him for the first time yesterday in the lobby of my hotel. He greeted me with a cheery 'Alright mate?' and a firm handshake, in a display of friendliness not always common among professional footballers. He seemed genuinely interested in what I was doing over here, possibly just curious to see a rare English speaker in his city. Although he couldn't stop to chat as he had to go off for treatment on his ankle, he said I should come down to training the following day for a chat. At that point neither of us had any idea that around six hours later the goalkeeper would be picking the ball out of his net having been beaten by Jesus Capi, just four minutes into his team Real Sociedad's home game against Real Betis. We didn't know that Betis' nippy young winger Joaquín would slide a shot beneath his body ten minutes later as that stricken ankle folded under him, or that La Real would eventually crash to a 4-0 home defeat in an important scrap between two struggling sides. Now it's the morning after the night before and Westerveld is feeling down. He won't be the only one. Real Sociedad are looking pretty fucked right now.

Rarely can a team have gone to such lengths to screw an intended angle on them. You see, I came to praise Real Sociedad de Fútbol, not to bury them. From a distance they seemed the perfect case to batter the theory that only big clubs can prosper in the Champions League environment. They qualified for the competition for the first time thanks to their exploits last season, when they failed narrowly to pull off the greatest underdog triumph in European club football for many a year. They finished a single point behind eventual champions Real Madrid in a league that they were in with a shout of winning until the final day, having led it for much of the campaign. It was a Herculean effort from a team who narrowly escaped relegation in the previous season. They had been working under a new coach, Raynald Denoueix, but had kept almost exactly the same set of players, the only exception being Boris, the first non-Basque Spaniard to be signed by Sociedad. Such was the team's extraordinary success that the fuss that might have been expected over this landmark signing failed to materialise.

Theirs was a rare story, a genuine manifestation of the football fairytale, particularly when you consider it happened in La Liga, widely considered as the strongest domestic league in Europe and therefore the world. Leading such a championship for most of the season from the world's biggest club and arguably even its best team - the *galácticos* of Real Madrid - is impressive on its own. When you consider Real Sociedad are a club of limited resources with a history of modest achievement (two league championships won consecutively at the start of the '80s being their giddy pinnacle), who have traditionally been only the second biggest club in the 3 million populated Basque Country behind Athletic Bilbao, it's nothing short of astonishing. I thought that football might not be capable of these types of shocks anymore, and I've come here to get to the heart of this fairytale.

San Sebastián is, though, a fairly appropriate place for a fairytale to unfold. It's something of a hidden jewel, tucked away just 60km from the French border on the north western coast of Spain. The main body of the city is set just in from a picturesque bay, with a beach that's inviting even when we turn up in early December. Despite being in winter, it's around 17° and you're still ok to get your feet wet without getting frostbite. The city's main social centre, the old town, is welcoming too. It's stuffed full of lively, hospitable bars, all boasting huge selections of tapas on their counters. In the main square, the busy but still elegant Plaza de Zuloaga, families meet for coffee while their small children kick balls around in a suspiciously accomplished way. It's not exactly small, but it's compact enough to feel fairly closely-knit.

Walking around the old town, you see plenty of shops sporting scarves, pennants and flags in Sociedad's blue and white stripes, as well as posters advertising the next home game. I wonder whether it's always been like this or if local pride has been stirred by recent achievements. Perhaps it's an extension of regionalistic pride given that San Sebastián is situated at the very heart of the Basque country. Whatever, the impression you get from these displays together with local papers and snatches of conversations in bars is that people are still proud of the club despite their dismal form so far this season.

My guide through this intriguing town is Phil Ball. Phil's an English football writer best known for his book 'Morbo', which is the only English language history of Spanish football ever written. He's fairly well qualified on the subject of Real Sociedad having lived in San Sebastián for more than 12 years, so I thought that I'd pick his brains on the club and Basque football in general. Far from settling for giving me a couple of vox pops on the team and the region, he's the very definition of hospitality, taking me for a swift half before coming to the game with me, and giving me a lift to the training ground the following day too. Helpfully, he thoroughly knows his stuff and tells a great story too.

Even with as thorough background knowledge of the subject as is conceivable, Phil struggles to fully explain why last season's success happened – along with the rest of the locals. 'No-one could believe it. Everyone kept expecting a slip-up but it just never happened.' It's totally understandable. The glories of 2002-3 were not the work of a dark horse. Real Sociedad weren't an unknown quantity, like a promoted side for example might be – as mentioned before, they had virtually the same players as the year before – and they couldn't even have been considered a decent outside bet. The victory over Valladolid on the penultimate day of 2001-2 which ensured they stayed up, achieved under a hastily-assembled temporary management team, was just the tip of the iceberg. Not for nothing does the club's official history define the period of 1999-2002 as the 'difficult years'.

The man who led them out of it was Denoueix, a bookish-looking Frenchman who had previously enjoyed great success at Nantes, where he had spent much of his playing career. There as first-team coach he won the 2001 French title to follow a pair of French Cups, having previously co-ordinated the club's youth coaching. In fact when the Basques made contact with Denoueix in summer 2002, he thought he was being offered a position at the head of the club's youth set-up, rather than the first team. His modesty also saw him get off on the right foot with the locals – when he came to buying a house, he bought in the countryside outside San Sebastián rather than on the city's harbour ('he showed a touch of class', as Phil puts it). Denoueix was certainly a break from the old guard. The club had scraped safety in 2002 after the sack ended John Toshack's unsuccessful third term at the club. Despite this – and two spells in charge at the locally-hated Real Madrid – Toshack is still regarded with a great deal of affection in these parts, and says himself he considers San Sebastián 'home'. Without resorting to 'Welsh firebrand' cliché, 'John Benjamin' (as he is known throughout Spain) was abrasive, self-assured and often confrontational.

Denoueix is about as far removed from this as is imaginable. Although he is much liked and admired throughout the club and its fanbase, 'the locals aren't too keen on his philosophical side', notes Phil – a quintessentially French trait that's thrown into sharper relief for being set in no-nonsense, say-what-you-mean Spain. Perhaps the coach's calm side was what allowed the team to flourish last season. Though it's been said that the team's success was achieved with the same players that struggled before, no-one has ventured that their improvement happened *because* of the lack of upheaval, rather than in spite of the lack of change. With a coach that believed in them, the classic short man/tall man strike partnership of Turkey's Nihat and the big Serb Darko Kovacevic flourished, with the pair hitting 42 league goals between them. The front pair had a lot to thank another stalwart for, the international left-winger Javier De Pedro, who laid on more goals that anyone else in the entire championship. Behind them, you had the intervention of Westerveld when required, a goalkeeper distrusted and unwanted at Liverpool, now revelling in his status as the team's very stability.

So how did Athletic react to their neighbours (and supposedly inferiors) lording it at the top of the table? Excepting the Real Sociedad title double in '81 and '82, looking up at their Basque counterparts was a position to which Athletic were highly unaccustomed. Athletic Bilbao aren't just the most successful club in the Basque country, but historically one of the top five most successful Spanish league clubs of all time. They're also one of only three clubs never to have spent a single season out of the top flight of Spanish football since the national league's inception, with the other two being Real Madrid and Barcelona, two of the only three clubs more successful than them in Spain (the other being Atlético Madrid).

'There wasn't anything particularly nasty in their reaction,' remembers Phil Ball. 'In fact, they were quite happy about it.' This isn't a complete shock. In fact, it stands to pretty obvious reason that Athletic fans would rather root for fellow Basques ahead of La Real's title rivals Real Madrid, seen within Spain as the Castilian establishment made flesh and still tarred with the stigma of being the notorious dictator Franco's team. Still, Athletic last won the league in 1984 (they won consecutive titles in the two years following Real Sociedad's back to back triumphs, curiously enough), and have only finished in the top five three times since 1986, suggesting that their continued status as Big Brother may be more perceived than real. Their neighbours from San Sebastián's success must have brought up the question of whether there had been a shift in power between the two geographically-close rivals.

The nature of the two clubs' rivalry may be curious to an outsider, but is perhaps more common to the football characteristics of the peninsula in that it is squarely based in regional politics. However whereas the rivalry between Sevilla and Real Betis for example may stem from an issue of social class, friction between La Real and Athletic has centred over the last 15-20 years on the argument – not unusually for such a proud region – over which club most represents the essence of Basqueness. This really began in 1989, when Real Sociedad brought Irish striker John Aldridge to San Sebastián from Liverpool, on the recommendation of former Anfield legend Toshack. He was the first non-Basque player to arrive at the club in 30 years. Athletic sneered that their rivals were selling out, and plenty of fans at the Atotxa were unhappy about it too.

Athletic took the moral high ground, but were hardly blameless in the equation. Having traditionally been the biggest club in the region, other Basque clubs besides La Real had long since complained that Athletic had swiped all the best players from the very limited catchment area by fair means or foul. 'When I interviewed the then-Real president (Javier) Esposito at the time (following the Aldridge transfer), he said to me 'what choice have I got?' while pointing over in the direction of San Mamés (Athletic's stadium),' remembers Phil. 'Athletic Bilbao 'preserved the Basque identity', they think.' While Athletic puffed their chests out with regional pride, Real Sociedad brought in more foreign players on the back of Aldridge's success. Both Kevin Richardson and Dalian Atkinson followed him over from England the following year, and this policy continues today with the presence of high-profile foreigners like Nihat, Kovacevic, Westerveld and the Norwegian defender Bjorn Kvarme. The San Sebastián side of the argument was reinforced when in 1996, contrary to an agreement between the clubs not to poach each other's players, Athletic aggressively (and successfully) pursued the signature of La Real's precocious young winger Joseba Exteberría. In protest, La Real refused official relations with their neighbours for the next few years.

Even before this the two parties differed in their personal definitions of what being Basque represented. 'This (ie the dispute over 'poaching') was more the result (of their differences) rather than the cause,' considers Phil. 'Real are the left-wing nationalist club, whereas Athletic have traditionally been the PNV (Partido Nacionalista Vasco, the original Basque nationalist party) club.' When I turn up at La Real's Anoeta stadium for the Betis game, I'm struck that all the security and door staff are wearing blue berets with the club crest. It later clicks in my head that this is some sort of Basque identifier, when I see the Bayonne team being led out by a beret-sporting guard-of-honour in January before they beat Bordeaux in the French Cup. Later on I also read in Mark Kurlansky's 'The Basque History of the World' that the beret was brought to widespread public attention by Basques – largely Carlists – during the First Carlist War in the 19th century (though its origins date from over 200 years before this). Kurlansky notes:

'Since the First Carlist War, the hat has not only become a central symbol of Basqueness but has also gained international popularity and is generally associated with the political left. Argentine leftist revolutionary Che Guevara saw no contradiction in using the image of the beret, because it is the hat of the underdog fighting the establishment.'

Even within the Basque Country, provincial identity is distinct - Bilbao is the capital of the province of Viscaya and Donostia (San Sebastián) the main city of Guipúzcoa. Despite this, the nature of the rivalry is rarely vicious. 'Basically, Guipúzcoan players are thought of as being thick and rich,' sniggers Phil. 'The stereotypes are pretty tongue-in-cheek.'

In case you were thinking that the unexpected reaching of the Champions League had at least made sure these Guipúzcoan players are rich, it's unlikely. Very little has changed. Once again, the personnel is more or less the same this season as it was in the previous one (Phil tells me later that the club's management were 'scared of doing a Leeds' – getting carried away and spending what they couldn't afford on the back of one good season). The only signings have been the South Korean Lee Chun-Soo, who's hardly cemented himself as a regular thus far, and the Frenchman Lionel Potillon. Whereas this approach worked for Denoueix before, it's proving a problem so far this season. The Champions League puts far greater demands on a squad, especially one not originally geared for competing in the upper echelons of league and European competition. On the eve of Wednesday's vital final group match - at home to Galatasaray - the players' mood should be like children sitting up waiting for Santa on Christmas Eve. In fact, trudging wearily towards their date with destiny, they're more like Dad steeling himself to carve the turkey through a raging hangover and surrounded by screaming kids.

The Gala match should be straightforward. It's at home (La Real already beat their visitors in Istanbul earlier in the campaign), and they only need take a point to join Italian giants Juventus in the second phase. The Real Betis game, though, showed every reason that it's not. There was something eerie in seeing the eleven in the blue and white stripes playing like the ghosts of their former selves. They were strangers to the vim and vigour of last season's side, seemingly stifled by the tension which a bad run produces. They've suffered some appalling misfortune, none more so than a fortnight ago when they managed to snatch defeat from the jaws of victory at Deportivo La Coruña. Leading by a Nihat goal going into the last 15 minutes, they lost to a brace – that's a brace – of own goals by defender Igor Jauregi.

They suffered again against the Andalucians, with Kovacevic having a legitimate goal wrongly disallowed for offside with the score still at 1-0. Then there was Joaquín's pair of goals, the aforementioned first followed by a second when the speedy winger beat Westerveld to the ball way out of his area before tucking the ball in. As these two goals in particular went in to the collective wince of the assembled press pack around me, the unmistakeable smell of fear – and, curiously, a big waft of ganja smoke as well - seeped from the pitch to the stands as the players' draining confidence lay naked in front of us. From the pitch to the stands is a long way too – since their last game at Atotxa in June 1993 against Tenerife, La Real have called the purpose-built Anoeta home. While being undeniably impressive, holding 32,000 and boasting top draw hospitality and media facilities, it lacks something in atmosphere, with a huge running track separating the stands from the pitch (and, I would imagine, making the view from behind the goals pretty atrocious). On a night when the chips are down, the players must feel like the fans are watching them from the moon. 'The Atotxa was much closer to the pitch, and had much more of a hostile atmosphere to visiting teams,' says Phil. 'And there's an athletics stadium next door, so they've only used the running track twice.'

You can't fault the supporters though. Even during a real belting, they pledge their loyalty to the players and staff who gave them so much last season. With the last half- hour of the game played out like a procession – Betis being 4-0 up after 59 minutes – the Anoeta faithful roused themselves to sing support for their team. At the press conference after the game Denoueix was visibly touched by this, composing himself before assuring that his players would 'continue working (for the fans).' It does however speak volumes for the level of expectation. Last season was an unexpected treat, but not the norm. Reality always bites.

So why have things gone wrong? Phil talks about the lack of signings – 'this gave out the message they didn't expect to get far (in the league or the Champions League)' – and the demands this has placed on the smallish squad, particularly citing the over-reliance on Kovacevic and Nihat. He also says the players said no to the idea of rotation, something that perhaps even hints at an undermining of Denoueix's authority. The performances in the Champions League have done justice to the ability that is in the team (give or take an excusable away mauling at Juventus), having beaten Gala, Olympiakos and even drawn with Juventus at the Anoeta. But the league performances have had a touch of after-the-Lord-Mayor's-Show about them, like the successful band struggling over that difficult second album. De Pedro is their season in microcosm. Having nailed his class to the mast so emphatically last season, his campaign has been one of niggling injuries and being in and out of the first choice line-up as he runs down the final year of his contract.

Their goalkeeper's suffering his ups and downs as well after last season's imperiousness. Sunday morning and Sander Westerveld has a face as grey as the December skies over the remote, tucked-away Zubieta training ground. 'Shit, I forgot,' he exclaims with a hint of Scouse brogue when I approach him. He looks like he just wants to go home for a sulk, facing up to the fact that he will miss Wednesday's game, the biggest of the season, due to the ankle that so betrayed him for the second goal yesterday ('it felt like a knife being stabbed in my ankle'). Everyone knows goalkeepers often play with injuries that outfield players couldn't, but in this case Westerveld has probably soldiered on to help the team through the sticky period when he could have done without it. 'I shouldn't have played,' he agrees with a resigned expression. 'It happened against Depor. I've been OK with it, but it hurts when I shoot the ball. It's been bad for five or six games and I probably won't play before Christmas.'

Missing out on the cruncher with Galatasaray will be particularly hard on Westerveld. If ever there's someone who's earned a crack at the Champions League, it's him. He was part of the Liverpool team who qualified for the Champions League in 2001, but never actually got to play in it. Manager Gérard Houllier lost patience with what he judged the Dutchman's unreliability after an error in a Premiership game against Bolton. He then humiliated the keeper by buying not one but two – Jerzy Dudek and Chris Kirkland – on the very same day to replace him. What the boss was telling the man from Enschede couldn't have been any clearer.

'I would have left straight away if I could have,' says Westerveld, mildly bristling at the memory, 'but I had to wait for an offer.' He'd always wanted to play in Spain and Toshack, always with half an eye on his old club, came in. 'I wanted to play in Spain, and I talked to Dutch players in Spain like (Roy) Makaay (then of Depor), and they recommended it. I joined Real because they were the only Spanish club that came in for me.' Westerveld is disarmingly honest. 'I was planning to stay for a year or so and then move on to a bigger Spanish club, but it's gone unbelievably well at Real. Last season we had an alright defence, I was playing well, and we had two strikers who could score important goals.'

His use of the past tense tells me this must seem like an age ago at the moment. What's gone wrong? 'We seem to need more chances before we score, and every time the other team has a chance it goes in,' he observes with a weary exasperation. 'We've only been second best to Atlético (where they also lost 4-0) and Betis. We've not really been outplayed by anyone else.' La Real look unlikely to qualify for the Champions League again through the league and let's face it, they're not going to win it, so whether or not this level of competition proves to be the exception rather than the rule, they'll want to live and breathe in every moment of this European campaign while they can.

'It's great,' enthuses Westerveld of the Champions League. 'Other competitions are good, but this has the best teams and best players and everyone watches it all over the world. And it means a lot having missed out with Liverpool.' It's easily gauged from him though how sapping even the extra six group stage matches can be for a team outside the big clubs comprising the usual European elite, mentally and physically. 'The quality's different – you can make mistakes in the league and still win, but not in the Champions League. Juventus away was hard – we had a bad start letting in two goals in the first seven minutes or so, but we came back well and at 4-2 (having been 4-0 down) had some good chances.' Not for a moment however has Westerveld lost sight of his club's place in the overall scheme of things. 'We talked about before the game and it's one that it wouldn't be too bad if we lost – they're one of the best teams in the world. The Champions League is great, but it's made it a bit difficult for us this season, because it's more games and we don't have such a big squad, so we can't rotate the team,' he acknowledges.

Playing for a club that doesn't have the luxury of Champions League football year after year – and therefore will in no way take it for granted – means a unique opportunity to realistically and accurately assess the level. What is the difference nowadays between playing in the Champions League, and in international football for example? 'Not much, because teams at both levels have the best players.' Maybe the Champions League has even overtaken international football in terms of quality. Although as an international coach you have an entire country's football talent to pick from, you still just have what you have. A big club, meanwhile, can go and buy a player if they feel they're short in a particular area. 'Yeah, I think you could be right,' muses the keeper. 'Like with Holland, we don't have a proper left-back, (Giovanni) Van Bronckhorst (who made his name as a midfielder) plays there. And of course the players play together every week, whereas internationals meet up only every couple of months.'

And therein lays the problem. While the big guns cruise effortlessly on with a seeming cast of thousands, the likes of Real Sociedad struggle to make do with what they have, spreading themselves thinly, like the student with two jobs trying to finish his dissertation at the same time. It's a true fairytale – beautiful, but no-one really wants to hear what happens after the happy ending.

Deportivo La Coruña

'Rubbish.' 'Very poor.' 'Why are the team playing this long-ball football?' 'Irureta should go. The team just aren't good enough.'

Ahhh. That's much better. After overdosing on reasonableness on my last couple of trips to Dortmund and San Sebastián, I'm delighted to see that the fickleness of the football fan is alive and well. I'm outside the Riazor, the home of Deportivo La Coruña, and as you can tell from my quick opinion poll, the locals are particularly sulky. You would never guess their team are admirably holding their own at the very top end of European football.

A Coruña doesn't feel like Spain. This is hardly surprising, you might say, considering that it's the second weekend in January. As I look out the window of the taxi taking me from the airport into town, the sides of the car are being sprayed with sheets of water from the road. The rain brings the lush, sloping green landscape on both sides of the car into sharp relief. It seems more like northern Europe. Spain is often referred to as a collection of fairly disparate parts, but the region of Galicia is especially isolated, tucked in the north-west corner well out of the way of the country's most heard-of spots. The more southern – and slightly larger - town of Vigo is almost in northern Portugal, but A Coruña is a fair way still from there and from the Asturias to the east. The city sits in a no-man's-land in the middle.

Accordingly, the town has traditionally been self-sufficient. Its charming main square, Plaza de María Pita, is named after the local heroine who led the (successful) efforts to resist British occupation, attempted by Sir Francis Drake in 1589. A Coruña and its surrounding area is perhaps better known for fishing. According to a study by the University of Santiago de Compostela, Galicia as a whole is responsible for the production of 40% of the fish consumed in Spain, making it 'the foremost fishing region in the whole of Europe.' But the area is still badly feeling the effects of the spill from the oil tanker Prestige in November 2002. This was a cruel blow to an area whose economy is still suffering from a similar disaster ten years previously, when the vessel Aegean Sea ran aground. The Prestige spill has affected more than 1,000 km of coastline, a catastrophe given that 18,400 people in the province of A Coruña (and nearly 50% of the population in small towns like Fisterra, for example) are reliant on fishing for their livelihood, according to the university's report.

From a sporting perspective at least, the locals are used to overcoming the odds. Phil Ball had told me that apart from Real Sociedad, Deportivo are the only club from a city with a population of 250,000 or less to have won the Spanish title. They've only won it the once, in 2000, but have never finished outside La Liga's top three since, an impressive achievement when you take into account the strength of the competition. Along with Valencia, Depor have earned the right to be ranked as equals in the Spanish game alongside the traditional giants of Real Madrid and Barcelona.

They have also become something of a fixture in the Champions League since they first qualified for the competition, as a result of that 2000 title win. Like in La Liga, the Galicians have now made themselves part of the elite. Last season's competition was the first in which they failed to reach the quarter-finals, losing out on head-to-head records with Basel and Juventus after finishing on level points with the pair in the second group stage. The fatal blow was particularly cruel – Depor's fate was sealed away at Juventus, when an excellent performance ended with them being mugged by Igor Tudor's winner in the fourth minute of injury time. This was made even more galling by the fact that they had led 2-0 against Juve at the Riazor only to be ultimately held to a draw.

At the moment Depor occupy an in-between position in the Champions League pecking order. They've made themselves a fixture in the competition, but are still relative newcomers. They could rightly claim to be part of the elite, but aren't on the level of the big dogs of Real Madrid, Manchester United and AC Milan. They aren't a team you would expect to win it, but they are the sort of team you would have to beat in order to win it. In short, the club is at a crossroads in European terms.

Depor have earned respect off the back of some impressive results. Their 4-3 win over Paris Saint-Germain in March 2001, having been 3-0 down just after half-time, is still the stuff of Champions League legend (it's the only time in the competition's history that a team has come from three down to win). They only narrowly failed to pull off a similar feat in the quarter-finals that same year when, having lost the first leg at Leeds 3-0, they pummelled the English at the Riazor but could only gain a 2-0 victory on the night. They've since stepped up a level. In the following season they beat both Manchester United and Arsenal twice (home and away) in the group stages before United gained their revenge, again at the quarter-final stage. After Depor's comprehensive victory at Highbury, Arsenal's Thierry Henry – a man not prone to hyperbole - described the visitors' classy playmaker Juan Carlos Valerón as 'the best midfielder in Europe'. They opened up the following campaign, in September 2002, by triggering Bayern Munich's group stage humiliation, humbling the German champions in their own back yard courtesy of Roy Makaay's hat-trick.

My own previous encounter with the Galicians in this season's competition, you might remember, was a different kettle of fish entirely from this. I do not exaggerate in any way when I say that Depor's display in Monaco in November was, without doubt, the most shambolic defensive display I have ever seen from a top-flight team in my 20-odd years of going to watch football. Monaco were undeniably great that night but seeing players like Manuel Pablo, Jorge Andrade and Nourredine Naybet playing like they had never met before was beyond baffling. What stayed with me even more than the memory of the game itself of that night was the shock of the Monaco players that they had managed to overwhelm their guests so emphatically.

It's easy to set aside the defeat in Monaco as a red herring, a freak, a one-off. Depor coach Javier Irureta wasn't the only man in Spain whose reaction was something along the lines of 'everything they hit went in'. Though there was some truth in this, the fact that they tried to dismiss it as a fluke and forget it meant that Depor weren't actually dealing with the causes of this humiliation. It was hard to believe that this could have happened to Super Depor, known for their organisation, reliability and their solidity as a unit, but failing to learn the lessons of Monte Carlo almost cost them their place in the second phase. Their final game was in Holland, against PSV Eindhoven, who they'd beaten comfortably (2-0) in Galicia back in September, and they needed only to avoid defeat by the same score to go through. Yet thanks to more shoddy defending, Arjen Robben's goal left them losing by exactly that score by the 48th minute in the Philipsstadion. In the end it took Albert Luque's thunderous 30-yarder to ease the nerves, and they went through despite losing 3-2 on the night, with PSV's John de Jong taking advantage of some further slackness at the back to give his side a consoling win in injury time.

That Depor expect, rather than celebrate getting into the second stage of the Champions League shows how far the club has come. Without wanting to trot out the old 'victim of their own success' line, it's clear that the supporters have quickly come to assume a great deal of success from their team over a short space of time. That spring 2002 win at Arsenal was arguably their finest result, and performance, in the Champions League to date. It's also highly significant in demonstrating the incredible rate of the team's progress. During the season when Depor won their first and only Liga, a mere two years before, they had been hammered 5-1 at the same venue in the UEFA Cup.

It's clear that Deportivo La Coruña have reached a ceiling. The fans sense it, as the Riazor's attendances for this year's Champions League group games tell us. The highest gate was 23,500 for the first home game, the visit of PSV. At the equivalent stage last year, the lowest gate among the three games, for the visit of Lens, was just under 25,000. The initial novelty value has started to wear off. It's also hard to imagine, though, exactly how the club could get any bigger. The Riazor has a capacity of 34,611. The club also has nearly 31,000 season ticket holders, an incredible figure in a city of around a quarter of a million inhabitants. Even if they had the money and the inclination to expand the stadium, where would the extra fans come from? And how can a city of this size sustain a team at the very pinnacle of European football?

If anyone can find the answer, it's Augusto César Lendoiro. It's Lendoiro who brought Depor from the provincial wilderness and made them into a major player. He was elected as club president in summer 1988, at the tender age of 33. His incredibly long (certainly by Spanish standards) reign at the helm is a testament not just to the strides that Depor have made under his stewardship, but to his intellect and constant innovation. Lendoiro is unusual among presidents for not being a mega-rich demagogue. Instead, he's someone who is very good at persuading others to part with their money.

Journalist Guillem Balague, Sky Sports' Spanish football expert, takes up the story. 'Lendoiro was originally the chairman of the city's hockey club, who became very successful (under him),' he explains. He had been something of a child prodigy. 'He first became a (company) director at 14 or 15 years old.' He was actually invited to put himself forward as president of Depor, and didn't hesitate. The club was in a mess when he arrived, languishing in the Segunda, with a hefty debt running into millions. He would not easily be discouraged, however. 'He was a man with a vision,' says Balague. Lendoiro brought a whole new dimension to the expression 'hands-on' – he set about increasing support and the number of *socios* (members) had risen to 17,500 by the start of the '90s. On the back of this swell, Depor gained promotion back to the top flight in 1991, where they've been ever since.

Lendoiro's successful initial brief had been simply to get rid of the club's debts, and to get them back in to the Primera. He wasn't, however, a man to stand still, and rather than settle for Depor being perennial strugglers tried to take the club on to the next level by importing high class foreign talent in the '90s. In 1992 the Brazilians Bebeto and Mauro Silva arrived in Galicia, with the former in particular being an instant success, racking up 29 league goals in his first season to be crowned *Pichichi*. The latter is still at the Riazor, a bona fide club legend. These two were just the start of an increasing influx of overseas players throughout the decade, with fellow Brazilians Flávio Conceição, Luizão, Djalminha and of course Rivaldo pulling on the blue and white stripes at various points.

The president was hugely successful in putting the club on the map. Sure, they may have developed a reputation as Spain's ultimate nearly men – notably for falling at the very last hurdle in 1994, when Miroslav Djukic missed the injury-time penalty which would have beaten Valencia and clinched their maiden league title in the season's final game – but they were certainly not provincial nobodies anymore. As the decade progressed, Lendoiro stretched to signing pricey players in increasing numbers as the money started to roll in from booming support and, more importantly, increased revenue from TV rights. Some fans started to worry that Depor were perhaps straying too far away from the club's origins, as the team became known as the 'United Nations', with half the squad consisting of foreign players from the mid-'90s onwards.

Regardless, the club had finally broken their trophy duck in 1995, beating Valencia (something of a touchstone in Depor's recent history) to win the Copa del Rey. Totally in keeping with the club's history, they even had an agonising wait for that, with the original game at Real Madrid's Bernabéu suspended amid torrential rain, in '*puro estil de* Hitchcock' as one Spanish fans' website put it, with 11 minutes to go and the scores level at 1-1. As is the norm in Spain, the two teams went back to the Bernabéu three days later to play out the remaining minutes, during which Alfredo put the winner past the veteran 'keeper Zubizarreta to clinch Depor's first trophy. Just to show how easy it could be, the second followed a few short months later, when Depor secured a two-legged Supercopa win against the league champions of Real Madrid in the very same stadium.

Looking back at the early to mid-'90s, the period's most striking feature is not the concept of Depor battling to challenge at the top but the absence of a certain coach. The impact of Javier Irureta has been so immense since his appointment in 1998 that it's sometimes hard to picture a time when Depor were without him. By the time the unassuming Basque took the reins – having been lured from Galician rivals Celta - much of the good work of the first part of the decade had been undone, but he immediately took the club back into Europe before winning the title in his second season. Much of his success came from having successfully imposed his own image on the team.

'Irureta made them very Spanish,' recounts Guillem Balague. The squad Irureta inherited from his predecessor José Manuel Corral had become bloated, containing 40 professionals, and underachieving. The new coach made the squad more streamlined and focussed. 'He brought them out of their identity crisis,' notes Balague, referring to the 'United Nations' period. Irureta had been synonymous with an ultra-defensive approach in his first years as a coach, and he got the team organised, though it would be unfair to say he replicated the teams of his formative coaching years at the Riazor: While the ranks still had their share of overseas talent, the team he shaped certainly wasn't flash. The key signing for the 99/00 championship season was Roy Makaay, an accomplished though unobtrusive Dutch striker, bought from relegated Tenerife.

Basically, Irureta is without question the outstanding coach in Depor's history. The evidence is overwhelming, both in terms of trophies and the club's firm establishment at the very top of European football, with a name respected throughout the continent. His greatest strength is, however, also his greatest weakness. His natural modesty has rubbed off on the team and made them effective, competitive and largely selfless, but in an age of saturation coverage and constantly hysterical overreaction, he can be cast as too permissive. This is largely nonsense – as one glimpse at the honours list should tell you – but incidents such as the 2002 clash at the training ground, where Irureta was head-butted by Djalminha, suggest that maybe he's just too nice a guy to make Depor into a superpower. When I ask Balague why he thinks Depor haven't converted any of their strong runs in the Champions League into a proper tilt at the trophy, he just shrugs. 'They just don't have that winning mentality.'

Another player who Irureta has had his problems with is Diego Tristán. To describe Tristán as an enigma doesn't quite do him justice. The Andalucian striker arrived from Real Mallorca in 2000, intended to supplement the title-winning squad. He already had form, in both senses, for goalscoring and gluttony. He put away 19 goals in his last season at the San Moix for a mid-table Mallorca side despite being a late starter in the professional game. He didn't turn pro until the age of 19, having barely even kicked a ball before he was 17, as legend has it. He was also famous for having narrowly missed out – twice – on a move to Real Madrid, firstly in 1998 when the capital giants scrapped a move with then-sporting director José Pirri saying that a player 'with his sort of lifestyle' would be unsuitable for the club. Tristán later replied famously; 'What do you want, a footballer or a monk?'

Tristán has frequently looked cast-iron class since arriving at the Riazor. Last season was the first in which he's failed to reach the 20-goal mark at Depor (he scored 19), and the season before that he notched 32 and finished as *Pichichi* (21 of those having been in the league). Yet even while scoring 23 in his debut season in Galicia, there were murmurs about his being a 'part-timer', on account of the fact that only three of that haul were scored away from home (and those were all in the same game at Oviedo). He and Irureta have frequently clashed over the player's attitude, and after several reports of him turning up to training late and/or 'dishevelled', the coach actually banned his striker from the training ground for a spell last season. So bitterly were coach and player arguing on the touchline after he was substituted against Real Madrid earlier this campaign that Tristán neglected to shake the hand of his replacement, the Uruguayan Walter Pandiani. Pandiani publicly criticised Tristán afterwards for his 'lack of respect'.

Everyone has an opinion on him – I've heard him described across Spain as everything from a 'genius' to a 'twat'. Look on the forum of any Depor fan site and you'll find that even when he's not in the team, he generates far more discussion than any other player. Some still pledge loyalty to him, while others would have him dumped in a moment if a potentially more reliable model was readily available.

Going into the Sunday home game against Racing Santander, the feeling about Depor, like with Tristán, is one of 'could do better.' This is despite last week's 5-0 crushing of rivals Celta Vigo away at the Balaidos. Celta, after a fantastic campaign last time out, are struggling terribly under the demands placed on them by their own first Champions League campaign. The difficulties of Depor's neighbours should serve as a giant reminder of just how far they themselves have come. Few in A Coruña, however, seem to share this perspective. The visit of Racing invokes trepidation. They may be mid-table but hammered Barcelona 3-0 in their last outing, and are no mugs on the road either. They have also won three of the last four games they have played at the Riazor. Hence the headlines on the free match day newspapers being handed out around the ground, proclaiming today as 'El dia de la bestia' (Day of the Beast). Today is also the 19th league game, marking the exact halfway point in the season and a good point on which to judge progress – the winter watershed.

It's a mild, overcast day. I sense that they see quite a few of these kind of days in this corner of the world. The Riazor is as beautifully positioned as any football ground I can think of, slightly raised from the end of the seafront, so I am able to wander up the beach to reach it. In common with the north-east coast of Northern Ireland, this would probably develop into a tourist mecca if it didn't rain so much. It's slightly surreal walking off the beach and up to the ground, but the atmosphere doesn't build too steeply once I'm directly outside the walls of the Riazor. There are plenty of people, but no roar of the crowd or smell of the greasepaint. Despite Depor's lofty place in the table as part of the top three isolated from the rabble, today's is clearly just another game. I tuck myself away by one of the corner flags, and it feels as if everyone else is doing the same. So stealthily does the ground fill that it's a shock to look up from the paper to see a busy stadium when the teams run out.

Tristán is in the starting line-up, despite only having three goals to his name so far this season, after making a scoring appearance as a substitute in Vigo last week. Watching a team warm up in a half-empty stadium is not always the most invigorating pastime, but watching Tristán's range of skills and tricks certainly shows why the one thing about him that is never questioned is his ability. In defence of his scoring record this term, the side have spread the goals around - Pandiani has seven (having only scored once since breaking a club record by scoring in each of the opening six games) and the winger Albert Luque has five. The team has even scored five more goals than at this stage last season – 31 against 26 – despite the loss of Makaay to Bayern Munich in the summer. Makaay scored 29 league goals alone last season, a figure approaching half of the team's total 67. Maybe losing the top scorer has encouraged more of a team effort.

Depor should be confident, knowing that after last night's results they can move within three points of Real Madrid and within four of leaders and 'winter champions' Valencia. But after Tristán fluffs an opportunity given to him by Luque's cross early on, Racing start to look every inch the away-day hustlers. They're organised and tidy in possession, taking the sting out of the game to the extent of giving it the demeanour of a soothing Sunday afternoon stroll by the sea – so much so, that it's something of a shock when the Racing left-back Ayoze crashes a long-range drive past a startled Molina and against the post in the 20th minute. Just to make sure we're now fully awake, the visiting midfielder Javi Guerrero repeats the trick shortly afterwards, lifting the ball over the prone 'keeper from all of 25 yards, only to see it come back off the crossbar.

Then the home team show their quality, scoring just short of half-time despite being second best. Valerón taps a short free-kick to Luque, whose venomous left-footer decides against knocking the bar off and settles for going in off its underside. The *Deportivistas* are finally lifted from their seats. On a day like today, it was always going to take something like this goal to rouse the faithful.

You have to assume that this will fill the home team with confidence and allow them to go on, with the goal presumably negating the effectiveness of Racing's counter-attacking style. Luque continues to be Depor's chief threat, lively and willing to take on defenders. After driving just over he sends in a delicious cross across the six-yard line that evades everyone before running to safety. This is the sort of moment where the loss of Makaay leaps back into the consciousness, as well as the temporary absence of the injured Pandiani. The lack of a killer touch comes back to haunt them. With ten minutes to go, Guerrero races on to a through ball before classily chipping Molina from just inside the area. Even the groans in the stands are stifled. After all, these things will happen when you only manage three shots on target in a home game.

So the *socios* sulk into the night, a whir of shaking heads and muttered barbs. Even the rather nice *Playa Club* (the club-run nightclub/café, tucked between the Riazor and the beach) is heaving more with disappointment than with people. The trophies from the triumphs of the past few years sit in a pristine glass case, staring out and teasing the customers. My opinion poll outside the ground says at least as much about the way Lendoiro and Irureta have raised expectation as it does about the turgidity of the performance against Racing. Monday's *Deporte Campeón* ('Galicia's Sports Daily') reveals as much in its conclusion that 'a team with title pretensions has to show more ambition than Deportivo did yesterday'.

Like all the regional Spanish sports dailies I've seen, *Deporte Campeón* speaks like a fan. When I see Monday's cover, I have to laugh. It's a priceless cover photo, taken just before kick-off, of the Depor team stood in a line applauding the *socios* in one of the stands. They all face the same way, apart from one man, with his arms by his side, seemingly off balance, facing in the opposite direction. He looks disorientated, and apart from his strip, as if he's just been dropped from a spaceship. That man is Diego Tristán. The headline simply says '*Perdido*' (Lost). They are crueller still inside, berating him for doing 'nothing' and demanding he stops 'living on his form of two years ago.'

That Tristán is the subject of such extreme views is perhaps unsurprising. He could be seen as an allegory of the club as a whole. So near, and yet so far. The fans and media, you feel, are overreacting. The season is only halfway through, and Depor are only six points from the top, as well as being in the second round of the Champions League (although facing a tough task against their nemesis, Juventus). Yet there's something missing this season. They've had some great years, but perhaps now they're fighting against the dying of the light. If you don't progress in football, it usually means that you're going backwards. If anyone can take the team onwards, it's Lendoiro, but with Depor's debts estimated last month to stand at a huge €178 million, he will have to be at his most creative. It feels like the club is approaching its limit. How far can A Coruña push its team?

Lokomotiv Moscow

It may be European for football purposes, but Russia still feels like another world. Despite the breaking down of cultural barriers in the last 12½ years, five hours' worth of flight still makes it as far away as Kabul. Walking through the large yet decidedly spartan arrival hall of Sheremetevo airport, it reminds me of one place in particular – Havana airport. Then again, perhaps this is just a perceived similarity in my mind, for obvious reasons. Speaking no Russian and not wanting to get fleeced by one of Moscow's notoriously-bent cab drivers, I've booked ahead. Moscow's main international point of arrival is some 40km from the centre of town and there's no train, with limited buses. I meet my driver, who speaks no English at all apart from the words '25 dollars' (everything is in US dollars for tourists), and he has me wait by the side of the car park before collecting me in a dirty grey Lada. I forgive myself for stereotyping.

Never again will I complain about the weather at home in England. I remember writing myself a note to 'get Moscow out of the way before it gets too cold', but I've singularly failed on that count. This is the true meaning of cold. When I arrive in the centre at around 5pm local time, night is descending and the temperature is dropping to somewhere between minus 15 and minus 20. And there's enough snow on the streets for me to fleetingly regret chucking out the beyond-unfashionable snow boots my mother sent up to me in my first year at university. So far, so true to the cliché, then. This is pretty much as I had imagined Russia when I was a kid.

You can never judge a book by its cover though. The extent of change in this part of the world since that momentous week in August 1991 (when one by one, Ukraine, Belarus, Azerbaijan and the rest declared independence, as the Soviet Union splintered) has been huge, and football has been as affected as any aspect of life. Overnight, the mighty and mysterious Soviet Union - the serious-looking blokes ubiquitous at major tournaments with the legend 'CCCP' emblazoned across their red shirts, European Championship runners-up as recently as 1988 - was no more, with the previous one entity being split into a mind-boggling 15 different football associations. Russia are now the only one of those 15 in the FIFA world rankings' top 30. Club football has suffered in kind. When the Soviet league split Dynamo Kyiv, the most successful club in the 50-plus years of the league's history (as well as the most successful Soviets in Europe), became part of a new Ukrainian league. Since then, only two Russian sides – Spartak Moscow in 2001 and Lokomotiv Moscow both last year and this year – have survived past the first round of the Champions League.

It's not surprising, given that pre-'91 Moscow had been under Communist rule for over seventy years, but the 2004 model Moscow still seems very much a work in progress. In the centre, the legacy of that era is unavoidable. The spires and rolling walls of the Kremlin loom large, and unsmiling army guards strictly police the opening hours of Red Square. Lenin's tomb is its spotless centrepiece. Lenin himself lies in a glass case with his eyes sewn shut, kept pristine like a waxwork by the then-pioneering preservation formula developed by Soviet scientists after his death in 1924. More army guards hurry you round the body and towards the exit. Yet for every symbol of old school Moscow, there's an indicator of Westernisation to clash with it. Behind Red Square is an air-conditioned shopping centre, where boutiques pump out garish Europop. I see a sports shop, bizarrely, displaying Wales' kit in the window, and a few people walking around in Wales ski hats. As fashionable as they may be, I know I wouldn't be keen on wearing leisurewear of the country who were trying to get my team turfed out of the European Championships[1]. Meanwhile, Ploshchad Revolutsii metro station has the inevitable McDonald's attached to its side. I guiltily join in by having a hot dog from a stand facing the Kremlin.

Jim Riordan knows what Russia, and Moscow, was like before the split better than most Western Europeans. He recently retired from lecturing at the University of Surrey, having previously written various works on Soviet sport. He first came to Moscow in 1961, sent on a scholarship by the British Communist Party. 'Moscow was so weird back then,' says Jim. 'Of course, it was still only eight years since the death of Stalin.' The plan was to stay for two years, but he ended up staying on as a translator until 1965.

Extraordinarily, Jim also became the first (and only) person from Western Europe to play in the Soviet league. 'The British Diplomatic Corps had a game every Sunday morning,' he explains. This is where he met Gennady Logofet. Logofet was a midfielder for Spartak Moscow. 'He was studying for a degree,' remembers Jim, 'and I think he fancied himself as a potential diplomat.' The pair got talking – 'and I mentioned that I'd played for the British Army,' Jim grins – and Logofet ended up inviting the Englishman along to training with the team at the Lenin stadium. Little did he know that his Spartak debut was just around the corner, in unusual circumstances.

'I got a very panicky call on Sunday morning, telling me to come down to the stadium immediately,' he recounts. 'The regular number five, a guy called Voronin, was blind drunk. They tried everything to sober him up, even throwing him in some Russian steam baths, but none of it worked. So there I was.' In the event, it all went pretty smoothly. 'I was lucky, the opposition weren't very good,' laughs Jim.

Spartak have always been one of Moscow's premier clubs, the workers' team, but at this point, Lokomotiv were not. The club was originally formed as KOR, the October Revolution Club, becoming defunct before taking off again under the patronage of the national railways (hence the name change) in the '30s. In the Soviet years, they only ever won two Russian Cups – in 1936 and 1957 – and have never had much of a fan base. The current team captain Dimitri Loskov was recently asked in a TV interview by a clueless hack whether he had supported Loko as a boy. Loskov laughed, with a perplexed look on his face, and answered in the negative. No one did. Lokomotiv have traditionally been Moscow's fifth club, behind the more traditional powerhouses of Spartak, Dinamo (the KGB team), CSKA (the army team) and Torpedo (the blacksmiths' team).

No one really talks about the old days. When I ask Jim about whether he still has friends in Moscow, he stops, and slowly considers. 'I'm hesitating, simply because of the last time I was there,' admits Jim. 'I saw Logofet, the man who originally introduced me to Spartak. I said hello, and he looked blank. You know, I said, 'it's me, Jim.' He just said, 'I'm sorry, I don't remember.' I spoke to someone else, another player. He just said 'I don't want to talk about it. I'm too bitter about the past'.' Such is the difficulty in reconciling Soviet history with the post-communist period that most just treat 1991 as Year Zero. 'I came to realise that these people are worried that people will be hating them, criticising them, for playing under communism. They're embarrassed.'

Today, Lokomotiv are no longer small fry. They may not be fighting off fans just yet, but they play in what is indisputably the best and most modern stadium in Russia, if not eastern Europe. The Lokomotiv Stadium is a state of the art facility in the Cherkizovo suburb of the city, currently with a 30,000 capacity, with plans in the pipeline to increase that by a further 10,000. In the 2002 season (the Russian season usually runs from March to November or December) Loko won their first-ever title in lifting the Russian Premier League, a feat which guaranteed a second successive season of Champions League participation, after having finished as runners-up in the previous year's league.

When I get into a cab late on Monday afternoon to head to the Lokomotiv stadium for a press call, the driver has no problem understanding where I want to go and we're swiftly on our way. God bless the international language of football, because generally speaking,

I'm finding the language barrier a difficulty. I have none of the freedom that I have elsewhere in Europe. With the alphabet being different, I can't even go into a shop or restaurant, point at a word and a make a piss-poor attempt at pronouncing it. I'm facing a few more Brits Abroad moments than I would like. I ask the taxi driver by mime where the seatbelt is. He just laughs – not the last taxi driver who will laugh at the seat belt question and my quaint regard for safety during my time here. The slapstick keeps on coming. I have half an eye on the time, and try to ask how long it will take to reach the stadium. The driver, perhaps not unreasonably, takes me tapping my watch and arching an eyebrow as a signal to floor the accelerator. I clutch the dashboard as subtly as possible and resolve to learn at least 200 words in every language I don't yet know.

When I arrive at the Lokomotiv stadium, I find it impossible not to be impressed. It's very new-looking – it was rebuilt just two years ago – and looks every inch the modern football arena. To get to the press room, I walk around the pitch, which looks in superb condition despite the inclement weather, although of course the domestic season hasn't started yet. Ahead of tomorrow night's Champions League second round tie between Lokomotiv and Monaco, the visitors' coach Didier Deschamps and his captain Ludovic Giuly are fielding questions. After, they brave the outside for a light training session on the pitch. Several of the French players are wearing head-warmers as they shiver through their paces. I love writing about football, but sitting on the home team's bench watching, this is one of the moments where I doubt my chosen vocation. Should my job really be watching a group of 20-odd grown men jogging around in minus 15? What the fuck am I doing here? I decide to sack it off to go and get some food and drink, but the Monaco team are a step ahead of me. Before I reach the exit Morientes, Rothen and co are virtually sprinting back down the players' tunnel.

So, I'm back to the struggle of communicating. Sitting down in a restaurant a block away from Red Square – selected purely for having an English menu in the window - it's like being on the Costa del Sol, ideologically rather than meteorologically speaking. I feel isolated, unwelcome even. Then again, even excepting the language barrier, you can forgive Moscow residents for erring on the frosty side at present. Just 17 days ago, the city was the victim of a horrific terrorist attack by a suicide bomber. The assailant blew up the second carriage of a metro train, going through a tunnel from Paveletskaya station in rush hour. It killed at least 39 commuters and injured more than a hundred, though the final death toll is unlikely to be finalised for a few weeks yet. Russia has almost become accustomed to this sort of tragedy. 46 people were killed in a similar incident last year on a train just outside the main station in the southern city of Yessentuki, not forgetting the explosion that levelled a Moscow apartment block in 2002, or the double bombing in the city in the space of a few days in September 1999. In December Nevio Scala, now Spartak coach, had a lucky escape when a bomb went off outside his hotel, killing five.

The claims of Aslen Maskhadov, the Chechen separatist leader, denying involvement are currently cutting little ice with the Russian premier Vladimir Putin. Putin has always refused the idea of negotiation with any groups thought to be connected in any way with terrorists, and is increasingly less interested in any discussion of the direction of his domestic policy. In this atmosphere, governmental statements have often shifted towards the xenophobic. The mayor of Moscow, Yuri Luzhkov, is talking of increasing efforts to stamp out illegal immigrants, and *The Observer* of February 8th also quoted MP Dimitry Rozogin (a Putin supporter) of demanding action against 'an ethnic criminal community that evidently supports the terrorists.' There is a definite climate of fear here, too reminiscent of past regimes.

It wasn't supposed to be like this. *Glasnost*, and the free market, was supposed to usher in the era of opportunity for all Russians, and those of former Soviet states. But it hasn't worked out like that. According to this year's estimates from Russia's own Federal State Statistics Service, 28.8 million Russians are living below the poverty line – a plainly unacceptable 19% of the country's population. Remember too that these are only the official statistics. Like - for example - Brazil, the money (and power) in Russia has been monopolised by a small proportion of people. These have tended to be entrepreneurs (or opportunists, depending on your perspective) who took advantage of the confusion following August 1991 to reinvent themselves in the new economy. As Jim Riordan wrote in his paper *Football: Nation, City and the Dream*, many of these were themselves in government:

'Seeing the inevitable end to their political power, a number of communist officials swiftly turned themselves into business people and, using their influence and contacts, purchased state enterprises at very low prices (about 20 per cent of their real market value) under the cover of privatisation.'

The most prominent of this new class of Russians are the oligarchs (owners of the oil companies). The oligarchs have started to invest in football – 'football clubs are outside Russia's normal tax systems,' Jim muses. This has resulted in the paradox that while the split of the Soviet Union initially weakened the strength of many of the old territory's football teams, the after effects are beginning to slowly bridge the gap between the Russian clubs and the top clubs of Western Europe more effectively than ever before. Spartak are sponsored by Lukoil, while the former police club Dinamo are now funded by Yukos, the biggest oil company in Russia. CSKA are hardly short of a rouble or two either. President Yevgeny Giner – a good friend of Chelsea head honcho Roman Abramovich – bought the club a few years ago, and has invested heartily. Giner may not be quite as flush as his now-London-based chum, but has still broken the Russian league's transfer record twice in the last year, first spending $3.7 million on the Czech Jiri Jarosik, then again when buying the Croatian striker Ivica Olic for $5.7 million. He also pulled off a coup in signing Russian international defender Sergey Ignashevich from champions Lokomotiv. Giner's millions ultimately saw his club win the 2003 championship[2]. It's a long way from the times which Real Sociedad's Valery Karpin (the first man, incidentally, to score for Russia after the Soviet break-up) speaks of when he remembers: 'With the money I earned at CSKA, I could not afford more than 10 packets of chocolate a month.'

Lokomotiv may not enjoy the oil connection, and certainly not the clout of CSKA, but theirs is no hard luck story. Their success has been strictly post-Soviet era. In the age of capitalist Russia, the transport industry has become very profitable, which 'The Railwaymen' have done pretty well out of. They were able to pay Marseille a fee estimated at $4.7 million last month to bring ex-Spartak striker Dimitri Sytchev back home. They also have, of course, the asset of the Lokomotiv Stadium, the first-ever purpose-built football stadium in Russia. The idea was to build a stadium that met UEFA and FIFA standards, aiding the nation's bid for Euro 2008 (though ultimately Austria and Switzerland's joint bid was accepted late in 2002). Shortly after the reconstruction was complete in summer 2002, the Russian FA announced it would be holding all the national team's Euro 2004 qualifying games at Lokomotiv. Russia usually played their games at Luzhniki (previously Lenin) Stadium up to this point, the main venue for the 1980 Olympics, shared by Spartak and Torpedo and holding over 80,000, but its status was complicated by the trial introduction of astroturf in June 2002. Besides, the Lokomotiv Stadium was a top grade facility; new, fresh, and showing the world the new face of Russia.

Lokomotiv the club's rise is mainly down, though, to good housekeeping. Real money, in the Russian Premier, tends to mean foreign influence – players, coaches etc. Lokomotiv have generally stuck to players from Russia, or the former Soviet republics. Only six of the current squad are from outside the former Soviet Union. Their plan is one of continuity. President Valeri Filatov has been in charge since 1992, and coach Yuri Semin has been in place since 1986, excepting a year-long stint managing New Zealand in 1991, a spell during which Filatov himself took over coaching duties[3].

Spartak were undeniably the first major force in the newly created Russian Premier. They won nine of the first ten championships from 1992 (the sole other winner being Alaniya Vladikavkaz in 1995), but

Lokomotiv were the team to break that stranglehold in winning the 2002 title. This was the logical conclusion to years of improvement, with the team having been runners-up in three successive years before the maiden win, as well as in the year that Alaniya won the title. Loko had made great strides in Europe too. In successive seasons, they made the semi-finals of the European Cup Winners' Cup. In 1998, they lost to Stuttgart, and the following year, they agonisingly went out on away goals to eventual winners Lazio. To put this achievement in perspective, the only other Russian club team ever to reach a European final was Dinamo Moscow, beaten by Rangers in the 1972 Cup Winners' Cup final. The only Soviet teams to win European club competitions have been Ukraine's Dynamo Kyiv, who won the Cup Winners' Cup in 1975 and 1986, and the Super Cup in 1985, and Dynamo Tbilisi of Georgia, who also lifted the Cup Winners' Cup in 1981.

Now Lokomotiv have also reached the Champions League's second stage in two successive years. Granted, they may have been a little fortuitous last season, sneaking through in a group stage where Barcelona so completely dominated that second place became theirs almost by default. Loko then struggled in the second group stage, losing all but one of their games. Yet if their overall record told of a little inexperience, the 'but one' equally told of their potential. They drew 2-2 with the holders Real Madrid at the Bernabéu, a game that they surreally led with only 15 minutes left, with only Raúl's goal preventing what would have been the most famous coup in the club's history. This season they have put their experience to good use, and though they again qualified by the skin of their teeth – thanks, ironically, to a late Dynamo Kyiv equaliser against Internazionale that prevented the Italians from leapfrogging them – they acquitted themselves well in a tough group. Loko did particular justice to their proud stadium, drawing with Arsenal, beating Dynamo in a seesaw game with a late goal from Costa Rica's Winston Parks, and hammering Inter in surely the best European display from a Russian side in many a year. Make no mistake, Lokomotiv are here on merit.

There can be no doubt how important the Champions League, and European club competitions in general, are to the recovery of Russian football. This is particularly true since the involvement of the oligarchs, people who are simply not used to second best. Just ask Valery Gazzayev. Having guided CSKA to their first title in 12 years (they previously won the final championship of the Soviet era in 1991), he was sacked in November and replaced by the Portuguese coach Artur Jorge. This was the price of Champions League failure, after CSKA crashed to a humiliating (and costly) defeat in the second qualifying round to Macedonian minnows Vardar Skopje. It's a fair bet that the sight of Lokomotiv's autumn success in the background didn't do Gazzayev too many favours.

For the moment, Lokomotiv are like men on the moon, striving to put down the Russian flag. They aren't strong enough to seriously challenge, and they know they won't be in the Champions League next year either, having lost their title and finished fourth in 2003. Success for former Soviet teams is scant, yet possible, as Dynamo Kyiv proved by reaching the Champions League semis in 1999 (narrowly missing out to Bayern Munich), and the quarters the year before. Loko can show Europe the increasing strength of the Russian game. And as commentators as Western Europe seem to say almost as often as 'goals change games,' 'no one will fancy a trip to Moscow.'

Either way, it's a good pre-season for them at the very least, as well as good publicity for both themselves and the nation as a whole. Lokomotiv's season doesn't start until next month, and Semin has made much of the disadvantage that this leaves his side at. I think he's being wily, and a kidder. Maybe his side lack proper match practice, having not played competitively since December 10th at Arsenal, but at least they're fresh. Semin must know that Monaco don't have the biggest squad, and they come here with a few injuries (notably their inspirational centre-back Sebastien Squillaci). The coach will be aware that a February trip to Moscow is the last thing the French want. He'll be instructing his players to go after the visitors from the off.

I saw the regulation Champions League metal turnstiles being erected 100 yards from the stadium walls when I was here yesterday. I've always thought they were superfluous, but now, stuck in the middle of a scrum of punters edging towards them, I'm thinking of them as more dangerous than pointless. Everyone has to go through these to get to the stadium – even the media, darling. Though I suppose others working in written and broadcast journalism may have turned up more than 40 minutes before the game. I wanted to come in on the metro, and sample a bit of the atmosphere. The underground system is another fantastic architectural legacy from communism. The stations are wonderfully ornate, decorated with marble, fine art, and in a few cases even chandeliers. Even at its busiest, I seem to feel an overwhelming serenity whether stood on the platform or on a train. This strange peace makes it even harder to get my head around the chaos of the recent tragedy. It's busy enough, with the ground set to be at nigh-on capacity for the game. Interestingly, the chants I hear are for 'Mockva' (Moscow) rather than Loko. With little traditional support, I guess that a lot of the people are just here to cheer on their compatriots, like the French were at Monaco. Maybe these two clubs from so far apart have something in common.

The press box is choc-a-bloc, even half an hour before kick-off. I dearly would have loved to have strolled in a few minutes before the start but unfortunately I had to go to the press office first to pick up my pass from the very helpful (and impossibly youthful-looking) press officer Alexander, and I have longer outside than I would have wished for. It's, well, pretty damn cold. This is the first – and hopefully it will be the last – time in my life that I have worn long johns. Having said that, I'd rather be watching than playing tonight. The effect of the chill is not helped, though, by the positioning of hospitality suites behind us. While I'm shivering so much that I can barely hold my pen straight, these smug, leather-jacketed bastards are larging it up five feet behind me, knocking back vodkas. The door to one of the suites opens and I consider walking in and abusing the free bar. I'm sure nobody would notice. Ever the professional, I decide no, and stay in my seat, shivering righteously. My 'phone bleeps. It's a text message from one of my friends at home. 'It looks pretty cold there mate!' Cheers.

A jolly-looking Russian man comes and sits next to me. I know he's a journo – I recognise him from the press call yesterday. He's the one who, at the end of training, ran to the edge of the pitch and hugged a bemused-looking Morientes while his mate took a photo. He looks like a chatter, so I'm looking forward to getting some more local knowledge. Unfortunately, a female reporter he knows (and is clearly trying to pull) sits down in the row in front and he dashes to sit next to her. So I go back to note-taking, and avoiding the bloke from *Monaco Matin* who I met yesterday – identifying me as a non-Russian, he backed me into a corner and wouldn't let me leave until I had named the entire Lokomotiv starting 11 for him to include in his report. Even though I made clear that I only knew about eight. It turns out one the players I told him would 'definitely start' has a long-term knee injury. Oops.

Much as I said I'm glad not to be out on the pitch, I didn't expect Monaco to start the game as if they didn't either. They look frozen, and ponderous, none more so than our old friend Dado Prso. He is as plodding as he was perfect on that November night against Deportivo. The skipper Giuly is not fully fit yet after breaking a foot and is only a sub, so Prso is meant to be replacing him in an unfamiliar right-sided role, with Morientes in the centre, as Monaco try to maintain their customary shape. But poor old Prso looks every inch a fish out of water, having one of those nights, with the ball skewing away from him like an eel at every attempt he makes to control. The visitors may lack their usual fluency, but at least they have the midfield players – Rothen, Bernardi, Cissé - to keep hold of the ball for spells.

It's at the back where Monaco are having their real problems. Squillaci is proving to be a big miss. Gael Givet is covering his position in the centre, while Hugo Ibarra is at right back. You wouldn't think one change would make so much difference – after all, the home side are missing their suspended South African left-back Jacob Lekgetho

- but Monaco are defending as if they only met one another the day before. In the first ten minutes, Loko's Georgian striker Mikhail Ashvetia (one I did correctly pick in the starting line-up) nips in after an abysmal mix-up between Givet and Julien Rodriguez, only to whack the ball high over the bar. Ashvetia fails to get another gilt-edged opportunity on target soon after. As much as the Monégasques look defensively uncertain, Semin has obviously (telepathically) taken my tactical advice on board, and Loko are drawing these mistakes with a high-tempo pressing game. They're suited to it, having all the technical gifts traditionally associated with Eastern European players.

Loko take a deserved lead just after the half-hour. The Monaco defence again fail to clear and the ball falls to Marat Izmailov. The youngster still has plenty to do, but expertly jinks past a brace of defenders before smashing a shot into the top of the net. And the press box goes absolutely apeshit. Everyone is on their feet cheering, and my friend in front takes the opportunity to give his female companion a bear hug. I'm not really used to this (and I don't just mean romance in football grounds), not only because journalists are supposedly impartial, but because in every other press box I've ever been in, the hacks sit there unmoved, blasé, and often barely paying attention to the game. This is something I never want to become. These people may be totally biased, but at least they're interacting with the game.

Izmailov is a fitting scorer. He and Loskov are increasingly bossing the midfield with their running and prudent use of the ball. Izmailov is a very young-looking 21 years of age, but has grown up quickly. In 2001, he went from turning out for the reserves in the third tier of the league to making the national side in the space of a mad five months. It must help playing alongside Loskov. He's the heart of Lokomotiv, a box-to-box midfielder who puts in the hard yards and frequently comes up with an important goal at the end of it. He was the Russian Premier's top scorer in 2000, and scored the goal in the final match of the 2002 season against CSKA that clinched that first title, as well as the one this season that earned a crucial group stage point in Milan against Inter.

Monaco now have a problem. Given that they look about as likely to score as it does to stop snowing, the goal has immediately made the game a damage limitation exercise unless they improve greatly. Their start to the second half is inauspicious. Lokomotiv have decided to go for the throat (good call again, Yuri), and really increase the pressure on their visitors. On the hour it pays off. Monaco struggle to clear a set piece, and a shot from the edge of the area deflects kindly to the Uzbek Vladimir Maminov, who drives in with goalkeeper Roma exposed. Deschamps' men are in real trouble.

The French coach drags off Prso, replacing him with the more nimble Shevi Adebayor. It would be stretching the truth to say this was a tactical masterstroke by Deschamps, but nevertheless his team manage to pull a goal back out of nothing. With twenty minutes to go, Rothen's left wing free kick is misjudged by the goalkeeper Ovchinnikov, and Morientes twists to guide home a clever header. The Spaniard is a class act. Starved of service, he is still alert enough to take the one half-chance that comes his way. The deafening virtual silence that greets the ball hitting the net (save the celebration of a dozen or so Monaco fans in front of us) tells you how crucial this away goal is.

Lokomotiv must be kicking themselves. They should be out of sight by now. They have a great chance to put some daylight between themselves and their opponents in the very final minute, when the substitute James Obioriah sprints clean through, with not a defender in sight. The Nigerian who recently returned from Cádiz has scored against Barcelona in this competition before, as well as in that famous game in the Bernabéu. But this time he fails to even force Roma into a save which the goal gaping at his mercy. If ever a moment in a match screamed 'I am a defining moment', this was it. It could be very costly.

Not that you would think it to see Yuri Semin holding court to the assembled media afterwards. He enters (and later leaves) to a round of spontaneous applause from the Russians in the room. Even if I could understand a word he was saying, I would find it hard to get past the satisfied grin that covers his lived-in features. Semin leans back in his chair in his casual leather coat looking very pleased with himself. In fact, he's carrying himself like he thinks he's a pop star. He does have every right to, however. He knows his team have been up against a very good side, and absolutely played them off the park. They may have passed up a chance to seal a quarter-final place – as Deschamps will admit a few hours later, 'we could have gone out of the Champions League tonight' – but hey, they're not going to win the trophy anyway. Whatever happens in a fortnight's time in Monaco, they have proved this year that they are a genuinely good team in Europe (I later discover Semin was saying that Loko did 'even better than I had hoped for'). The reactions of the Russian media during and after the game show how much this means to them. Not only is the Champions League a platform to show the wider world that the Russians are competitive in Europe again, but it shows the strength of Moscow itself. After the events of the last few weeks, the city and its people can recover, eventually.

If only the future of Russian football was that simple. As the 'New Russians' pour money into the Moscow clubs, further success in the Champions League is surely not too far down the line. Lokomotiv show that giant strides have been made in a relatively short period of time. But will it last? I read in Wednesday's *Moscow Times* (the English language newspaper) that yesterday, while Lokomotiv showed Europe the new Russia, Vladimir Putin was flexing his political muscles. He sacked Prime Minister Mikhail Kasyanov and his cabinet, even before next month's election, metaphorically shrugging at the democratic process. Significantly, Kasyanov was the last remnant of Yeltsin's government, and had criticised Putin's probe of Mikhail Khordokovsky, head of Yukos and critic of the Kremlin. Money or no money, it's increasingly clear that the oligarchs need to keep Putin on-side to survive.

Russian football is quickly becoming – no pun intended – a game of roulette. With the stakes ever higher and the window for opportunity getting smaller, there is little margin for error. 'The Moscow teams are completely taking over,' says Jim Riordan. 'The clubs that are there at the moment can't (all) survive, and one or two will fold – Torpedo, or Moskva maybe.' Like the villain Dog in *Lock, Stock and Two Smoking Barrels* says: 'It's a dog-eat-dog world out there.' Lokomotiv will just have to hope they have bigger teeth than the rest.

AC Milan

I can't remember staring out the 'phone like this for ages. It's like being a teenager again. I tell myself, the more you look at it, the less it's likely to ring. I switch on the laptop again. If I get really stuck in, I'm bound to get a call when I'm really involved. It's reverse psychology, in the same way that smokers lighting a cigarette when waiting for the bus is. Yet whichever way I approach it, I know deep down that I'm destined to be disappointed.

You see, I'm chasing Clarence Seedorf. At least, it's starting to feel like that. Little did I know when I casually let it slip to a friend in the pub that I was going to be interviewing Seedorf tomorrow that six months on, I would still be waiting for tomorrow. So far, I've talked to some very interesting people on my journey through the Champions League. But Seedorf is the one I've wanted all along. With all due respect to his footballing abilities, they're not really what makes him such a big draw. Fans have been more drawn, naturally enough, to the likes of Patrick Kluivert and Marc Overmars for Ajax, Raúl for Real Madrid, Andriy Shevchenko for Milan and Dennis Bergkamp for Holland – the flair players. None of those, however, has achieved what Seedorf has. Clarence Seedorf is the only player in the history of the game to have won the European Cup or Champions League with three different clubs.

The first time I really thought about this fact was in the immediate aftermath of the third of those wins, Milan's victory over Juventus at Old Trafford in last year's final. The ITV on-pitch reporter grabbed

Seedorf just a few short minutes after Shevchenko had stroked in the winning penalty in the shoot-out (being one of the very few English speakers on the pitch, poor old Clarence was always liable to get collared). The reporter had barely finished asking the standard opener - about how Seedorf felt about the victory - when the Dutchman broke down in tears. The midfielder had enough to be proud of on that night anyway, but considering that he had only just turned 27 years of age, let alone that he had something of a reputation in his earlier years (notably as part of the 'Ferrari Set' at Real Madrid), the achievement was little short of astonishing.

To briefly put aside the fact that the penalty shoot-out that night put the game out of its misery, Milan were the deserved winners of last year's Champions League, certainly when considering the competition as a whole. Most of the European press outside Italy lampooned the final as being some sort of slow death by *catenaccio*, the worst final contesting the Champions Cup since 1991's yawn-a-thon between Crvena Zvedza (Red Star Belgrade) and Marseille. You could say that at least in that final, one of the teams was trying to win it during the actual match. Yet in the case of the all-Italian showdown, it's hard to see how such a high-stakes game between two such close domestic rivals would have gone any other way. The intensity of the occasion demanded the utmost in caution from both sides. Perhaps we're doing Seedorf a disservice in assuming that his tears reflected his own personal feat. Maybe it was a simple release of tension, after 120 chanceless minutes and a shoot-out where nerves were jangling to the point where five of the ten penalties failed to find the net, including that of Seedorf himself (just as in Holland's Euro 96 quarter-final against France, where he had the crucial kick saved by Bernard Lama).

In years to come, people will remember nothing of Old Trafford 2003 save Andrei Shevchenko sending Gianluigi Buffon the wrong way from the spot, the kick that returned the trophy to the San Siro for the first time in nine years. The 1994 final had been 2003's diametric opposite, with Fabio Capello's peerless side annihilating Johan Cruijff's

Barcelona. While UEFA's official all-time ranking list (based on points, actual since 1992 and theoretical before, accumulated over the competition's history since 1956) places Milan third behind Real Madrid and Bayern Munich, the *Rossoneri*'s latest win gives them a total six titles, beaten only by Real Madrid's unmatchable nine. This puts them clear of Bayern, Ajax and Liverpool (four each). Given that the El Real won each one of the first five competitions and that the final four of Milan's wins are since 1989, the Italians are at least as synonymous with the Champions Cup in the modern era as their Spanish counterparts.

A fresh Monday morning in March at the San Siro may be a long way from match day, but it is a good opportunity to get up close to this history. It doesn't take much of a look through the stadium's museum (which covers both AC and Inter, who also use the stadium, of course) to affirm that Milan are one of those rare clubs for whom only overwhelming success is recognised. Domestic honours, like the silver plate emblazoned with gold stars that commemorate Milan's first ten *scudetti*, jostle for space with European trophies, cigarette cards of stars of yesteryear like Cesare Maldini, and international shirts (including one from Cesare's son, the current captain Paolo). The star of the show, though, is at the very front. As you walk in, you find yourself directly facing the sixth Champions League trophy. I've seen the trophy at close quarters before in the Camp Nou's museum in Barcelona, but for some reason it looks so much more vivid here. It's flanked by one of the white shirts worn by the players that night, signed by all the squad from the game, and a previous Champions Cup trophy (though I guess after you've won six, one is pretty much the same as another). Yet it's the 2003 version, decked in its red and black ribbons, which leaps out at you.

It's fitting, because although Milan are undoubtedly one of the, say, five biggest clubs in the world, they haven't won much in the last few years. The 2003 Champions League was actually their first trophy of any kind for a whole four years, although the *Rossoneri* also won the Italian Cup a few days after the final, and have since won the showpiece Super Cup final against Porto. Such is the power of their name that it's hard to believe. In some ways, it's not dissimilar to the truth of the legendary Milan side of the late '80s and early '90s. Centred around the Dutch triumvirate of Ruud Gullit, Frank Rijkaard and Marco van Basten, it's a side which, particularly in the light of the Old Trafford final, the club's current charges have been held in unfavourable comparison with in some quarters. When that Milan side won the *scudetto* in 1988, it was the first time the club had won the trophy in nine years, and only the third time since 1962. After '88, it took the Dutch and their colleagues four years to get it back.

With the passing of time, the little matter of a domestic title here or there becomes less and less important. Gullit-era Milan are remembered as one of the great club sides because of their domination of the Champions Cup. They won in 1989 with a pummelling of '86 winners Steaua Bucharest (4-0, with Gullit and Van Basten scoring twice each), and again the following year with a more narrow victory over Benfica, with Rijkaard this time netting the winner. These wins and their manner cast a Milan-shaped shadow over the whole decade in the competition. The shock loss against Marseille in '93, and the '94 whipping of Barcelona are – internationally - associated with the reign of the three Dutchmen, such was their influence, even if the reigns of Arrigo Sacchi and Capello are quite distinct for Italian fans. This is despite the facts that Gullit didn't play against Marseille, and both he and Rijkaard had left by the time of the '94 final in Athens (Van Basten was still at the club, but had already started to succumb to the ankle injury which would finish his career, and played no part). While league titles make big clubs, the Champions Cup makes the biggest clubs.

Such is Milan's cruise towards the retention of their European crown that they've been able to put plenty of energy into getting back the domestic championship. The impression is that they're getting irritated that they haven't won it for a while. None more than coach Carlo Ancelotti, one would imagine. Ancelotti played in midfield for

Milan himself between 1987 and 1993 (not that you would guess it from the generous paunch he's carrying forth into his mid-40s), and played in the European triumphs of '89 and '90. Subjected to the sort of customary scrutiny reserved for prominent ex-pros stepping into coaching, Ancelotti had developed a media image as a 'nearly man'. Last year's Champions League was the first title he garnered in ten years of coaching, a spell that started as assistant to then-national coach Sacchi - and has taken in stints at Reggiana, Parma and Juventus – before he returned to the San Siro in 2001. Ancelotti now has three trophies in the bag of course, but he also has the chance to quash those barbs for good by clinching the *scudetto*.

Milan are well-placed, currently five points ahead of second-placed Roma, who had been leading the table pretty much all season until being usurped in late January. The stats are slightly misleading - the *Rossoneri* have not exactly swept to the top with typical Milanese majesty. On the contrary, it's been an attritional few months. While Milan have been grinding out results such as last month's 1-0 win at Lazio, and the derby win against Inter where they came back from two down, Roma have been far more fluent, beating Siena 6-0 and then winning 4-1 at Parma, shortly after caning champions Juventus at the start of February (4-0). Milan have maintained their lead with more than a dash of Ancelotti's characteristics from when he was a player – organisation and discipline.

It's a far cry from the way I remember them winning the Champions League. Certainly in the early stages, the word 'swashbuckling' would have done Milan little justice. Their first two away performances in the first group stage – a 4-0 humbling of Deportivo La Coruña, followed by a stylish win at Bayern Munich courtesy of Pippo Inzaghi's brace – were especially eye-catching, showcasing all the attacking rhythm we've come to associate with the red and black stripes. In both group stages, they won the first four matches, allowing them the luxury of carelessly tossing away their final two in both cases. They even stood on the brink of elimination in a thrilling quarter-final against Ajax (the sort of tie that's surely the very essence of the competition) before substitute Jon Dahl Tomasson's goal in the fourth minute of injury time gave them a 3-2 win, following a scoreless first match.

But if I think a little harder about it, it wasn't all Serginho struts and Inzaghi finishes. Again, like with the Dutch era, it's a question of perception, conveyed by a few key matches. In the second group stage, they managed just five goals in their six games (with four 1-0 wins, no less), before the 0-0 in the first leg of the quarter-final in Amsterdam. We've already touched on the grind of the all-Italian final, but Milan had already gone through the difficulty of a semi-final derby against Inter. After drawing the goalless 'home' leg, a Shevchenko goal in a 1-1 draw eventually saw them to Manchester on the away goals rule. This Milan side are no strangers to rolling up their sleeves and digging in.

In the past, the Italian media had often linked Ancelotti's perceived over-cautiousness to his role as a runner-up. Yet his reserve is exactly what has brought Milan's traditional flowing football further along the trophy trail. This season's group phase performance had more in common with last season's approach to the knockout stages. It was an object lesson in masterful economy, with a trio of 1-0 wins and a goalless draw at Celta Vigo doing the trick. They could afford to coast the end of the group again, losing the final match against Celta at the San Siro after putting out an under-strength side (much to the chagrin of third-placed Club Brugge). Even an earlier shock home defeat to Brugge couldn't disguise Milan's superiority. Inzaghi's emphatic strike in match one against Ajax, Kaká's inspired late winner at Brugge and Shevchenko's fabulous finish to sucker Ajax again in Amsterdam all pointed to the same thing - they are the champions of Europe because they have the killer touch when it matters. Still think Ancelotti's a silver medallist?

Of course, their opponents only feel the full effects of these devils in sports casual because of the team's extraordinary tightness. If the 2003 Champions League showed us anything, it was that the spine of this Milan team is as rigid as of any in recent memory. Clearly, it's no coincidence that the competition was won in Alessandro Nesta's first season at the club. He may have cost €25 million, but if there was ever such an instance as a sure thing in football transfers, then this was it. When one of Roman Abramovich's first acts as Chelsea owner was reportedly to authorise a €50 million offer for Nesta, it was a well-expressed statement of intent. Nesta is worth every bit of the expense because he is quite simply the best there is. Adding him to a defence already counting Maldini, Kaladze and Costacurta amongst its numbers made breaching it nearer impossible than improbable. On top of this, Rino Gattuso was growing into a full embodiment of the fearsome, combative midfielder that he had always promised to be. In goal Dida, back from a few loan spells and with his confidence recovered from some earlier high-profile mistakes (such as the one which gifted Leeds' Lee Bowyer a late winner in the Champions League back in 2000), was also showing his worth, a progression that culminated in his crucial role in the Old Trafford penalty shoot-out. He saved from David Trezeguet, Marcelo Zalayeta and Paolo Montero on that night in Manchester.

So how did the AC Milan who won next to nothing for most of the '70s and '80s become the living legend of times since? One man's shadow looms large over this period – Silvio Berlusconi. Unlike with most football club moguls, you'll already have a knowledge of the man and his background (and almost certainly an opinion about him too). To recap, Berlusconi has not only been the club's owner since 1986, but also wields an virtual monopoly on commercial broadcasting through his Mediaset empire, part of a group of business interests which have made him Italy's richest man (and among the top 30 richest people in the world). Oh, and since 2001, he's been the Prime Minister of Italy as well.

Berlusconi started to become successful in the '70s through construction before branching out into commercial property development. He moved into the television business in the early '80s, the decade that later saw him take the reigns of the red and black half of the San Siro. Milan were ailing, still weak in the aftermath of the betting scandal which led to the club being relegated from Serie A for the first time ever in 1980 (the lingering effects saw them relegated again, this time via earned league position, in 1982). He dramatically changed the club's infrastructure from the bottom upwards – the Milanello training facility, for example, was a trailblazer and remains the team's own private world to this day. He appointed the hitherto little-known Sacchi as coach, bought Gullit, Rijkaard and Van Basten to combine with Italian stars like Maldini, Franco Baresi and Roberto Donadoni. In short, he made Milan the European giant it is today.

Not that he's to everybody's tastes. The *Rossoneri*, naturally, have loved him. Berlusconi is a man who would never allow trifles such as diplomacy or tact to impede his passion and drive. The very characteristics that have so often proved problematic in his political career are a boon in appealing to the football public. His political approach is teeming with sports language. He rode to power at the head of his *Forza Italia* ('Go on Italy,' basically) party, and his personality is every inch that of the modern football businessman. Since coming to power (having previously been Prime Minister for seven largely disastrous months in 1994) three years ago, Berlusconi has set about securing his position in the most brazen ways imaginable. Dogged since the '80s by (unsubstantiated) stories of Mafia links, he has been convicted of tax fraud, false accounting and bribing tax officials (although these charges were all later overturned on technicalities). When he came to office further charges awaited; but Berlusconi had no intention of taking these lying down. In fact, one of his first moves was to pass a bill decriminalising false accounting. Last June, Italy's upper house approved legislation from the Prime Minister that would make the PM, the president, the speakers of both houses of parliament and the chief justice immune from prosecution. So the court case against Berlusconi for bribing judges - which he failed to turn up to twice, with his aides saying he was 'too busy' - was more or less dead in the water.

The suspicion was the hastily introduced immunity law was passed to save Berlusconi the humiliation of attending court at the same time he would be assuming Italy's six-month presidency of the EU, at the start of July. The prospect of his tenure at the head of the EU was enough to horrify many in European politics on its own. Sure enough, his gaffe-laden, brash style – personally, I've always thought of him as a cross between Prince Philip and Arthur Daley - was typically unchanged. On only his second day in the job, he suggested to German MEP Martin Schultz that he would suit the role of a Nazi concentration camp guard in an upcoming film. Naturally, he flatly refused to apologise afterwards. Having spent most of his working life calling the shots in the boardroom, why would Berlusconi embrace diplomacy now, when he's well into his 60s?

Though he assumes less of a hands-on role in the club now he is a full-time politician – vice-president Adriano Galliani, his trusted deputy for nearly 20 years, conducts Milan's day-to-day business – Berlusconi is never more than a soundbite away. Even the stoic Ancelotti has had to grin and bear his share of presidential meddling. The president is known to have made suggestions to previous coaches on team selection - perhaps most famously when he successfully 'encouraged' then-incumbent Alberto Zaccheroni to tuck in Zvonimir Boban behind the Oliver Bierhoff-George Weah front pair in 1999 – and the coach winning a Champions League title isn't going to dissuade him from that. Berlusconi has reminded Ancelotti on more than one occasion of his obligations to be true to Milan's footballing heritage, most notably when he told his coach that the team must always play with two strikers – 'it's common sense!' It was even reported in *The Times* by Owen Slot that an Italian political journalist published a book of tactical sketches by Berlusconi, intended to guide Ancelotti. The president sees no clash. 'It's my team, after all,' as he modestly remarks, something he obviously had in mind when he pulled out all the stops to sign Rivaldo from Barcelona in summer 2002, despite Ancelotti not being keen. The Brazilian's impact was minor, and he ended up us an unused sub in the Champions League final. He returned to Brazil with Cruzeiro in

January, after Milan cancelled a contract that had 18 months left to run.

One thing that coach and owner are united on is the importance of the Champions League. Ancelotti conceded during last season's group stages that given the choice of winning Serie A or the Champions League, 'I'll take up the second option.' Put simply, he said, 'AC Milan belong to Champions League history.' While Berlusconi would have approved of such a grand statement, his interests in the Champions League stretch beyond mere football prestige. There is no doubt he is a supporter, as the fans themselves are aware – many turning a blind eye to a prominent right-wing figure leading their traditionally more left-wing club – but Milan is the ultimate tool in international prestige for him. That's why the maintenance of the *Rossoneri* as one of Europe's biggest, best and most exciting clubs is so important to Berlusconi personally.

Berlusconi repeated his call for two up front before the second round, first leg tie away at Sparta Prague ten days ago. A wary Ancelotti heeded his call, pairing a barely-fit Inzaghi with Shevchenko, to little effect as the team were held to a goalless stalemate (which left them totalling a miserable four goals from their first seven Champions League fixtures of the season). The lack of an away goal leaves them with a slightly-harder-than-routine second leg against the Czechs on Wednesday. It should be straightforward, but any slip, like the concession of a goal to the visitors, and they could be in trouble.

Should they take their league form into Wednesday, there shouldn't be a problem. Milan have won an impressive 18 of their 23 Serie A fixtures so far, and lost just once. It shows you how good Roma have been that it took their rivals so long to depose them at the top. It was Milan who ended the then-leaders' unbeaten record in winning at the Stadio Olimpico just after the winter break. This is the game that alone articulates how Milan have flourished since winning the Champions League. Despite missing Inzaghi and the similarly injured Nesta, they played with a stunning incision and quality, absorbing the home team's early pressure and breaking. Two world-class Shevchenko strikes, either side of an Antonio Cassano equaliser for the home side, may well mean that evening will be looked back upon as the turning point in the title race.

While Shevchenko could be rightly described as the greatest striker in Europe at this moment, Milan's cutting edge from this season has come from a perhaps unexpected source. When they paid São Paulo an estimated €7 million for 21-year-old Ricardo Izecson Santos Leite in August, it looked like Berlusconi and Ancelotti were investing for the future. The player's enormous potential was plain, but he had world-class competition for his place in the shape of his legendary compatriot Rivaldo and Portugal's Manuel Rui Costa. Just over six months later, the man known as Kaká is the darling of the *Rossoneri*, with his influence great enough to marginalise both his competitors and prompt the club to dispense with Rivaldo altogether. When he arrived, the youngster was at pains to outline his willingness to play anywhere the coach desired, but his is a rare attacking talent that demands to allowed to roam behind the strikers. He has instinctive movement, two good feet, an eye for a killer pass and finishing skills to match. The signings of veterans Cafu and Giuseppe Pancaro have been more than useful, but it's Kaká who has made Milan 2004 look so sleek and deadly.

The movement and murmur of the game is everywhere on the walk down to the stadium - through stalls selling replicas, red and black seat cushions and flags – and bound tighter by the crackle and odour of grilling meat in the fresh March air. On a drizzly, grey Sunday afternoon, the San Siro lacks the presence that it has at night matches, having a touch of the multi-storey car park about it. Yet it's still imposing, its outside (which, strangely, seems much bigger than the inside) reminding you of the scale of the club whose home it is. The game against mid-table Sampdoria feels the breath of the Champions League on its neck. With Wednesday's game waiting, Milan could do without this, but can't afford to take it lightly with Roma waiting for a slip-up. Both Nesta and Inzaghi are fit to return, a timely boost that also allows Ancelotti to give Shevchenko a rest before Wednesday. Tomasson, the dependable Dane, plays up front with Inzaghi.

We sit in the downstairs seats behind the goal, which makes you feel in the thick of the action, if a little wary – flares constantly fizz over our heads, stirring the memory of the story that everyone's heard about Inter fans pushing a scooter off the top tier. Sitting next to me is an enthusiastic man, in his mid-60s, who clocks us as non-Milanese immediately. Establishing that we're English, he soon takes us under his wing despite the exhaustion of my ten words of Italian in the early stages of the conversation. He gives a crash course on the politics of the Italian game; roughly, that Milan are the best, and that Juventus have all the referees in their pocket, which he indicates with a particularly firm gesture, one which you may think twice before repeating in front of women and children.

Sampdoria have a modest yet proud history, numbering a Serie A title (plus a few near misses) and five Coppa Italia wins amongst their achievements. This is their first season back in the top flight after four long seasons in Serie B, and they're holding their own. They are certainly no mugs on the travels either. They stroke the ball around confidently, which is only to be expected when you have midfielders of the quality of Aimo Diana and Italy international Cristiano Doni. Milan's class, however, is evident in the way they suddenly create the beautiful out of the ordinary. The game is ambling along at, well, Sunday afternoon pace, when the ball finds its way to Andrea Pirlo, some 25 yards out, just past the quarter-hour mark. Pirlo takes the briefest of looks up before swerving a bolt of a shot in off the inside of the goalkeeper's left-hand post. Pirlo is the least-lauded of the midfield three on show today (Gattuso and Seedorf being the other two) but is a class player growing in stature. And he definitely has the trademark Milan verve about him.

The visitors have no intention of standing back and watching in admiration, however. As Milan press again, a swift break puts in Doni with just Dida to beat, and the midfielder easily tucks home. Samp have brought around 8,000 fans from Genoa, and they go nuts, their cheers echoing around the cold silence of the other three sides of the ground. Milan are not going to be able to coast like they want to. To their credit, they buckle down as they have so frequently since the turn of the year. Before half-time, Pancaro whips in a cross from the left and Inzaghi gets in front of his defender to send a diagonal header into the corner. The striker wheels off in his trademark celebration (ie near-hysterics), as well he may. Following his injuries, this is his first goal since the beginning of October.

Milan must have conserving energy for Wednesday in mind. Intelligently, they realise the best way to this is to go for the throat, finish the game off, and then take it easy. Three minutes after the break, the ball is picked up by Kaká, drifting out to the left. Although he's some thirty-five yards from goal, his body language promises directness. You can almost see his eyes light up from the stand, as he jinks inside teasing the defenders in his path. He beats a couple, then pulls the ball onto his right foot before delicately bending a sidefoot shot into the corner. The first real roar goes up from the *Rossoneri*, hailing their star. Even the old guy next to me is almost lost for words. He simply turns to me, and nods. '*Perfecto*.' I couldn't have put it better myself, mate.

This is good news for Ancelotti. He gets to give both Inzaghi and Seedorf a breather (although the Dutchman is later said to be carrying a minor injury), and Shevchenko gets a twenty-minute run-out, in which he fires a shot against the 'keeper's legs. More importantly, Milan are that much closer to what would be a seventh *scudetto* in the Berlusconi era. His men are looking menacing despite rarely getting out of second gear. Sparta may be bringing a clean sheet with them, but they have it all to do on Wednesday.

I never did get to speak to Seedorf. After being blown out the umpteenth time, I decide to admit defeat. In retrospect, I'm almost glad. Don't get me wrong, his unparalleled record in the competition deserves respect. But the essence of AC Milan in the Champions League is so much bigger. Real Madrid, Manchester United and Ajax are all intrinsic to the Champions Cup's history, and its appeal. Milan, however, are the club that feels like its modern face, the most powerful link between the two incarnations – the European Cup and the Champions League. The club's website rather grandiosely describes the club as 'a synthesis of sport and entrepreneurial values.' Never has that been a more relevant aim than in the age of the Champions League.

Porto

Hmm. I thought that I'd got the hang of the Champions League press conference, but obviously not. The UEFA media rep walks into the press room, and welcomes us all - 'and especially representatives of the French media who are here today.' He then proceeds to inform us, in perfect English, that no questions will be either taken or answered in said tongue. As the people here for ITV seethe and fluster, I take the more practical step of frantically jotting down translations of my notes into French, so they can be translated into Portuguese for someone who can speak English to answer.

That someone is Porto's coach José Mourinho. His story is pretty well known by now - originally employed as Bobby Robson's translator at Sporting Lisbon, he impressed Robson so much that when the Englishman went to Porto, and then on to Barcelona, he took Mourinho with him. Robson had enough trust in the young Portuguese, having seen him at work, to start giving him scouting missions to carry out on his behalf. This was Mourinho's way into coaching, and at 41 he's already one of the most coveted managers in Europe today. Moreover, he caused a huge stir on his last visit to England, having had a very public verbal joust with Sir Alex Ferguson in the run-up to his team knocking Manchester United out of the competition. Without wanting to demean the tie's playing merits, this was a battle far more interesting than the football itself. Ferguson, the grand master of mental warfare, was clearly rattled and annoyed by this charming, educated young pretender, who belied his comparative inexperience as he calmly baited the Scot - with more élan than many far senior to him could dream of being able to employ - in measured and precise English. While Ferguson complained of officials failing to clamp down on Porto's diving in the first leg – moaning 'they always do it, don't they?' in the tone of a xenophobic pub bore – Mourinho offered in a deadpan expression that he too would be upset if his team had been taught a lesson by a team which 'cost a tenth of the price'. This guy really had something about him.

Mourinho again looks confident and relaxed sat before the media on the day before his side's quarter-final first leg tie against Lyon. He answers questions from the French media without needing the help of the translator sat next to him (cue a few clearly impressed whispers of 'il a compris!' from just behind me). Then he's asked how the preparation for this game will vary from the build-up to the matches against Manchester United. A wry grin creeps across his face as he quietly answers, almost to himself, in English – 'No mind games.'

The quarter-final presents a vastly different challenge for Mourinho and his team. Not only is there the need to recompose themselves after the high of springing a shock on one of the perennial favourites - despite the coach's *sang froid* before the game, his memorable celebrations at the final whistle told of a team who had invested untold effort into the outcome - but this has the look of a tight tie. Of all the quarter-final pairings, the one between Porto and Lyon is probably the hardest to call. All the other ties have clear favourites; Real Madrid should beat Monaco, you would expect holders AC Milan to be too strong for Deportivo La Coruña and Arsenal have the power to see off Chelsea. It's not only the potential closeness of this match up that makes it the most interesting.

This is also a game that harks back to the original idea of the European Champions Cup. Of the four ties, this is the only one between *bona fide* champions of their respective countries. Having both been surprise packages thus far, it's a great chance for one of them to get into the semi-final. The two cities themselves are fairly comparable too - like

Lyon in France, Porto is the second largest city in the country. It's based around industry and commerce rather than tourism. The locals say that 'while Coimbra studies, Braga prays and Lisbon shows off, Porto works.' It's unpretentious and feels very liveable. The city's best known for food and drink. Vila Gale, just across the impressive Ponte Luis I bridge from the dead centre of town, is an adjoining suburb famous for its port lodges. Though fish is rife throughout Portugal and here, as in all other towns, you see *bacalões* (salted cods) hanging in shops, the rest of the country knows the city's residents as *'tripenos'* (i.e. tripe eaters), such is its omnipresence in the city's cuisine. When I go to one of the many workers' cafes in the centre on my first night there my stomach isn't feeling too strong and I try to avoid it, asking instead for '*filhete de peixe.*' Either the waiter's Spanish is not as good as I'd hoped (possible) or they just don't have any other fish, as 15 minutes later I find myself with enough mini-fillets of tripe sat in front of me to sink a galleon.

It's great to experience a city that doesn't tart itself up for visitors but on the other hand something you never clock on the roadside city centre maps are gradients. And Christ is this one hilly centre. With the combination of these peaks and the Rio Douro (literally, golden river), separating the centre from Vila Gale, this was surely a veritable stronghold in times gone by. It's a good metaphor for FC Porto at home. They've won all their home games so far this season save the Champions League group match with Real Madrid and have won their last 29 domestic home matches in succession, first at the Estadio das Antas and then at the Estadio do Dragão since their move there - its official inauguration was on 17th November last year.

It would be, however, misleading to group Porto with Lyon in the 'upwardly mobile' category of the Champions League. Porto have history. Theirs is a genuine European pedigree that far predates the UEFA Cup win over Celtic in Sevilla last May, which stands out as the highlight of Mourinho's relatively brief but explosive reign. They won the European Cup in 1987, beating Bayern Munich in the final, with legends like João Pinto and Paulo Futre in the side, under the stewardship of coach Artur Jorge. Though they only have a semi-final and a couple of quarter-final appearances to boast since the start of the Champions League in 1992, they've been as regular participants as any of Europe's big names have. At the start of the season, only six clubs could boast more Champions League appearances than Porto, and those clubs were Manchester United, Real Madrid, Bayern Munich, Barcelona, Juventus and AC Milan. Statistically, they're one of the ten best teams since the Champions League started and as far as Portugal goes, they're streets ahead of the nearest competition (Porto had won 82 Champions League points to the start of this season, while Benfica are the next best with 17). This is where the comparison with Lyon emphatically ends.

Most of those Champions League points were accumulated during the '90s, a hugely successful decade for Porto in which they won the Portuguese title eight times - you could even make a case for them being the Portuguese Manchester United (I'm sure Sir Alex would love the comparison). They suffered something of a millennium bug however, and they hadn't won the title since 1999 when Mourinho took over from Octávio Machado halfway through the season, in January 2002. The new man salvaged UEFA Cup qualification from that campaign before winning the league/cup/UEFA Cup treble in his first full term, having given a club that had lost its way a firm kick up the backside.

Those years of relative mediocrity must have really hurt the fans. This is a real football city, in the mould of Newcastle or Marseille. There's another club in the city – Boavista - but you rarely see their colours anywhere and it's an uneven rivalry. They don't have Porto's history, having won the title just once, and Boavista are currently trailing so far behind their neighbours in the Portuguese Superliga that Mourinho and co would need binoculars to see them. People in the town are proud of their major club and excited by the team.

I first get an idea of this when I arrive at the airport the day before the game. I'm in a hurry to get the press conference so jump in a taxi straight to the Dragão, suitcase in tow. The driver is a portly, jovial guy in his mid-forties and I've barely sat down when he asks '*Fala Português?*' (Do you speak Portuguese?). I tell him no, '*pero hablo bastante bien español*' (but I speak Spanish quite well), so he shrugs his shoulders and decides '*Ah, igualmente, eh?*' (it's the same difference) before letting out a filthy, raucous laugh and nudging me in the ribs for the first of many times on our short journey.

They say that you speak to the taxi drivers if you want to get your finger on the pulse of a town. Or perhaps if you just fancy a parochial, xenophobic rant through a stream of half-truths than would make a tabloid editor blush. This guy seems OK though. We have a lively discussion on football generally and Porto's chances, the driver 'correcting' my Spanish into Portuguese as we go. When he gets over his disappointment that I don't know David Beckham personally, he tells me that he's confident that Porto will go through. Interestingly he doesn't talk about any of the players until I bring up the names of the likes of Deco, Costinha and Benni McCarthy, but just talks about the coach. 'Mourinho's the man,' he asserts. 'He's got them playing very well,' which gives you an indication of the extent to which the club's success has built around the cult of his own personality (Mourinho's, not the taxi driver's).

I'm a little disappointed when we reach the stadium before he can tell me which members of the Porto playing staff/board/youth team have been in the back of his cab in the last week. Yet my first lesson from the locals has taught me that Porto have got the punters talking. As I get out and pay, the driver can't resist an admiring glance at the very impressive new stadium. 'It's something, isn't it?' he coos with an almost paternal pride. The Dragão (Dragon - Porto's nickname is the Dragons) is just off the main motorway into the city, and has been built just down and across the road from the site of Estadio das Antas (named after the suburb which it's in), about a goal kick away. The new stadium is one of a number that have been constructed for the European Championships, taking place in Portugal this summer.

Paul Le Guen, the Lyon coach who's even younger than his opposite number, having just turned 40, also holds his press conference there, later on in the early evening. He displays his normal modesty and quiet charm, which is thrown into sharp focus compared to Mourinho's own more familiar brand of confidence as displayed earlier in the day. The two coaches form another initial point of comparison between the two clubs that's actually quite misleading. The two are relatively young and inexperienced, doing exemplary jobs under big club pressure, but Le Guen doesn't dominate proceedings in the same way as Mourinho. This is perhaps partly explained by their comparative football backgrounds - Le Guen was an accomplished player, representing Brest, Nantes and Paris St-Germain with distinction as well as wearing the blue of France 17 times. Mourinho had not much of a playing career to speak of, turning out in the Portuguese lower leagues until he realised 'that I wasn't going to make it' at 23. Due to his lack of playing pedigree, Mourinho has had to work a lot harder to be able to count on the respect of his players.

After Le Guen's finished, his team have an open training session on the Dragão pitch, and I get my first glimpse of the stadium from the inside. It certainly fulfils the promises that a look from the exterior gives you. The swirling flourishes of the frames which circle the stands give the stadium a necessary grandeur, but you also have the feeling of freedom granted by the space between the two. It's certainly a massive improvement on the newer grounds in England, the meccano-style efforts at Middlesbrough and Sunderland being examples which spring to mind, which are so lacking in personality that if you were dropped blindfold into the centre circle, you'd struggle to know which one you were in. Having never visited the Estadio das Antas, I can't say if it's an improvement or not, and it's usually a wrench for the fans when a club moves, but the place smells of innovation and progression, a marker of a brave new era. It speaks volumes of a club going places.

While standing half watching the Lyonnais amble through some light training, I'm approached by a man asking me if I'm French. He's trying to find out where the Lyon players are staying in town. I'm not and I don't know, but in a place and situation where being English is more of a welcome curio than something to mutter embarrassedly under your breath, he perks up visibly with interest and we begin a conversation.

· Paolo is in his late 30s, bespectacled, and of average height with the slightest paunch. With him is Monica, maybe five years younger, of similar height with wavy blonde hair. They're from Rio ('the real Brazil', as Paolo makes a point of stressing) and have lived in Porto for ten years. Both speak perfect English. Paolo's very chatty - unsurprisingly, as he commentates on all Porto's matches for a local radio station. I start to realise that he was the guy asking Le Guen intelligent, searching questions in faultless French - certainly the coach looked more engaged when answering him than any of the French journos. He's also very keen to know what I think of the Dragão, and I tell him how impressed I am. He says how great he thinks it is and how important it is as a source of pride to the city and its residents. After decades of playing second fiddle to Lisbon, Euro 2004 is a chance for the world to see what Porto has to offer.

That's part of why the Champions League is such a big deal to Porto this year. They're not just attempting to re-establish themselves in the European elite, but while doing so, they're flying the flag for Portugal ahead of Euro 2004. They have earned the right to consider themselves as Portugal's representatives. On top of last season's treble - where they took the title by 11 points from nearest rivals Benfica - they are unbeaten in the league so far this season after 26 games, and are seven points clear with two games in hand. They're also in the Portuguese cup final again. Many of Portugal's most recognised players - Figo, Rui Costa, Pauleta - play abroad, so they are making people across Europe take Portuguese club football seriously.

Competing in the Champions League is important, but beating Manchester United has raised the bar. This took them from competing in the Champions League to achieving in it. The scenes provoked by Costinha's dramatic last-minute goal at Old Trafford which put the

Dragões through showed that this was a real watershed moment for the manager, his team, the club and the city. The sight of Mourinho tossing aside his trademark cool to go sprinting down the touchline, punching the air to join his celebrating players when the goal went in - as well as his brazen victorious salutes in front of the United fans as he headed for the tunnel at the end - will undoubtedly figure in the most prominent images of this season's competition. 'I am quite fair to both teams,' insists Paolo of his commentaries. Even as Porto's captain side-footed into the net at the last in Manchester? A confessional grin creeps across his face. 'Well, maybe I went a little crazy, just that once.'

With success, Porto have started to take themselves more seriously. I get the impression Paolo regrets this a little. 'I travel on my own when I go abroad,' he says of following the team to report on their European away games. 'I used to travel with the team, but now they don't like you talking to the players. It's all very formal and a little awkward.' Speaking to him, it's apparent that he's at least as well travelled in Europe as me. He talks engagingly about visiting Belgrade and how dramatically it's changed, politically and socially. In a way Paolo is typical of his adopted city. People are switched on, with an enthusiasm for and knowledge of global events that's not so apparent in some other European countries. I see a lot of language skills on display too, with bus drivers speaking fluent English to tourists.

The feeling around the city on match day though is pure Portuguese. People are really taking up the theme of celebrating their city, through the club. When I get up, I notice on TV that in Mercado Bolhão, the city's main market, a daytime show is holding an FC Porto-themed party. When I get down there in mid-morning, it's in full swing. Middle-aged women take time off from their shopping to wave blue-and-white scarves and flags, and they clap along as a succession of silver-tongued (and haired) crooners saunter through some Portuguese easy-listening classics (all the housewives are singing along). If they gave the audience on *Richard and Judy* free beer and cocaine, it wouldn't be half as much fun as this. When I pop in to my hotel mid-afternoon to drop some things off, it's still in full swing. Around the city, loads of people on the streets are wearing scarves and many shops have been done out in the club colours. It's proper cup fever. God knows what the place would be like if they made the final.

When I arrive at the Dragão around an hour before kick-off, it's already buzzing. The streets on the approach to the stadium are thick with people and the bars on the Avienda Fernão de Magalhães teem with mainly middle-aged men, many with their kids. The younger people seem to get down to the stadium earlier. As I walk down the sloping approach road to the stadium, I feel a tinge of sadness looking at the building site to my left, what's remaining of the old Estadio das Antas. Just the one stand is still there, but just looking at its stained concrete tells of years of history - drama, triumphs, failures. I wonder what must go through the hearts and minds of the men in the bars on Fernão de Magalhães every time they walk past on their way to the Dragão. Paolo told me that what's left of the old place is due to be 'detonated' in a fortnight.

Tonight is only the second time a European tie has been played at the Dragão, the first having been the first leg of the tie against Manchester United last month. The full beauty of the stadium comes into focus from high up in the press stand. The view of the pitch is great but it's not that which is most striking. It's that you can see the traffic zipping by on the freeway through the huge spaces between the ceiling structure and the seating. You can also see supporters walking around the ground on their way in. Most football grounds are completely enclosed with the only natural light coming in from directly above, so it gives you a rare perspective of life going on around the stadium, so often the hub of its community. In the half-light of dusk, it's a breathtaking sight.

Surroundings like this crave not just an entertaining team, but an awesome one. While Porto may not be quite there yet, they certainly look as if they're building an admirable dynasty. My first concentrated look at Mourinho's team was in last season's UEFA Cup final. The game panned out pretty much as you would have been led to expect, with the

Portuguese displaying the greater technique and finesse and the Scots fighting hard. This point of view is outrageously patronising to Celtic - sure, they're well organised and work hard, but they've their fair share of genuine quality too in the likes of Larsson, Thompson and Sutton. It was testament to Porto's collective and individual talent that they made their opponents look so workmanlike in comparison. Their attacking demanded attention, manifested through the guillotine-sharp striker Derlei and the prodigiously gifted midfielder Deco. They served up more of the same in their thrilling first phase win in Marseille.

In the last round against Manchester United, the compactness of the Porto team was highly notable. They weren't without their forward threat, but they didn't go gung-ho in the way that I expected they might, which would have played into the hands of such experienced Champions League opponents. They had the look of a team not just with talent to spare, but of one that would be very hard to beat, a quality they could need against a Lyon side that has looked highly impressive themselves in the Champions League so far this season in brushing off challenges from the likes of Bayern Munich and Real Sociedad. Lyon's president Jean-Michel Aulas made a point of emphasising before kick-off, though, that this was 'the worst possible draw' for his club. 'They are much stronger than us.'

The French aren't overawed despite their president's feelings. The first half unfolds as a cagey affair, played out in the manner of two teams who have a lot of respect for each other. It's captivating without exactly being end-to-end stuff. Benni McCarthy, the South African who is proving a very able replacement for Derlei (who suffered a serious knee injury around the turn of the year), put a couple of beauties past United in the last Champions League game here. He's not having his best night here though, and fritters away a couple of presentable first-half chances. The best chance falls to Lyon's nippy winger Sidney Govou, whose fierce drive after a good move deflects marginally wide with Vítor Baía beaten in the Porto goal.

Lyon are looking comfortable enough as half-time approaches.

Porto are seeing a lot of the ball, as you would expected for such an adept side playing at home, without forcing the pace too much. Then they get the type of lucky break that turns a game this hard to call. A diagonal ball by Maniche finds McCarthy loitering with intent in the penalty area, and again the striker miscues, but the mishit strikes the on-rushing Deco and flies into the corner of the net. 'Keeper Gregory Coupet automatically throws up an arm, appealing vainly for offside, but it's more in hope than expectation. It's a moment that not only lifts the whole stadium, but knocks the stuffing out of the visitors.

Although their strength comes from their solidity as a unit, Deco is pivotal to most good things that Porto do. A player who's the very definition of flair, he's adored by the fans. In Julío Magalhães' *t'Antas Glórias*, a recently published retrospective of Porto's years at the old stadium, he's named by the author as one of the top five players ever to have graced the place - the final chapter *Os génios* places him next to the likes of Futre and Cubillas. He's influential on so many levels - his set pieces are always dangerous, and he has the vision to open up a defence. The opposition know he can also beat two or three players at a time so he attracts potential tacklers every time he picks up the ball, leaving spaces elsewhere on the pitch. Not forgetting, of course, that he's simply very good at keeping the ball, something valuable when you're a goal up.

If I had a euro for every time I've heard that scoring just before half-time 'is the best possible time to score', I'd own Brazil by now, but in Porto's case the cliché couldn't be truer. Having got themselves in front they know that Lyon will be coming at them, looking for an away goal, which suits the home side down to the ground. Le Guen tries to improve his side's ability to hold on to the ball by bringing on Vikash Dhorasoo - one of the most prudent users of the ball you will ever see - for Juninho. This however means they are short of Juninho's set piece expertise, surely a must-have in an away game against a side as solid as this. Instead Lyon ending up giving away far too many free-kicks around their own penalty area, giving Deco plenty of opportunities to find his own range. Coupled with the scope for greater directness that the visitors' efforts to press give Porto, Lyon are living on a knife-edge.

Mourinho has introduced Lithuanian man-mountain Edgaras Jankauskas up front, replacing the young Brazilian Carlos Alberto, to occupy Lyon's back line further, and presumably to take advantage of one of Deco's free-kicks too. Going into the last twenty minutes, it's the poised centre-back Ricardo Carvalho that does just that, heading in a curling Deco delivery from out by the corner flag. From the players to every last spectator, there can't be a mind in the stadium that doesn't think the game is up for Lyon tonight.

If you wanted a perfect example of a 'professional job' in the Dictionary of European Football Platitudes, this would be it. Like their hugely impressive coach in whose image they are so resplendent, this Porto team are wonderfully controlled, disciplined and, well, professional. Towards the end of the game, the young guy reporting for UEFA is compiling his ratings next to me. 'That guy playing number 6,' he suggests. 'Costinha. Yeah. He didn't do much, did he?' It's a typical viewpoint, if plain wrong. No-one ever notices him, because he's just efficient, protecting the defence and winning the ball so Deco, Alenichev and McCarthy can do their stuff. 'He's never been a fans' favourite, but he's really appreciated by his coaches and the other players,' his great friend John Collins tells me later, a team-mate of Costinha's during their spell at Monaco. Going by the current side, Costinha is a very Porto type of player.

Paul Le Guen is probably as downcast as he's ever been seen after this. He looks totally deflated, and describes it as a 'very hard result.' Going home to France without an away goal is bad enough, but he now knows – if he didn't before - what a tough nut Porto will be to crack. When he casually strolls in around ten minutes later, José Mourinho is of course perfectly poised, no different from the man presented to us at midday yesterday, dutifully talking of it 'only being half-time in the tie'. I don't think that there's a person in the room who would really believe this, whether they heard it in Portuguese, French or English. It's clear that if this team can maintain its coach's poise, it could take something special to stop the people of Porto losing theirs, and partying some more.

Real Madrid

I'm beginning to think I'm some sort of jinx. First there was the Moscow metro bomb just before I went there, and now Madrid has suffered its own equivalent, the Atocha bombings. Though we're post-Soviet Union and Cold War, there's still little to emotionally connect most British people with Russia - the Moscow bombings were deemed only worth a day of headlines - but the reaction to the 'M-11' bombings (as they're referred to in Spain) has shocked me. As Western Europe's worst terrorist attack of recent times, it's the horror that's brought the reality of terrorist violence closer to us in the post-Iraq climate. Yet still the reaction was - though supportive and sympathetic - muted next to that which characterised September 11. It may be hard to fathom why when you consider that José María Aznar staunchly backed Bush and Blair's pro-war stance, but then you start to think how we really look at Spain. We don't share a language, we rarely think of ourselves as actively European and it's just a holiday destination for most. With Britain being a country that so closely aligns itself with (and sees itself as a version) of the US, we might as well be a million miles away from Spain rather than two hours' flying time.

I guess my attitude's different, but I felt it more than that. Actually it scared the living shit out of me. I know Madrid better than New York, but it wasn't just the feeling of global terrorism moving geographically nearer. It's facile, but maybe football is why I feel so much closer to Spain, Italy, France and Germany than the States - it feels like a mark of culture.

If anything else characterised the difference between the UK/US axis and the Spanish, it was in their reaction to the attacks. While the admittedly grieving and shocked Americans resolved to bomb seven shades out of their Middle Eastern country of choice in recompense, people from all regions of Spain - a country supposedly just a loose collection of diverse states - took to the streets in their millions to demonstrate for peace. Then, in the subsequent elections, they dismissed Aznar, who endorsed the war despite the opposition of 80% plus of the population before trying everything he could to pin M-11 on ETA, from office.

The spirit of unity fostered by their defining event of modern times is everywhere. When I arrive exactly a fortnight after the attacks, posters on Metro platforms speak of continuing through adversity and being there for each other. A huge white banner with photos of rescue workers, medics, firemen and police covers the front of the town hall in the Puerta del Sol, with the simple message – '*Gracias a todos*' (Thank you to everyone). It's hugely moving.

The RFEF (the Spanish FA) decided almost immediately against cancelling the following weekend's fixtures, despite the country being in the middle of three days' official mourning. *Jornada 28* was largely acted out in a ghostly atmosphere of solemnity, no doubt seeming pointless to many. Atlético de Madrid's captain Carlos Aguilera had admitted that his team had 'no desire to play the game' that his side was obliged to fulfil at Real Sociedad that weekend. Not dropping the baton has been the way to cope though, and without getting too sanctimonious about it all, it's fair to say that football, as the obsession of so much of the peninsula, is playing a part in the lengthy healing process. 'The first weekend was strange, but there was some sort of recognition that football goes on,' says Sid Lowe, an English journalist based in Madrid. 'You could also argue that the new government coming in (two weeks later) was a watershed. As psychologists might say, it represented a sort of 'closure'.'

To the outside world, the capital's football begins and ends with

Real Madrid. It's understandable - it's the world's biggest football club after all - but tough on the two other clubs, Atlético de Madrid and the smaller-still Rayo Vallecano. Significantly, Bayern Munich offered to play El Real in a charity match in the aftermath of M-11, as if they alone represent the city. Planning eventually started for a fundraiser for the victims' families between a side made up of a combination of Real and Atlético players and a rest of the world team.

There's a notable contradiction between the now established image of Real Madrid as flamboyant entertainers and the city's traditional image as the bastion of conservative Castilla. Madrid often comes off in an unflattering light, particularly when it's measured against Barcelona, which it's thought to be less fashionable, arty and cosmopolitan than. This is an image that most Catalans don't hesitate to encourage. Though these generalisations aren't without a degree of truth, what often goes unmentioned is that Madrid has little of Barcelona's aloofness and self-regard.

It looks like we're slipping into Spanish social and political cliché already. But I think it's necessary to reiterate. The notion of El Real as 'Franco's club', something still regarded as fact in much of provincial Spain, is something that will meet with blank looks if you drop it in conversation in the pub in London. Real Madrid is routinely defined purely by its 21st century image - the 'Harlem Globetrotters of football' blah. The older slight is inescapable here though. La Liga is openly political, and acknowledged as such by the fans. Especially in the regions more specifically marginalised during General Franco's dictatorship - ie the Basque country and Catalonia - there's no doubt that El Real are still the club shaped in the image of *El Generalissimo*, they're still given favours by the establishment and referees (as during the dictatorship) and there's still nothing better than putting one over on the 'forces of darkness'. This is not typical 'big club' jealousy. The inference is not simply that El Real are favoured so much because they're a big club, but because they represent the very essence of the Castilian establishment.

This view of El Real - and particularly the idea of their extensive catalogue of honours having been aided and abetted by the bias of match officials - is as far as can be from the global perception of the club as it is today. El Real's now-prevailing image as a team of heaven-sent footballing mavericks is probably the biggest triumph of president Florentino Pérez' near four-year reign at the Bernabéu. It's in this period that Real have overtaken Manchester United as the world's most marketable club, thanks to the simple trick of signing the world's current most prestigious footballer every summer. They stand out like giant neon dollar signs, from the signing of Luis Figo in summer 2000 (when Pérez was elected) onwards - Zidane, Ronaldo, Beckham. You couldn't say that Pérez' tenure has radically overhauled the traditional values of Real Madrid, but it has altered the club's direction. But more of that later.

To figure out what El Real's 'traditional values' are, you have to speak to a dyed-in-the-wool *madridista*. Someone who lives and breathes the club, who represents its very essence. Someone like Emilio Butragueño. *El Buitre* (The Vulture), having been brought up as a fan -'on the very first day of my life, my father left the hospital and came to the stadium to make me a member of the club'- played for his boyhood idols 450 times between 1984 and 1995, and scored 180 times. Within a minute or so of meeting him, you can tell what this has meant and still means to him. 'Frankly speaking, I didn't think I was going to be a professional player. Not even when I was playing for Castilla (El Real's second team, currently in the Segunda B). In fact, not even after I got the (first-team) opportunity.' There's an image of Butragueño the awestruck fan for a second. 'I considered Real Madrid like another world- so good, so extraordinary that I thought I didn't deserve to belong to it.' The rarity of hearing a legend speak like this is quite humbling. You almost feel the need to put your arm round him and reassure him what a great player he was.

Butragueño mentions the importance of 'history' and maintaining the club's 'values' a lot. He embodies what playing for Real Madrid means, or should mean. Received wisdom is that Butragueño, as part of

La Quinta del Buitre, helped to shape El Real in the image that they're perceived today. *La Quinta del Buitre* roughly translates as 'The Vulture Squadron' (as Phil Ball has it in *White Storm*, the only English language history of the club). It was how the group of Butragueño, along with Martín Vásquez, Michel, Manolo Sanchíz and Miguel Pardeza, came to be known - a group of players from *la cantera* (the youth set-up) all coming through at the same time. The anomaly is they never fully formed the core of the side, and played together for the first team just the once, but what they represented for *madridistas* is important as their introduction ushered in the reign of one of the club's most successful ever sides.

'We have very demanding fans. Very demanding.' Butragueño thinks back to that late '80s team that won five consecutive league titles. 'They are used to seeing great performers, talented players, and they are used to winning. But at the same time, the *way* you win is very important. Our style has to be very offensive, and you have to offer something beautiful, every game.' The aesthetics are important to Butragueño. Making chat before we start the interview proper, I mention that I went to the Real Betis-Sevilla derby while visiting a friend in Sevilla a few weeks before. He searches for the right words, musing 'Hmm,' in the tone of a disapproving parent. 'It was a fairly... ugly game,' he decides, contorting his enduringly youthful features. 'From the visual point of view, it (the '80s team) was a very attractive team. We had very talented offensive players. People came here with the comprehension that they were going to have a very good time. The knack to being unpredictable, to do something different every game or even every five minutes is very important.'

We're sat in a conference suite in the club's plush offices at the Bernabéu. Facing me is a large framed photo of Pérez receiving the 'Team Of The Century' trophy from Sepp Blatter and João Havelange as part of FIFA's millennium celebrations. There's plenty of history around us - glass cabinets house framed and laminated tickets from some of the biggest occasions from down the years, including the 2002 Champions

League final against Leverkusen. A replica of the trophy won that night in Glasgow sits adjacently. Wherever you are in the Bernabéu, it's impossible to get away from the European Cup/Champions League. Legendary president Santiago Bernabéu (that's right, the one who the stadium's named after) was part of the committee that helped create it in the '50s, from an original idea by a *L'Equipe* journalist. El Real won it for each one of its first five years, and it underpins the club's claims to being the greatest in the world. 'A huge part of their identity is based on the European Cup/Champions League,' says Sid Lowe. When doing the stadium tour - where you seem to read text every five or so yards along the lines of '...and this is what makes Real Madrid the world's greatest club'- you're left in no doubt that it's a considerable piece of the club's history.

'The main one, I think,' offers Butragueño. The one black mark on his virtually perfect career is the lack of a European Cup triumph. Having won 6 European Cups by 1966, the ensuing period was – continentally speaking - spent in the wilderness. The magical side of *La Quinta*, Hugo Sanchez and co couldn't quite top off their reign with the *séptima*. 'Right.' Butragueño takes a big gulp of water and shuffles in his seat. I may have touched an old, yet still raw wound. 'At that moment, you had to win your national league to aspire to win the (European Champions) title. At that time it was tougher, because there was only one team per country, apart from the defending champion. Now you end, I don't know, 20 points behind the champion, and you can participate in the (Champions League) next year.' He swiftly qualifies this statement, careful not to bite the hand that feeds. 'But I think it's fair, because if you want to create a great competition, the best teams have to be there.'

Trying to pass into club immortality became an addiction. 'At that point, we won the Spanish league five times in a row, so it meant five opportunities to achieve our goal, our main goal. It was like an obsession for us, because the European Cup is the most difficult and the most prestigious competition in Europe. When you are competitive, you want to test yourself in an uphill situation.' Of all the if-onlys, it's the narrow semi-final defeat to PSV Eindhoven (the eventual winners) in 1988 that rankles the most. Sure, they missed out in the semi-final again the following year, but in truth they were belted by an exceptional Milan side. 1988 was the ultimate should-have-been.

'In my opinion we were unlucky. In my opinion we were the best team in Europe. We made the mistake here in Madrid (where they let in the away goal that would ultimately decide the tie), we didn't play well. In the second match in Eindhoven (a goalless draw), we deserved the ticket to get through to the final.' So if there was one thing you could change about your career...'Of course. That was a scar forever, you know?' And The Legend is not a man prone to overstatement. There's no doubt this sense of unfulfilment is felt by the *socios* too. 'Real Madrid's fans remember that period very well, because it was a splendorous period for the club. People were very excited with the team. Extraordinary period. But at the same time, people remember with deep sadness, because we didn't win the European Cup.'

So is this what the recruitment of the *galácticos* is about? Buying Zidane, Ronaldo, Figo and Beckham for the same team (not to mention already having the likes of Raúl and Roberto Carlos) is like using a sledgehammer to crack a nut in terms of competing for domestic titles. You don't get all these together in the same place unless you're hell-bent on world domination. And the European Cup/Champions League, as the most visible competition in the world is, as Butragueño admits, Real's 'obsession.' 'For us, it's the main competition. Real, in my opinion, has incredible prestige all over the world *because* of the Champions League, *because* of the European Cups. I think these titles have a lot to do with our presence all over the world. It doesn't mean the league or the King's Cup aren't important to us, they're very important. But we are an international club, so we have to look abroad.'

Not an international club that forgets its roots though. One of the cornerstones of Pérez' presidency has the policy of composing the team of 'Zidanes y Pavónes' (Francisco 'Paco' Pavón being a graduate of the *cantera*), a mix of world stars and local boys, a more explicit realisation of what *La Quinta* gave the club in the '80s. According to Butragueño, this mixture is imperative in maintaining 'Real Madrid's values'. Though they 'strive to be one of the best teams in the world', they need these young players. 'When Ronaldo or Zidane comes here, they have to understand what Real Madrid means, (in terms of) observing the habits and customs of the club. If we didn't have the local players, it could be very difficult for us to explain everything to them. Raúl, Casillas, Gutí and now Pavón, Bravo, Mejía, (to) all these players, Real Madrid is not only a football team, it's part of their life.'

Sid Lowe is unconvinced. 'It's about marketing. It's also the only way to afford these superstars.' Pérez' election pledges in 2000 were simple. He would bring the world's best players to the club, and clear the club's debts (estimates ranged from £150 million to way over £200 million). While public institutions as El Real had traditionally been cut ample financial slack by Spanish banks and the government, UEFA had warned clubs during the tail end of the '90s that they would have to prove financial solvency in order to participate in their competitions, making El Real's debt a potentially crippling problem. One of Pérez' first actions as president – after completing the promised purchase of Figo - was to sell the training ground, netting the club an estimated €510 million (around £350 million) and putting them firmly in the black. The argument over the legitimacy of this sale is still raging on, with the ADED pressure group only last December criticising the fact that the city council's decision to reclassify the ground - from sporting use to development property - was signed off by one of the club's own lawyers, Tomás Ramón Fernández. Pérez had been as good as his word, but he has always been sparing with financial details. A study (albeit one by a university in Barcelona) detailing projected earnings by the club mentioned that they would be receiving €100 million from the communications company Telefónica. The club itself failed to mention that this figure would be spread over 10 years.

The president has therefore needed to be innovative in his spending.

While the *galácticos* pick up an estimated €6 million annually- after tax- the likes of Javier Portillo and Pavón take away €150,000. Although I'm sure these young men are, like Butragueño, fulfilling a childhood dream in turning out in the famous white shirt, can such a disparity be healthy? There's not just the issue of dressing-room morale, but the persistent feeling that, well, if you pay peanuts, you get monkeys. Carlos Queiroz was a low-key choice to replace Vicente Del Bosque as coach last summer, presumably hired as a yes-man to crack on with the coaching while Pérez handled the grown-up stuff. 'Things were a bit stuck under Del Bosque,' says Guillem Balague. 'Queiroz promised something fresh, with new techniques and approaches.' Yet Queiroz it was who began to question the feasibility of the 'Zidanes y Pavónes' model.

'He was more ready to admit than Del Bosque that the team needed a defender,' says Lowe. Queiroz was dismayed when the power brokers failed to complete the signing of Argentine defender Gabriel Milito - with El Real citing a 'knee problem', he was allowed to join Real Zaragoza instead - and let defensive midfielder Claude Makélélé leave to join Chelsea. The coach's reluctance to trust the *cantera* and thus honour the model infuriated Pérez and put him on shaky ground almost as soon as he'd arrived. 'At the beginning of the season, Queiroz admitted privately that it would be a 'miracle' if Real won anything this season,' Lowe remembers. 'The *cantera* is fine in principle, but he recognised they have to be good enough, and some of the youth-teamers just aren't good enough.' The moment which perhaps embodies this most came when Queiroz substituted the young defender Rubén - in floods of tears as he left the pitch - just 25 minutes into November's humiliating first-half beating at Sevilla.

Guillem Balague doesn't think that the model itself is essentially flawed. 'With 'Zidanes y Pavónes', there is no one without the other. It's the only way to have these stars.' While Sid Lowe observes that Real's identity is based on the European Cup/Champions League, he stops short of saying that Pérez' accumulation of stars is particularly with the aim of chasing the trophy; 'I don't know if the star thing's really about that.' Butragueño's circumspect acknowledgement that they 'give us international prestige' leads us towards the reality. It all comes back to the m-word - marketing. Balague argues that this was the hub of Pérez' vision when he took the job. 'He looked abroad to countries like England, where you would see far more people walking down the street wearing Barcelona shirts than Real ones, and said to himself: 'We have the biggest name in the world. We should be doing that.' He started the process of making customers out of fans.'

So how does sticking to the model affect El Real's chances in the Champions League? The world footballing public views it from a slightly different angle than the one presented by Butragueño and Pérez, but it's a romantic view. It assumes El Real as a creation of ad-hoc brilliance, where the stars just rock up and play, a loose and fluid collection of geniuses, unfettered by dull modern concerns like tactics and formations. While this exaggerates, all clichés carry a modicum of truth. 'Real forgot the natural law of the game,' insists Balague, talking about their difficulties in recent weeks. 'You can't play fantasy football for a whole season.' The feeling persists that the pursuit of stars has begun to eclipse rational thought and organisation, something that the arrival of Queiroz was meant to put the brakes on after the *laissez-faire* regime of Del Bosque ('a kindly, cuddly club man', as Sid Lowe describes him).

But the coach has no squad to speak of - the lack of strength in depth is laughable compared to some of their domestic rivals, like Depor or Valencia, let alone their European ones - and therefore has no scope to rotate during a long season. Even if Queiroz wanted to rotate his starting eleven, he would be 'slaughtered' if he did so, reckons Lowe. The *galácticos* are what Real Madrid is about to 90% of the world, so playing competency, or the matter of resting to stay fresh, doesn't come into it. You just don't leave Zidane on the bench.

Walking down to the Bernabéu a few hours before kick-off against Sevilla is like making a visit to a footballing theme park, or a footballing Madame Tussaud's, with people slowly shuffling round as if in reverential awe. As I come out of the metro on to the corner of El Paseo de la Castellana the coach carrying the Real squad whips past in the evening rain, and we catch glimpses of Zidane and Beckham. There aren't any hearty cheers or outbreaks of singing, but a few mild shrieks and 'is it really them?' type gasps, the sort of reaction you might expect from pop fans spotting their idols pre-gig.

Inside, the Bernabéu fills up slowly and by kick-off is just under three quarters-full according to the official crowd figures, although you would swear it was less than that. Like the San Siro but more so, you can't avoid describing the Bernabéu as touristy. On the metro I was surprised by how many English voices I heard - stag parties, lads' weekends away etc. It hasn't always been like that, said Sid Lowe, so I see it as one of the clearest effects of the presence of the *galácticos*. As anywhere, all the atmosphere originates from behind one of the goals (in this case the lower Fondo Sur) but it really is just these few thousand, if that many, who are on their feet, singing for their team. Maybe they see themselves as a small band of die-hards trying to keep the *madrileño* spirit alive, like a group of village conservationists.

The rest of the famous ground just murmurs. Granted, they're not playing Barcelona, but there's been plenty of edgy build-up to the game in the press this week. El Real have met Sevilla three times already this season, in that hammering they took at the Sanchez Pizjuán in the league that we mentioned before, and more recently in a two-legged Copa del Rey semi-final. Real just made it through - having taken a comfortable enough two-goal lead down to Andalucia for the second leg, they let in a first minute goal and hung on despite having Zidane sent off before half-time. The Frenchman had retaliated in frustration to some over-friendly attention from his man marker, the Sevilla captain Pablo Alfaro. His red card caused Real's sporting director Jorge Valdano to charge into the referee's room uninvited and harangue the official for letting his player receive such treatment in the first place (an action which is unlikely to quell any provincial assumptions about the nature of the club's relationship with officialdom).

It's Alfaro that most of the pre-match sparring has centred around. Dr. Alfaro is actually medically qualified, though at the weekends he's an old-fashioned centre-half whose most famous recent exploit was sticking his finger up an opponent's arse while defending a corner. By which standards Zizou got off fairly lightly. The mild hysteria in the week's sporting tabloids peaked on Friday with both *Marca* and *As* carrying a front-page photo of a crazy-eyed Alfaro clenching a scalpel between his teeth, which the comparatively refined Queiroz thought of as 'in very poor taste'. This has obviously had some effect on the public - the cat-calling every time Alfaro receives the ball is just about the only reaction they manage during a drowsy first-half. In the event Alfaro doesn't prove too good at handling the attention - he looks every one of his 36 years (and perhaps more), nearly gives away a goal with an awful backpass and is substituted by his coach Joaquin Caparrós at the break.

By this time El Real are already two up. The industrious Santiago Solari sweeps them in front early on from a telegraphed Beckham pass, and Ronaldo's first meaningful touch is a goalscoring one as he heads/shoulders in Beckham's trademark whipped cross in first-half injury time. Looking at Beckham, it's hard to tell whether he'll last the distance as a true *galáctico*. Even though he's been here for nine months now, he looks like a child eager to impress. He chases everything, does twice the running of anyone else on the pitch, and gets after the referee loads - which is interesting considering that he apparently speaks next to no Spanish - seemingly in an attempt to assert himself. The strange juxtaposition between his effortless passing and his breathless hurtling around the pitch has characterised his game for a long time, but it looks out of step in this context. Sid Lowe later says to me that 'it's almost as if he looks to his team-mates sometimes asking 'Why don't you care as much as me?'', which rings true.

While Beckham ostensibly has the profile of a *galáctico* - the beauty, the fame, the skill- he doesn't quite have the swagger, or the effortlessness.

After Sevilla pull a goal back in the second half from a penalty, Real are riled from their semi-torpor and show us some of that trademark style. Beckham's midfield partner Gutí sweeps a breathtaking ball through to Zidane, who teasingly waits for his moment before choosing to bring the Bernabéu to its feet, gently lifting the ball over the diving Esteban. Shortly after, Ronaldo jinks around two defenders after a flowing move and after his shot is pushed away by the overworked 'keeper, Michel Salgado arrives to slap an emphatic shot high into the net.

This is the Real Madrid that the fans have come to see, and that tradition demands. With the score at 4-1, we get the *olés* after each pass from the crowd. Looking back at my notes from the night, it says '4-1. Fancy flicks and fanny taps.' But it would take a hard heart not to enjoy it. They're playing to the gallery, with Zidane pirouetting through a series of drag-backs and turns for his adoring public. It's reminiscent of what they did to Monaco in the Champions League quarter-final first leg the Wednesday before, where after a poor first-half which left them a goal down, they came out and took the French apart, eventually winning the match 4-2 (despite conceding a late goal to one of their own, the on-loan Fernando Morientes). It's what Butragueño was talking about when he said the team could sometimes finish a game in five minutes.

And it's what being a *galáctico* is about. Ronaldo dispossesses the defender Oscar in injury time and takes an age before tucking home the fifth - a delay that I later hear was while Ronaldo asked Esteban where the 'keeper would like him to put the ball. Esteban said left, and the Brazilian obliged. It's absurdly cheeky, and tells you something about what the modern-day Real are about. It's more inspiration than perspiration. Maybe the fledgling midfield partnership of Beckham and Gutí leaves the team short on defensive cover, but it was so fluent tonight. Maybe Zidane isn't on the ball that much for someone widely regarded as the best in the world, but every touch is an event. Maybe Ronaldo ambles around the pitch looking hopelessly out of condition, but when he gets a chance, it's nearly always a goal.

The catchphrase of the week has been of Real's '*Ronaldodependecia*' in the Spanish sports papers, and it's not hard to see why. The circumstances of his move from Inter have seemingly redefined him in the eyes of the football media. During the 2002 World Cup, people took delight in his comeback and cherished his gifts, but since leaving Italy under a cloud – and 'selling out' those at Inter who helped him through his injuries, he's taken constant stick over his weight and his attitude. The Catalan daily *El Mundo Deportivo* (admittedly never slow to have a snipe at their capital rivals) routinely refers to him as *El Gordito* (Fatty). But as Sid Lowe points out, it's Ronaldo's goals and Iker Casillas' saves that have kept Real afloat through some decidedly dodgy performances. They're why, despite everything, they're top of the league and heading to Monte Carlo for their quarter-final second leg this week as hot favourites. It's the goals and wins which live in the memory, while the performances are quickly forgotten. It's unusual that the world's most fêted team should look so vulnerable at the same time as being the dictionary definition of dash. But they made history, and they made it their way. They're not likely to let anyone tell them now that way is wrong, are they?

Leeds

'You can stick a fork in 'em, Clive. They're done.'
*Rodney Marsh to fellow Sky Sports panellist Clive Allen, when asked by
Allen about Leeds' prospects of avoiding relegation, February 2004*

And they say that clubs never give their fans anything. Elland Road
is busy, if not exactly buzzing, certainly more than it normally would
be on a weekday night. Leeds United's home match with Leicester City
is the one from this weekend's fixture list that has been deferred to the
Monday night for live broadcast. In between punters cramming fast
food in their faces, queuing for programmes and texting friends with
meeting arrangements, there's a steady stream flowing into the club
shop. It's every inch the modern football superstore, with the usual
range of gear for all the family – DVDs, mobile phone covers in club
colours, name and number printing press for the kids - much of which
is currently cut-price. Nevertheless, it has something of a ghostly air
about it, like the rest of the area around the ground, despite being
so busy. Maybe it's the vibe coming from the fans, a tangible air of
trepidation rather than anticipation. And the huge, painfully germane
'SALE' signs currently annexing the front windows of the shop clearly
aren't helping either.

Most football supporters are balanced enough to generally accept
the peaks and troughs that are part of the package. Nobody, however,
could blame Leeds fans for being utterly bemused by the course that
their club has taken over the last three years or so. That's how long it's

taken from Leeds to tumble from Champions League tyros (and semi-finalists) to Premiership prize turkeys. The free-flowing, energetic young team nurtured by David O'Leary fell apart as abruptly as they had burst on to the scene in the first place. As Leeds United has been exposed as the classic house built on sand, that vibrant side has morphed into an unrecognisable, pale shadow of its former self. The team's fortunes have unravelled concurrently with the club's finances. Especially in the last 12 to 18 months, every tabloid exposé charting Leeds' latest step towards financial ruin has been matched by a new disaster on the pitch.

The sad, incontrovertible and not especially secret truth is that Leeds United represent the worst-ever example of Champions League-related profligacy. The bare facts are that when then-chairman Peter Ridsdale gave O'Leary the go-ahead to sign Robbie Fowler from Liverpool at the end of November 2001, it took the club's spending to an outrageous £96.3 million during the Irishman's reign, which began almost exactly three years before – the sort of spending spree that would make our old friends at Dortmund blush. And hey, at least the Germans won something first before getting stuck into the transfer market with such gusto.

That said, if it was potential you wanted, that Leeds team had it in spades. With O'Leary's name (and Ridsdale's) so inextricably linked with Leeds' financial meltdown, it's easy now to forget how quickly he moved to create a thrilling side in the initial flush of his tenure. He took over, initially as caretaker, in October 1998 from George Graham, his manager at Arsenal when he was a player, who subsequently invited O'Leary to become his assistant at Elland Road. Martin O'Neill had been the board's first choice to succeed Graham, but when the Leicester boss refused to break his contract, O'Leary was given the nod. A young coach, O'Leary had none of his predecessor's cautious attitude towards road testing some of the club's highly rated youth players, and quickly made the likes of Harry Kewell, Jonathan Woodgate and Alan Smith mainstays of his first-team squad. The energy and attacking verve of the team moulded by the manager were all the more striking when contrasted with the frugality that Graham's teams were traditionally associated with.

Though O'Leary guided his team to fourth place in the league in 98/99 – the club's highest finish since their 1992 championship win - it was in his first full season that they really built their reputation. Leeds edged out Liverpool to seal third place in the Premier League on the season's final day, sending them into the third qualifying phase of the Champions League, and an opportunity to hit the big time. They already had a taste for Europe, having reached the UEFA Cup semi-final that same season, before going out to Galatasaray in tragic circumstances. The night before the first leg in Istanbul, two supporters, Christopher Loftus and Kevin Speight, were attacked and killed during trouble in the city centre. With the players' minds understandably not really on the job in hand Leeds slipped to defeat, and went out after a drawn return leg in West Yorkshire.

This Leeds team - and their manager – never did things half-heartedly as a matter of course. In retrospect, a club going into the Champions League with this attitude was like a naked flame being thrown at an oil slick, in both good and bad senses. When people shake their heads in disbelief of Leeds' frivolous ways during the O'Leary/ Ridsdale boom years, they're forgetting how thoroughly exhilarating Leeds' entrance into the Champions League was. Qualification for the group stages was a great achievement in itself. Leeds had negotiated a tricky qualifier against 1860 Munich despite suffering a string of injuries to key players, coupled with suspensions. This had mushroomed into a genuine injury crisis by the time of the first group match at Barcelona, where the English looked every inch callow youths, and made their way home with a 4-0 hiding and their tails between their legs.

It must have been some education. From that point on, it was Roy Of The Rovers stuff all the way. The youngsters fashioned a perfect response in the following game with a dramatic home victory over AC Milan, with Lee Bowyer's last-minute shot squirming through the hands of visiting 'keeper Dida in the driving Yorkshire rain. In the following game, they dished out a thumping of their own, putting six past a stunned Besiktas team at Elland Road. A Dominic Matteo header in the final group match, the return against Milan, won the point which saw Leeds edge out – you wouldn't believe – Barcelona to seal a place in the second group stage.

They looked out of their depth again in the initial stages of the second set of group matches. Just like against Barcelona, they faced the other Spanish giants of Real Madrid at Elland Road with a severely depleted side. Injuries had become a recurrent theme in the season and had badly hampered Leeds' efforts to keep pace in the league – they had sat down to Christmas lunch at a miserable 12th place in the league. El Real were in no mood to sympathise, and the scratch home side were given the run-around by the defending champions, who helped themselves to a comfortable enough 2-0 win. Leeds had more in the locker than anyone expected, though. By the time they faced the return in Madrid they had already qualified for the quarter-finals, courtesy of a famous win in Rome against Lazio (which helped to hasten their coach Sven-Goran Eriksson's departure to take up the England job) and a brace of wins over Anderlecht. The second win over the Belgian champions was the one which got Leeds real respect from the rest of Europe. Anderlecht had an enviable home record in the competition (100% for the season) but the visitors displayed all their power and flair in Brussels, going three up by half-time and finishing with a 4-1 win. The extent to which their naturally ebullient game was being further expressed was evident in that game in Madrid, where the visitors took the lead through Alan Smith before narrowly going down (3-2), only thanks to a goal that Raúl handled into the net, unnoticed by the officials.[1]

Leeds took this confidence into the quarters with them, giving the Spanish champions Deportivo La Coruña a real hiding in the Elland Road first leg, and taking a seemingly impregnable three-goal lead out to Galicia 13 days later. There the tyros showed they had tenacity to go with their skill, withstanding a real hammering from Depor (the home side had 20 shots on target to Leeds' none) to go through 3-2 on aggregate. That put Leeds in the barely believable situation of facing a Champions League semi-final against Valencia, losing finalists in the previous campaign. In that tie, their lack of experience finally caught up with them. After a goalless first leg, the Spaniards asserted their authority on their own turf, cruising through 3-0 at the Mestalla, though again Leeds were the victim of an errant hand, this time from Juan Sánchez while scoring the opening goal.

But Leeds had vastly exceeded expectations, and really arrived on the European scene in the process. It seemed as if their thorough preparation was paying off. They had already been thinking ahead for the Champions League, buying Mark Viduka and Olivier Dacourt for the 2000/1 campaign, at a joint cost of around £13 million. O'Leary had spent before, with the previous season's 19-goal top scorer Michael Bridges having joined from Sunderland for £5 million the year before. In fact, such was the player turnover under the manager that when Robert Molenaar left for Bradford in summer 2000, not a single player signed by George Graham was still at the club. The purchases that summer were, however, on a different level. The reinforcements during the season itself were startling, none more so than the November 2000 capture of Rio Ferdinand, with a then-British record £18 million being shelled out on the West Ham defender. The fee also made Ferdinand the most expensive defender in the world, with his fee being a whole £5 million more than Roma had paid Boca Juniors for Walter Samuel earlier that year.

The Ferdinand signing was a statement that Leeds would stop at nothing to build on their success, and it was now clear that their aim was to cement their place at the very top both domestically and in Europe. West Ham were clearly loath to sell Ferdinand, and had set a prohibitively high price tag to keep him, which (presumably to their astonishment) Leeds actually paid. Harry Redknapp, the West Ham manager, admitted the offer had been 'too good to turn down.' Just a few weeks later, Leeds then signed Robbie Keane on loan from Inter Milan for the remainder of the season (Ridsdale, ironically, mused at the time it would be 'imprudent' to buy him outright so soon after the Ferdinand deal). They would then have the option to make the Irishman's transfer permanent for the price of £12 million, which of course they later did.

When Leeds started on the serious spending spree, it appeared to be a mere footnote to their ever-more-fluent Champions League performances. Admittedly, this all happened before the current world football recession bit, but the Ferdinand purchase was the first that made people register that the club were really spending – this even though the Rio deal made it over £65 million spent in two years of O'Leary. When Leeds finished 2000/1 in fourth place – with only the top three good enough for the Champions League at the time – it was shrugged off as a minor hiccup in the team's relentlessly upward trajectory. The spending carried on, with Keane's move becoming permanent and both Fowler (£11m) and Seth Johnson (£7.5m, rising to £9m conditional on appearances etc) joining in the autumn.

O'Leary's presentation of himself and his team was maybe a little disingenuous, certainly one dimensional, but gave Leeds a very clear public persona. Think Leeds, think young and dynamic, with team acting as an extension of manager. Anyone faintly familiar with Premier League coverage of the time will have lost count of the number of times O'Leary referred to his 'babies' (fair enough if referring to the likes of Smith and goalkeeper Paul Robinson but a bit of a joke in the cases of expensive buys like Ferdinand and Keane). The dynamism came not just from the manager but from Ridsdale too, not only the architect of the squad of O'Leary's fantasies – as he acknowledged himself in his now-infamous and oft-repeated quote that the club were 'living the dream' – but also the most visible of Premier League chairmen.

On the back cover of David O'Leary's book about the club (more of which later), the blurb grandly describes him as 'arguably the most charismatic football manager in Britain today'. Another way of looking at it is that both manager and chairman were drama queens – though hardly the only ones in the circles of top level English football - prone to grand gestures which simply accentuated the hype surrounding the team. The football media, of course, lapped it up. O'Leary and Ridsdale were a dream come true for them, presenting something new, with a dashing, youthful vigour and an up-and-at-'em attitude which offered the prospect of breathing new life into a competition already being choked by Manchester United's near-monopoly. And besides, they made great copy too, being the ultimate rent-a-quote pairing. You could forgive O'Leary – after all, isn't that half a manager's job? – but bearing in mind that at least, say, five out of ten tabloid sport readers would have struggled to name the chairman at Old Trafford, Ridsdale's profile was becoming suspiciously high and his constant presence in the nation's back pages increasingly cloying.

Public profile is the recurrent theme in the Leeds United story of this period. The first full season under O'Leary -1999/00 – was the one that really shaped the club in this time, during which the team made headway in Europe and suffered the Istanbul tragedy. It also began the sequence of events that would regularly keep the club's name in the front pages of the newspapers for almost two years. The main points are well known - in the small hours of a Wednesday night in January 2000, following a fight outside the Majestyk nightclub in Leeds city centre, a student named Sarfraz Najeib was chased through the streets before being subjected to a sickening beating by a group of young men, which put him in hospital for a week. By March, Jonathan Woodgate and Lee Bowyer were both charged with affray and causing grievous bodily harm in connection with this, along with two of Woodgate's friends, Neale Caveney and Paul Clifford. Reserve striker Tony Hackworth was later also charged with the offences, while defender Michael Duberry (himself a £4.5 million buy from Chelsea in 1999) was charged with attempting to pervert the course of justice.

Besides being a complete public relations disaster, the trial would prove to be an enormous drain on the club, in terms of time and emotion.

The case against Hackworth was dropped midway through due to lack of evidence. Then, in April 2001, the ten-week trial collapsed after the publication of an interview in the *Sunday Mirror* with the victim's family, which the judge, Lord Justice Poole, felt could unduly influence the jury. The upshot of this was a retrial - though not for Duberry, who was acquitted of his charge - which didn't come to a conclusion until December 2001. Bowyer was cleared of all charges, but Woodgate was convicted of affray (along with Caveney) and Clifford got six years for GBH.

Some say the court case precipitated the Leeds collapse, and while this is overstating, it certainly didn't help. Leeds put on a disciplinarian public front, fining Woodgate and Bowyer six and four weeks' wages respectively for flouting club rules – basically, for running around the city centre drunk, which they indisputably had done on the night of the incident[2]. That was just about all they did right in the wake of the trial. Peter Ridsdale told the media that: 'I was asked by David O'Leary this week whether I would consider signing Lee (Bowyer), knowing what I know now. The answer is: 'No, I wouldn't.'' This was unbelievably stupid. Whatever Ridsdale's personal feelings may have been about him, it's hard to see what airing them in public would achieve, save alienating one of the club's best players. Bowyer is someone who continues to provoke strong feeling, particularly in the light of an ugly 1995 altercation in a McDonald's branch that he *was* convicted of, just after moving to Leeds. The fact remains, however, that he was found not guilty of all charges in the Najeib case (although he faces the threat of a civil action from the Najeib family, a claim that is still unresolved at the time of writing).

On top of this, it came to light that O'Leary would release his own take on the last few years, the embarrassingly-named *Leeds United On Trial*, in the following month. The book was clearly heartfelt and not without its merits in terms of its honesty, but it was deeply misguided. Running through passages of a football manager dissecting months of legal argument, you do wonder how on earth it was that someone didn't talk O'Leary out of it. At best, it was painfully ill-timed. It's hard not to imagine the club's players and supporters feeling totally sold out by their boss. Bowyer clearly did. The fan website *leedsutd365.co.uk* put it best: 'Whereas Wenger and Fergie are criticised for defending the indefensible behaviour of some of their players, we had a chairman and manager that couldn't defend a player found innocent by a jury. They have a lot to learn. Starting with keeping their mouth(s) shut.'

Woodgate, however, largely escaped public vilification. This was despite the club's shockingly insensitive announcement that they were awarding their defender a new five-year contract, almost doubling his pay, barely a fortnight after he was sentenced to 100 hours of community service. This served to completely trivialise the fine the club had been so keen to be seen imposing on the player. Contrast this to Bowyer's role as pariah. What most affronted people was the difference in the way the two most high-profile defendants handled the case. Woodgate was a mess. The official line during that first trial was that he was 'injured', something that O'Leary admits in his book was not strictly true. He certainly wasn't fit to play. The weight had dropped off Woodgate dramatically. On the way to court appearances he looked gaunt and drawn, with hollow cheeks and grey skin. The press and public took Woodgate's obvious worry as some sort of act of contrition.

Bowyer, meanwhile, rolled up his sleeves and carried on. He found his release on the pitch. Quite simply, the man was in the form of his life. Bowyer was the pivot around which Leeds' Champions League challenge revolved. Although he couldn't play away games for obvious reasons, he made his presence felt in matches at Elland Road. He dashed from court by chauffer-driven car (and even helicopter, on one occasion) to make night matches, most notably when he hit a late winner against Anderlecht in February after a day in the dock. Most took the same line as Agent Dave Kujan in *The Usual Suspects*. 'If you bring in two guys for a murder and you put them in the cells for a night, the one sleeping in the morning is your man. He knows he's caught.' As far as the press were concerned, Bowyer had form. He snarled, he was defiant and determined, and therefore, he was guilty.

As Leeds went into 2002 with the court case behind them, it was looking rosy on the pitch even though, true to form, some seemed to have learnt nothing from the episode, with Robbie Fowler arrested on suspicion of criminal damage at the club's Christmas party. Fowler and Mark Viduka were among the goals in a 3-0 drubbing of West Ham on New Year's Day, a result that took Leeds to the top of the Premier League. Yet the cracks in the foundations were already there. The court case had made lasting marks on morale. Duberry had been forced to testify against Woodgate, having originally covered up for him (hence his being charged). Examination of television footage of a reserve match featuring the pair during the retrial had captured Woodgate telling Duberry: 'You've killed me.' The two were no longer speaking. Although it was expected that Bowyer would be offered a new contract, he was still smarting over the club's near-vilification of his character post-trial.

On top of this, Leeds had an injury crisis, again. Form slumped – it was March until Leeds won again after the West Ham game, and only wins in the last two games helped them into fifth place, as Newcastle secured the newly granted fourth Champions League spot fairly comfortably in the end. Yes, you read that right. It would be a second successive season out of the Champions League, something that the club hadn't budgeted for in the heady days of Milan and Depor coming to West Yorkshire. Ridsdale kept talking, but the talk was now about selling players. He was again rash and indiscreet, openly musing that any takers could have Olivier Dacourt for £15 million, and that Harry Kewell would be sold by Christmas if he failed to sign a new contract, with only two years left on his remaining one. If the chairman wanted to give an impression of a desperation, this was the way to do it.

One they definitely didn't want to sell was Rio Ferdinand. As well as being an excellent player (and now captain), he was symbolic of Leeds' status in the top bracket of English football. But Ferdinand's outstanding displays in the 2002 World Cup in Japan and South Korea, coupled with the now-common knowledge that the club had stretched itself to the limit financially, made wagging tongues inevitable. O'Leary's next big statement – that he wouldn't sell Rio, or anyone else - was his last, as he was sacked at the end of June (officially - results not good enough/ unofficially – for breaking with the board's party line). Terry Venables, fresh from helping Bryan Robson get Middlesbrough to safety but without solo management experience in the top flight since 1991, was surprisingly appointed. It was straight in at the deep end. As well as the Ferdinand situation, Bowyer had stated his intention to leave, and a £9 million fee was agreed with Liverpool, only for the deal to fall through. This raised the very real possibility of Bowyer seeing out his contract's final year and walking away for free on a Bosman.

One of Venables' first acts at the helm was to consider who would replace Ferdinand. Manchester United knew that Leeds needed the money, and got their man for £30 million. It was a big blow, to the club's ambition as much as anything else, hurting the fans all the more for having to sell to their hated rivals from over the Pennines. Little did they know at this point that the money would probably save the club. It seems now almost like an act of charity. It's amazing in retrospect to think they paid that much, rather than driving the price down.

That's because a procession soon followed Rio out of the Elland Road door, but at more competitive prices. Venables won his first two games – against Manchester City and West Bromwich Albion – and a sweet victory over Manchester United put his team top of the early table, but it couldn't last. Robbie Keane left for Spurs for £7 million (a loss of £5˙million), and a crushing defeat by Arsenal was the start of five successive home losses. By Christmas, Leeds were out of Europe (beaten in the UEFA Cup by Málaga) and 16th in the league. A raft of departures followed in the new transfer window, with Bowyer off to West Ham for a paltry £100,000, Dacourt loaned to Roma and Fowler sold to Manchester City for just £3 million upfront, with another £3 million dependant on appearances. Leeds were over a barrel. They were desperate to sell, so they weren't only shipping out players at huge losses, but in the cases of Keane and Fowler, they were continuing to subsidise their huge wages in order to ease the burden. The club still paid Fowler £10,000 per week after his departure.

Then came the blow to push Venables to the edge. Despite persistent rumours of interest in Woodgate, the manager seemed to have been reassured that he was going nowhere, having been 'assured' that Fowler's departure had removed the need for any more. It was a grim-faced Venables that sat beside Ridsdale at the news conference announcing the defender's £9 million departure to Newcastle. It had been bad before, but selling one of the 'crown jewels' (ie Woodgate, Smith, Robinson etc), and so clearly against the manager's wishes? It's not often that you can say the savvy Venables has been sold a line, but he had been left horribly exposed.

He was soon put out of his misery, sacked in mid-March with the team still teetering precariously in the bottom six. The speed of the turnaround had been astonishing. With all due respect to Peter Reid, his appointment until the end of the season, having been sacked by ailing Sunderland in September, showed how far the club's stock had fallen. Leeds survived – with Reid reportedly picking up a £500,000 bonus by the terms of his highly-incentivised contract - largely due to Viduka's goals (14 in the final 11 games). A shock win at Arsenal on the penultimate day where both he and fellow Australian Harry Kewell showed quality secured safety and harked back to better times.

Ridsdale had gone by then, leaving ten days after Venables, on the same day that the club announced an enormous £78.9 million debt. He was always likely to be the ultimate scapegoat, and his successor as chairman, Professor John McKenzie, wasted little time twisting the knife – in April he released figures including board members' travel expenses, and famously the £20 monthly rent Ridsdale paid for the tropical fish in his office. This was presumably to show the fans that the new regime would not tolerate such gluttony. Well, it was a bit late for that. McKenzie pledged to get the club 'back on track', but seemed to lack the nous required of a top flight chairman. He was heavily criticised over Kewell's departure to Liverpool in summer 2003. Desperate for the deal for a player with just a year left on his contract not to collapse, Leeds paid £2 million of the agreed £5 million received straight to Kewell's representatives. This for a player talked about in the £20 million bracket a few years before.

McKenzie may have been a little naïve, but huge losses on other deals would be out of his hands. Ridsdale had financed some purchases during the boom years with the help of Registered European Football Finance (REFF), run by Ray Ranson, the former Manchester City and Newcastle defender. REFF acted as a player-lease agency, putting up the cash for players against future revenue. Of course, this means if Leeds sell a player bought under this footballing hire purchase system, such as Viduka, they would receive a mere fraction of the money paid by the buyers. What money they did get would be a drop in the ocean. Leeds were running out of saleable assets.

Reid was doing his best. While O'Leary had the cash and prestige to tempt players with the promise of the Champions League, his second successor would have to make do with loan signings, such as the Marseille trio Salomon Olembe, Lamine Sakho and Cyril Chapuis, and frees like Chelsea's Jody Morris. A dreadful pre-season, which included defeats to Burnley, Hull and Shelbourne as well as a furious row between the manager and Viduka, was not ideal, and after a decent start to the league season, a 4-0 thumping at Leicester (incorporating an appalling debut performance by Brazilian World Cup-winning loanee Roque Junior) signalled the beginning of the end. McKenzie agonised very publicly over Reid's position, even asking supporters' groups for advice, before firing him after a 6-1 humiliation at Portsmouth in November.

All of which pretty much brings us up to date. Eddie Gray – erstwhile player, manager, coach and all-round great servant – is caretaker-manager, with special dispensation to continue from the Premier League despite holding neither a UEFA Pro Licence nor a management diploma. The team are still mired in the relegation zone, which they have been since late October. And you can add to the debt a pay-off due to Reid (£800,000) to go with those due to O'Leary and Venables (£2 million each), and Roque Junior, the disastrous loan signing whose contract was terminated (£1.2 million).

There is, however, a glimmer. Last month, on Friday March 19, a locally-based consortium took over the club, led by insolvency expert Gerald Krasner, in a deal which saw the plc and holding company wound up and a new holding company take over its assets with reduced debts. In effect, the club's liabilities, which stood at £100 million in October (including a record pre-tax loss of £49.5 million), have been cut to around £20 million and major creditors including Gerling (the insurers backing the REFF deals) have been paid off. That this was at all possible was thanks to the work of ex-Chelsea chief executive Trevor Birch who stoically persevered through all the rumours and failed takeover bids - including one being planned by McKenzie, who had resigned as chairman in November. Throughout January he secured the almost-weekly creditor standstill agreements, and eventually the £5 million needed to assure the club could trade until the end of the season[3].

The club are 'off life support', as Krasner puts it. They're not out of the woods though, and now owe £15 million to ex-Watford chairman Jack Petchey, who helped finance the takeover, plus a sizeable VAT bill, estimated at over £10 million. Of course, the best financial tonic would be to stay up. Krasner's consortium insist they have factored in the possibility of relegation, but whatever he insists, going down would be a body blow to the finances. Even allowing for the 'parachute' payments received by clubs relegated from the Premiership, the overall loss is around £15 million a season. Krasner moved quickly after the takeover to insist that Leeds will not be leaving Elland Road 'as long as I'm chairman'. Ominously, he didn't rule out selling it and renting it back.

At least the team managed a win in his first game, against fellow strugglers Manchester City. They did, however, take a hiding at Birmingham last week, and beating Leicester tonight is a must to stay in touch at the bottom. Following the weekend's results, a win would put Leeds on level points with tonight's visitors and just two behind fourth-bottom Portsmouth, albeit with a vastly inferior goal difference. If they get beaten? With just seven games left after tonight, it doesn't bear thinking about.

We tuck ourselves into the home end - behind the north stand goal - and despite the seats, it's not such a modern experience. For starters everyone stands, but you can tell why Ridsdale looked so far into moving when his grand plan was in full swing. Even though 40,000 can fit here, it feels as if we're tightly packed in. There's more of the retro feel when 'Marching Altogether' plays over the tannoy as the teams come out, and you feel like you're breathing in a bit of history. It makes me think how Leeds got away with such wanton spending at the mere sniff of success. The main reason occurs to me - it's because there's no hint of *nouveau riche*. Leeds have the history, with the great team of Giles, Hunter, Bremner, Lorimer and co in the '70s even reaching a European Cup final (in 1975), where they lost to Bayern Munich in Paris. The club's name had so often been associated with success in the past that you suppose this is why the alarm bells didn't ring when Leeds so suddenly rose to high-rolling prominence again.

Flicking through the glossy £3 programme brings us back to reality. An advertisement inside advertises limited edition 20-year season tickets, an incredible concept, not to mention a leap of faith given that in the last few months, supporters have probably wondered whether the club would last another 20 weeks. The club is still desperate for cash. Looking at the line-ups on the back of the programme reminds us of the previous regime's waste. There are 40 players in the Leeds squad printed there, including loanees such as Sakho and Camara that Gray never picks, the perennially unfit (Johnson, Bridges), and the unwanted (Batty, Wilcox).

The fans are still defiant. They've been through enough to know that at least they'll be here at the end, come what may. The team are lifted by their vocal support, and get a great start when Duberry (suddenly a first-team regular) heads home from close in on 10 minutes. Just a few minutes later, they double the lead, with a piece of quality that reminds you of where this team came from so recently. Didier Domi and Jermaine Pennant (the two Reid loan signings that Gray includes) combine, the latter heading down the former's cross, before Mark Viduka sends a beautifully executed overhead kick into the corner. Elland Road rises in joy, relief, hope and nostalgia of the not-so-distant past. Paul Robinson, a remaining 'jewel' of the youth academy along with Alan Smith, makes a couple of decent saves before the half ends, notably from Marcus Bent's daisy cutter, but Leeds look fairly comfortable, considering what's riding on the fixture. They are playing to their ability, not their league position.

One notable fact in the Leeds decline is the amount of *schadenfreude* that their predicament has met with. It's hard to find a single football supporting friend or acquaintance who feels sympathy for Leeds. For those raised on '70s football, they'll always be 'Dirty Leeds', the uncompromising, cynical, no-frills winners. For others, there's the association of more right-wing elements of their support in the '80s. I know that Leeds have done a lot as a club in the last 8 to 10 years to be part of the community and combat racism. This makes it all the more disappointing when a mindless minority shout abuse Leicester's Muzzy Izzet whenever he gets the ball. It's the four-year anniversary tonight of the Istanbul tragedy. It's an understandably emotional subject (there's a impeccably observed silence before kick-off) but only an utter idiot would think heckling a Turkish international is the way to honour the feelings of the victims' friends and relatives.

Leeds have the chance to wrap it up just into the second half, when Smith's shot is kept out well by Walker. It's going well, and given the calamities of the last 18 months, probably too well. The faithful must smell a rat. 13 minutes remain when Leicester sub Paul Dickov turns to pull one back. Tension takes over faces in front, behind and to both sides. A few shiver. Only two minutes later, the visitors repeat Leeds' earlier double whammy, when Izzet crashes a 25-yard volley into the top corner. Devastating though it is for the large majority of decent home fans, you can't help appreciating one in the eye for the bigots.

There's only one expression on every face you look at. 'We've blown it.' The unthinkable is met more with resignation than horror. But if there's one piece of the old, dynamic Leeds left, it's Alan Smith. He's shown his more reticent team mates the way all night, with his usual industry, work-rate and skill. Four minutes remain. James Milner crosses from the left, Viduka chests down to Smith, 10 yards out. His shot isn't the most precise finish, but it's bludgeoned with conviction and slides under Walker. The north stand goes nuts. You just have to look at Smith's face to know. He is them, and they are him.

Viduka makes one last (and not especially welcome) contribution, petulantly kicking the ball away to earn a second yellow card of the night and suspension for the crucial game with Portsmouth. They need all hands on deck. In the scheme of things, it's more an annoyance than a hammer blow. Leeds have had enough of those to know what they feel like.

At last, it looks like the shock is starting to wear off. They won't trouble the Champions League again for a long while, but if they're ever going to remember the good times in the competition with uncluttered fondness, rather than for the wrong reasons, they had to come out of it, and face reality. They've started to realise where they are, and that they need to deal with it right now. Or those great Champions League nights of just three years ago could turn out to be part of the most expensive campaign that the competition has ever witnessed.

Juventus

This is no fun. I've just done a quick mental tally of the total cost of the 22 players on the pitch. I make it to be over £200 million (although when you bear in mind that Buffon and Nedved cost nearly £60 million between them, maybe this is a conservative estimate). Not that you'd guess – well, what sort of match reduces you to doing this? The stands are grey and largely empty. It's cold for mid-April, and the chill is metaphorical as well as literal. The season has a month to go, but for Juventus the end can't come quickly enough.

Il Nuovo Stadio Delle Alpi has never been loved by its public, but it is a particularly depressing place just now. *La Vecchia Signora* (The Old Lady, as Juve are widely known) have all but given up the *scudetto* ghost. With six games to go, the team is in third place, just one point behind Roma but a whopping ten behind leaders AC Milan. The second leg of the Coppa Italia final against Lazio is to come, but Juve are 2-0 down from the first leg and have it all to do. Besides, it only offers the chance of a minor consolation prize for a shabby season. Second best is next to nothing for this club.

It's a very different scene to the one at the same point last year. Juventus were cruising to the league title and still in the thick of the Champions League, midway through a quarter-final clash with Barcelona, a tie which they eventually won thanks to Marcelo Zalayeta's extra-time winner in the Camp Nou. They still had the season's pinnacle to come, a thrilling semi final win over Real Madrid, where in one glorious (and uncharacteristically well-sold) Delle Alpi night they hammered the European champions, and thumbed their noses in the face of those who continue to insist that Italian football exclusively deals in slow-paced, defence-obsessed misery. They had probably the hottest player on the planet in the shape of their Czech midfield genius Pavel Nedved. Fine team performance though it was, it was indisputably Nedved who inspired them to that win over El Real.

The line between success and failure is skinny, and nobody knows that better than Juve. Since that crushing penalty shoot-out defeat in the 2003 Champions League final, they have been living through the mother of all hangovers. Marcello Lippi, Juve's coach, stood up as a leader should after the final. He insisted his side were still 'the better team', and pointed out that in sauntering to successive *scudetti*, Juve had garnered a combined total of 27 points more than Milan over the last two seasons. Lippi also insisted that his team would be back to win the final next year to make up for the disappointment of Old Trafford.

Those words ring hollow twelve months on. The soon-to-be-deposed champions are trailing in Milan's wake, both in terms of style and substance. Last month, they suffered the disastrous week that this disappointing season has long threatened. Firstly, they were dumped out of the Champions League at the second stage, courtesy of a home defeat by Deportivo La Coruña to match the first-leg one they picked up in Spain a fortnight before. That was on Tuesday, and was followed on Sunday by an equally deflating loss, again at the Delle Alpi, and this time against Milan.

If anything, the disappointment after the second game in that awful spell was perhaps even greater than the first. Sure, Juve had been turgid and uninspired in the Deportivo defeat, but their loss had still registered as a shock in Europe. It was the sheer inevitability of the Milan defeat, though, that really confirmed some harsh truths. Namely, that Juve were losing their title to the same team who took a trophy from them back at Old Trafford, as the *Rossoneri* moved six points clear. A still more resonant message was in the manner of loss. Milan were superior in every department, coasting into a three-goal lead (on Juve's home territory, lest we forget) with the less-than-prolific Clarence Seedorf helping himself to a brace, before Ciro Ferrara netted a largely irrelevant consolation near the end. Lippi's own Champions League final postscript had been a reasoned, as well as a passionate, defence of his team. But the body of its argument was now no longer true. Juve were now irrefutably inferior to Milan.

Which, as we've already established, will not do. After all, this is the club that is famously reputed to have sacked Carlo Ancelotti, Lippi's predecessor as coach (and now Milan boss), at half-time in the final game of the 2000/01 season, by when it had become clear that the team would only finish second behind Roma. Even amongst giants, the Juventus trophy haul is incredible. The 2003 title was the 27th in the club's history. To put this into perspective, Milan have won 16 and Inter 13. The *Bianconeri* also have two Champions' Cups (going on to win the European/South American Cup in both cases), three UEFA Cups, a Cup Winners' Cup and two European Super Cups. They've garnered the Coppa Italia nine times, and the Italian Supercup four times for good measure.

Juventus' history may have begun with the club's founding in 1897 by a group of students, but the rise to establishing themselves as one of the dominant forces in world football was largely authored by corporate power. In 1923, the Agnelli family took over ownership of the club. Edoardo Agnelli, whose father Giovanni had founded Fiat (actually an acronym for *Fabbrica Italiana Automobili Torino*) at the very end of the 19th century, was the new regime's first president. Juve became stronger almost instantly. Fiat was a huge company, 'run almost as a state within a state', as a 2003 article in The Times put it, enjoying a virtual monopoly on the automobile market domestically and also doing a roaring international trade. Winners of just the single Italian title in the pre-Agnelli era, the club had won a further six *Scudetti* by 1935[1], including five consecutively from 1931.

Edoardo's son, named Giovanni like his grandfather, had a mostly-enviable life from birth in 1934 well into the 1950s. Though qualifying as a lawyer (hence the nickname *L'Avoccato*, which stuck with him for life) and serving a spell in the cavalry during World War II, he was, basically, born to be a playboy. He lived on a generous allowance left by his father, travelled and was well educated, speaking several languages. He mixed in high society circles, and was linked to glamorous women of the era, like Rita Hayworth and Anita Ekberg. Though appointed vice-chairman of Fiat in 1945, he wasn't too hands-on initially, and the first impression he really made in business was when he became Juve president in 1947. In the eight years he was in charge, Agnelli started to establish the club as a real power, and even after stepping down wielded considerable power, consulted on choices of coach and player purchases as a matter of course.

Famously witty, charming and mannered, and with the weight of Fiat behind him, Agnelli had influence of an extent beyond the wildest dreams of most major global captains of industry. He was pretty much an unelected statesman. Fiat was huge – when Agnelli took over at the top in 1966, the company had a whopping 60% share of the domestic market, as well as shifting huge amounts of foreign exports. This would come down to an estimated 40% by the time he stepped down from the company, but he branched out internationally, establishing factories as far afield as the Soviet Union and South America, and taking over competitors such as Volkswagen. The extent of his political involvement is often the source of fierce debate. Agnelli was close to becoming a candidate for the 1976 general election, but it never happened in the end. Some would say he already had enough political power. It was increasingly hard to see the seam between Italian industry and Fiat. As almost an Italian royal family and often compared to the Kennedys, the Agnellis were omnipresent, but Gianni (as Giovanni was usually known) ensured they were no figureheads. He never stopped cultivating high-level contacts, and broadened his influence into the media, taking control of two big-selling dailies, *Corriere della Sera* and Turin's *La Stampa*. Tallied up, he was in control of a quarter of the companies on the Milan stock exchange. He died in January last year.

Gianni's younger brother Umberto – *Il Dottore* (The Doctor) - was more closely associated with the club in the modern era. He had succeeded Gianni as president in 1956, when only 22, and in a seven-year tenure, the club won the title three times and also bagged the Coppa Italia twice too. During that spell, he also served as head of the Italian Football Federation (from 1959 to 1962). He brought in some of the club's better known players, such as the Welsh legend John Charles from Leeds. Umberto returned to Juve in 1994 as honorary president, and has been a frequent presence in the media, never slow to speak up if the direction of team affairs isn't to his liking.

With such enormous clout, Juventus' success was always going to attract jealousy, if not downright suspicion. They're virtually a direct Italian equivalent of Real Madrid. Loaded, successful, and supposed to have a helping hand from up on high. Given the Agnelli hold on politics, like Gianni's (successful) move to limit Japanese imports to Italy in order to protect Fiat's profits, it's not beyond the realms of possibility that Juve might have been the recipients of the odd piece of preferential treatment. The old guy who sat next to us in Milan (at the Sampdoria game) was pretty clear, even in a language I don't speak. 'Juventus have the referees in their pocket.' Not so much a suggestion as a given for supporters of their Serie A rivals.

This dominance, however achieved, has never extended to Europe. They have a decent haul of European trophies, but considering the stature of the club domestically, you feel the honours list is a touch underwhelming. In particular, the Champions League hasn't been kind to Juventus. Reaching four finals in the 11 years since the competition was revamped is good going. That only one of those finals has ended in victory tells of a great deal of misery. The run of three successive finals, from 1996 to 1998, is especially galling for them. Favourites in all three, they only won the first, and even then they only beat Ajax in the Rome '96 final on penalties – so it was a whisker away from being so much worse.

They are, however, one of only two teams to lose twice in the final, amongst their five Champions Cup final defeats overall (Benfica being the other). Even their first European Cup victory – which, having made them the first club to have won all three major European trophies, should have been a peerless triumph - was tainted. The 1985 win over Liverpool in Brussels will forever be remembered for the Heysel stadium tragedy, rather than the final itself. During disturbances between rival fans before the match, a terrace wall collapsed and in the ensuing crush, 39 people (32 of them Italians) lost their lives. The most hollow triumph in European Cup – and probably football - history was sealed by a dubious second-half penalty converted by Michel Platini.

To look at the photos of Platini lifting the Cup, it seems utterly bizarre that the game even went ahead. The reason it did is that the authorities feared more violence in the stands if the game was pulled, and many of the involved players have since said they didn't want to play but were forced by UEFA. In one respect it worked. There was no more trouble after the game. That said, what might have happened if Juventus lost, given both that it was mainly Italians that were the victims (although Juve fans were not entirely blameless), and that their fans far outnumbered the English? Naturally, this has given rise to many a not-so-far-fetched conspiracy theory re the penalty that won the game. That the players – many of whom claimed to have no idea of the extent of the tragedy – paraded the Cup at the end, and that the club arranged victory celebrations for the return to Turin is something wholly more unbelievable. There is no plaque at the Delle Alpi in respect of the dead, and nor was there at the Stadio Comunale (Juve's ground until 1990).

Heysel was a dreadful choice for the final, a crumbling old relic that was an accident waiting to happen. It has since been completely reconstructed, with virtually nothing remaining of the 1985 version. It has even been renamed, as the Stade Roi Baudouin. Yet there's little there commemorating the victims – something that's strangely in keeping with the final that's never remembered for the football, and so desperately hard for people to acknowledge at all. Platini himself, now a FIFA bigwig, dismissed out of hand the idea of going back there in an official capacity during the Euro 2000 championships, jointly held in Belgium and the Netherlands.

In the wake of all this, you can see why the 1996 win over Ajax was so joyfully received. It was the feeling of a twenty-year-old weight lifting from collective shoulders. Just before the final, Gianluca Vialli admitted as much. 'As far as the club is concerned, Juventus have never won the European Cup[2].' Vialli was the epitome of Juve's elation that night, tears streaming down his face amid the celebrations, having lifted the trophy. Though a final being decided on penalties is never ideal, the Stadio Olimpico final was everything Juve could have wished for from a Champions Cup victory. It was a terrific game, played out against worthy and skilful opponents – who happened to be the holders – but with the eventual winners being entirely deserving.

Though the '96 final is mainly remembered for the grace of the young Alessandro Del Piero (only 21 at the time), the finishing of Fabrizio Ravanelli and the penalty-stopping heroics of Angelo Peruzzi, there was real substance to Juve's style. The image of the captain Vialli leading them to triumph, in what turned out to be his last game before leaving for Chelsea, is perhaps the most potent of all. Sure, he was gifted and glamorous (particularly in the context of the English Premier League at the time), but he was a grafter too. In his own words, Vialli had often been used as the national team's 'donkey' in his 59-cap career with the *Azzurri*. He was a real fighter. Vialli was born into a super-rich family in Cremona – with his father the multi-millionaire head of a building firm, he grew up in a 60-room mansion. Rather than simply be kept or score a cushy number in the family business, Vialli hauled his way to the top with single-minded determination, starting in Serie B with his local team (Cremonese) before making his name with Sampdoria, eventually (briefly) becoming the world's most expensive player when moving to Juve in 1992 for around £12 million. In short, he embodied that Juve team, a marriage of swagger and steel.

The team that took the field to defend that title in Munich the following year were undoubtedly their predecessors' superiors, on paper at least. They had already recaptured the *scudetto* from Milan and were hot favourites to retain their trophy. To the team that beat Ajax the year before, add Zidane, Boksic and Vieri. Even the mighty Del Piero was only deemed worth a place on the bench by Lippi. They had steamrollered Ajax (who had, admittedly, lost a few of their top players by then) in the semis. What followed was a shock to say the least. Though Juve enjoyed plenty of possession, a well-organised and classy Borussia Dortmund beat them with less fortune than many a sycophant would have you believe. Juve were a truly great team who were supposed to seal their immortality – and celebrate the club's 100th year - with the ultimate bauble. Even though their conquerors had been German champions in the two years preceding the final, it was considered, as Henry Winter said in the *Daily Telegraph* at the time, 'one of the great upsets in the history of the European Cup final.'

It certainly seemed to have a major effect. A year later in the Amsterdam Arena, Juventus again went into the final as newly-crowned Serie A champions. Again they were hot favourites, this time against Real Madrid, who had finished in fourth place in their own league, out of the Champions League places. Again Juve choked, with Predrag Mijatovic scoring the game's only goal and condemning them to a demoralising second Champions Cup final defeat in the space of a calendar year. Significantly, Juve failed to win a trophy of any description following this setback for the next four years.

It goes back to where we were earlier, the narrow line between glory and the gutter. The Juventus of the mid-to-late '90s could have been, should have been, maybe even were one of the greatest sides of the modern era. Instead, Del Piero somehow failed to fulfil his destiny in becoming the world's greatest player, Zidane (no doubt scarred by the loss of three successive European finals, having lost the 1996 UEFA Cup to Bayern Munich with Bordeaux) upped sticks for Madrid and Lippi was fired in 1999. With every passing year of missing out, Juve veer towards becoming European football's equivalent of the

England cricketer Graeme Hick - the flat-track bully that raises merry hell domestically, but lacks that certain *je ne sais quoi* at the highest echelon.

If failure seems a harsh word, we just have to remember that Juve's well-established resources mean that they have everything in place to affect total mastery over Europe. The Agnellis would generally stop at nothing to brush aside the opposition. Many accusations have been thrown down the years, and works like Alan Friedman's *Agnelli And The Network Of Italian Power* pull few punches. Friedman's suggestions of 'sweetening' are difficult to substantiate, but the facts are that Giovanni Agnelli built alliances wherever it suited him, even selling 10% of Fiat to the Libyan dictator Muammar Gaddafi in 1976. In early 2002 LAFICO (The Libyan Arab Foreign Investment Company) shelled out around £14 million for a 5.3% stake in Juventus. Gaddafi's son, al-Saadi, immediately announced his intention to expand the stake to 20% (it currently stands at around 7.5%). This led to the 2002 Italian Supercup between Juve and Parma being held in Tripoli, a move again raising the question of the club exerting high-level influence. The Libyan connection eventually caused a tangible problem last summer, when Nike announced in August that they were unable to produce replicas of Juve's Champions League shirts this season as the carried the sponsors' logo of Tamoil – the Libyan state oil company. Last season's Champions League kit was also sponsored by Tamoil, but as Lotto (an Italian company) made the kit, it didn't matter. US trade sanctions against Libya started in 1986 and still prevent any commercial connection with the country.

If they had been able to sell the shirt, it would probably be on special offer by now. Even then, takers around the Delle Alpi today would most likely be limited to tourists. The match day atmosphere for the Serie A visit of Lazio is more on the side of stale routine than even mild excitement. It's quiet. The background noises are murmur rather than singing, and chatter rather than shouting. It's calm enough to take a leisurely walk around to the north-eastern side of the stadium, where there's a nice view of the Alps. It's out of step with what I'd been told to expect of the stadium – i.e. bloody horrible – but it's more wilderness training camp than teeming cauldron of football passion.

The Delle Alpi (literally, 'of the Alps') is a big problem for Juventus. It opened in 1990, built for the World Cup held in Italy that year. It seemed hexed from the very start. During the building process, the cost trebled from the original estimate, and the project ended up costing in excess of $100 million (about £70 million at the time). It compared unfavourably with the Stadio Comunale in the eyes of the fans. The sightlines were poor in some areas of the Comunale, but it was in the centre of Turin - the new stadium was a 25-minute bus ride out of town, in a semi-industrial wilderness - and it was home. Besides, it quickly became apparent that the view at the Delle Alpi was much worse. Due a design fault, you couldn't see from a few thousand seats. Hence if you look at the club records, the stadium has never been filled, even when 'sold out'. Even Gianni Agnelli slagged it off, complaining about the athletics track which kept the stands a hefty distance from the pitch. Oh, and the track itself wasn't built to competition standard and so has only ever been used once.

The board realised this was an unsustainable situation and in 1999, announced plans to knock down the existing ground, building a new stadium, museum and leisure complex next door in a $200 million-plus project. After protracted haggling and a fair amount of brinkmanship between the club and the city council, Juve were able to buy the stadium for €25 million last summer. The plan now is to build a new stadium within the boundaries of the current one, holding between 35,000 and 40,000. Work is slated to start in a year's time, with the stadium ready for 2007.

It seems a practical solution, but there have already been murmurings of discontent from some fans about the capacity reduction. This is all very well, but the average attendances here have fallen for five years in a row, and the club have sold 5,000 less season tickets than last season, according to local sources. Champions League attendances were not great last season, but have completely stiffed this season. Despite the team's good form in the group stages, the crowd figures failed to reach 20,000 for any of the games (best was 17,246 for Real Sociedad's visit) and less than 25,000 turned up for the season-defining clash with Deportivo La Coruña. The club have a point in thinking that a full medium-sized stadium makes for a better atmosphere than a half-empty big stadium.

Half-empty is about what it is tonight. It's hard to blame the casual supporter for giving it a miss. It's chilly, there's no longer a championship to play for, and it's not unreasonable to assume that both Juve and Lazio will be keeping their powder dry for the second leg of the cup final. Although in Juve's case, just getting a team out is hard enough. Injuries have blighted their season, and there's no Montero, Ferrara, Zalayeta or Del Piero tonight. Since the Depor defeat they've won one league game out of four, a fairly unspectacular win over relegation-fodder Modena, and been beaten by Inter last week to go with the home humbling from Milan.

You have to give credit, though, to the fans that have turned up. It's noisier than the San Siro in here, by a long way, for the duration of the game. All the chanting is coming from the Curva Sud, behind one of the goals. Although quite a long way behind one of the goals, this being the Delle Alpi. Juve fans are widely mocked in Italy as a bunch of lame-brained glory hunters, who can't even be bothered to turn up to watch their own team. But these *tifosi* are the real deal. This is certainly no tourist haunt.

The game, then. Whatever the opposite of zestful is, Juve are it. It's hard to blame Lazio for the quality of the viewing. They've had their well-documented financial problems that have brought the club to its knees (even if they do retain players of the quality of Jaap Stam and Stefano Fiore). Besides, don't you know anything about Italian football? It's never up to the away side to make the running. Sadly, Juve don't seem capable of it. David Trezeguet – not back long from injury – is isolated up front with precious little support. Hopeful diagonal balls consistently attempt to seek him out. Nedved, meanwhile, is also just back from an injury lay-off, and looks unrecognisable from his normal self. If ever one player personified Juve's slide in the last 10-11 months, it's him. Banned from the final having picked up a caution in the second leg against Real Madrid, he was sorely missed at Old Trafford. It wouldn't be overstating at all to say that one yellow card changed the destiny of the 2003 Champions League. Struggling with fitness and form, the Czech has hardly been the same since. It's a sad sight, and as the half-time whistle blows, not even the merest whisper of applause greets the players. People can't even be bothered to boo them off.

This is, without doubt, the worst game I've seen on my travels this season. While the journalists next to me – who showed their community-spirited side in the interval by passing out drinks and snacks from the complimentary buffet through the gate to the punters – loudly set Turin to rights, my eyes wander down to the touchline. Marcello Lippi cuts a lone figure. He's one of the last old-fashioned coaches to stand on the perimeter chain-smoking, staring impassively into the middle-distance, a bit like the Argentinian Cesar Luis Menotti. I remember Lippi's pledge last year that he would quit if Juve didn't win the Champions League this season. Could he soon be reaching for his last cigarette? After a woefully misplaced pass by Alessio Tacchinardi, a fan from behind throws a nut in frustration that whizzes by my ear. That's the last time I give any half-time food away.

Lazio work hard and are well-organised, but Juve shouldn't be struggling against a side like this. I've finished adding up the players' transfer market worth. People are sidling off to the exits, and I'm putting my notepad away. We're in the last few minutes when Mauro Camoranesi at last whips in a quality cross from the right and Trezeguet rises to head home from about 10 yards. It's simultaneously relieving and vexing – relieving, because at least everyone didn't come out for nothing, and vexing, because they showed enough class in five seconds to amplify still our chagrin at being subjected to the previous 88 minutes of misery.

Juventus need to put this season to bed. Their fans at least have the consolation of knowing that the club can't take two seasons like this in a row, and are likely to get in some heavy-duty personnel in the summer to get it right. But regaining Serie A won't be enough. Renovating the stadium won't be enough. To get the excitement flowing again, the fans need a real exploit, something that will grab them by the shoulders and shake them. The Champions League itch desperately needs scratching.

Bayern Munich

Germany is still full of surprises, even if Munich isn't quite as alive as Dortmund was on match day. OK, it's a Sunday, but it has the feel of just an average Sunday to it. Closer to the Olympiastadion, though, there's much more of the kind of revelry which makes me think back to how much I loved my last trip to this country. There's a full-on beerfest around the stadium's perimeter, with hordes of opposing fans mixing together, drinking, laughing and singing, inside and outside a big marquee. There's a stage with an MC inviting all comers to have a go at a penalty challenge. The bonhomie is, nevertheless, totally out of sync with events on the field. Bayern's fans may be drinking all around the ground, but the players would be lucky to get served in the last chance saloon at the moment.

If Bayern weren't Bayern, they'd already have written this season off as a disaster a while ago. They look like losing their Bundesliga crown, having trailed surprise packages Werder Bremen for the majority of the season, and they were put out of the Champions League at the first knockout round back in March. Yet while they may be parodied by their detractors as the prima-donnas of 'FC Hollywood', they have a resilient streak a mile wide. Last week's reverse at Borussia Dortmund was the first in six league games since the Champions League exit. They are never down for long. Bayern Munich is not just one of the world's biggest football clubs, but one of its most indomitable.

In fact, Bayern are perhaps more closely identified with the perceived characteristics of their nation than any other club in world football. Marseille may be taken to represent France by overseas fans, or Manchester United England, but Bayern's whole identity – as a results machine, however unfair that perception may be – mirrors what the very fabric of German football is assumed to be. In the 1999 Champions League final, where Bayern had victory snatched from them right at the last, pubs, bars and clubs the length and breadth of England weren't just celebrating United bringing the trophy back to England for the first time in 15 years. Patriotic pride pushed many football fans' deep dislike of the freshly crowned English double-winners to one side for the night, and it was the excuse for all manner of frolicking in *schadenfreude* that night too. For them, it wasn't just United versus Bayern that night, but England versus Germany. The roles of the two teams regressed into stereotype before our very eyes – the slick, controlled technicians against the spirited, enthusiastic yet somehow naïve hustlers. English joy that night stemmed from United mugging Bayern just as Germany had mugged England in 1990 and 1996.

This is a crass mentality, of course. But that Bayern – as ubiquitous a presence in the Champions League as the French inscription on the silver of the bauble itself – can be perceived as such hints at what a huge shadow they cast over the rest of German, and European football. The aura surrounding the club's very name makes their fallibility this season all the harder to take in. Sure, you can't win the league every year, as goalkeeper Oliver Kahn rather forcefully pointed out to a critical journalist last week, but the shock this season has not so much been Bayern's failures but the manner of those failures. Personally, I would have wagered any sum you would care to name on both of two bankers. Firstly, Bayern having a big hand in the latter stages of this season's Champions League, in response the dismal group stage flop last time out, and secondly, coasting the domestic title again (they finished 15 points clear at the top last season, as well as winning the Cup) for good measure.

That they haven't was partly the luck of the draw - getting Real Madrid in the first knockout round is not a tie that too many with

Champions League aspirations would hanker after. They were unlucky in the tie itself, going out after a single goal loss at the Bernabéu followed a 1-1 draw in Munich, a first leg in which they outplayed their opponents and should have won comfortably. Oliver Kahn inexplicably let Roberto Carlos' 40-yard effort squirm through his grasp and over the line shortly before the end, prompting speculation about the state of the keeper's eyesight and giving the Spanish an undeserved equaliser. But for Bayern to even require the decidedly mortal concept of luck shows how far beyond their expected level they had fallen. In truth, they never looked like mounting a serious challenge before that. Bayern's form in the group stage was scratchy at best, with the team playing as if they were still harbouring the uncertainties of the previous season's blow-out. They were lucky to scrape a win in the opening game at home to Celtic, which was won by a fluke when Roy Makaay's speculative cross drifted straight in just four minutes from time. The draws retrieved from the trip to Anderlecht and the return with Celtic were not without fortune either and sandwiched a home defeat by Lyon, a result made all the more galling as the winning goal was scored by reluctant Olympiastadion departee Giovane Elber. A second slim home win eventually saw Bayern qualify in second place (hence the tough knockout round draw), with a Makaay penalty seeing them home against Anderlecht.

That Olympiastadion clash against the Belgians was notable for more than just seeing Bayern through. It was something of a landmark in being a rare sighting of Bayern struggling to so much as break even. It certainly made Uli Hesse-Lichtenberger raise an eyebrow. 'You could see they were afraid against Anderlecht. It was very un-Bayern-like.' Bayern scoring a goal and then shutting up shop would have been one thing, but scoring from a penalty (and a questionable one at that) and then hanging on against a side that may have been underrated, but was nevertheless not in the same class, was something else entirely. The iron men were quivering. It looked like the 2002/3 Champions League campaign had more of an effect on them than anybody could have thought.

Before we start on that line, let's be totally clear on one thing. Last season's European campaign was nothing short of an absolute disaster. Bayern are incontrovertibly one of the very elite Champions League clubs. They went into last season with a 21st-century record of having been semi-finalists, winners and then quarter-finalists. They were a draw that nobody would fancy and the only question mark against them in a group stage context would be a simple 'first or second?' That Bayern were not just eliminated (from both the Champions League and the consolation UEFA Cup spot for group third place), but humiliated was as unexpected for the rest of European football as it was unacceptable for the club itself. The campaign began badly, with then-opponent Makaay's hat-trick for Deportivo La Coruña handing them a home defeat in the opening game, before they were crippled by back-to-back defeats in the home and away double-header against Milan, and eventually finished off by Makaay's last-gasp goal handing them a loss in the return in A Coruña. It's not unfeasible that the damage done to Bayern by Makaay's goals is what persuaded the club to part with up to €18 million for the Dutchman - though it should be pointed out that he added a further five goals in the competition to the four he got against the Germans.

By the time it was all done and dusted in mid-November, Bayern were most emphatically out, finishing bottom of Group G with a pathetic two points, six less than third-placed Lens and a massive ten shy of the qualification positions. That, at this point, they were already streaking away in their domestic league at this point just made it more painful. It's not as if anyone in the group hammered Bayern either, adding to the feeling that their own carelessness was to blame. In the home and away games against both Milan and Depor, Bayern pulled back a deficit before giving away a winner, with three of the four coming in the last 10 or 15 minutes. They also shelled a lead in both games against Lens. Elber, the highest-scoring overseas player ever in the Bundesliga as well as being in the Champions League's all-time top ten, didn't manage a single goal after netting in the opener against

Depor. The expensive new signings Michael Ballack and Zé Roberto singularly failed in bringing their sparkling Champions League form from Bayer Leverkusen, who they had helped take to the previous year's final. They didn't manage a Champions League goal between them in 02/03. Elber later recounted how a furious Franz Beckenbauer 'told us we were just about good enough to get into an asylum for old-age pensioners'. Through all their ups and downs in the Champions' Cup, it was hard to remember a Bayern team putting up such a spineless show.

It's incredible to think that they found themselves in this situation barely 18 months after Stefan Effenberg lifted the trophy in the San Siro. If ever there was a portrait of the narrow line between success and failure at this level, then it was in the contrast between the 2001 final and the 02/03 campaign. Statistically speaking, the margins between the two instances were negligible, with Bayern only victorious after a penalty shoot-out following a 1-1 stalemate in the first 120 minutes. But that win was pure Bayern, one which many would have seen as a typically ugly triumph. They recovered from going a goal down to Valencia in the first five minutes and from Paulo Sergio missing the shoot-out's very first kick, in a largely attritional game lacking a goal from open play. Even knowing the Spaniards were a well organised and highly accomplished side in a second successive final, a side with a solid defence (in fact, not so different from their opponents), even when Mehmet Scholl missed a penalty in normal time with the Spaniards leading, it never felt like Bayern were going to lose. The 2001 Champions League winning side had a real presence about them.

So where did this image of Bayern as the kings of grinding out games start? Besides the dubious linkage with the national team, it's not difficult to see from the sides of the modern era we're most familiar with, particularly in the context of European competition. Key players starting the 1987 European Cup final included the likes of Lothar Matthäus, Andreas Brehme and Dieter Hoeness (Uli's younger brother), players you would be more likely to categorise under 'perspiration' than 'inspiration', while the 1999 Champions League final side had not just the sturdy likes of Jens Jeremies, Thomas Linke and Matthäus (again), but the giant Carsten Jancker. Since the mid-'90s, they've been able to count on one of the world's best and most imposing keepers in Kahn, as rare in stature and talismanic value for Bayern as Peter Schmeichel was for Manchester United. Even the Brazilian Elber has seemed to play, and score, with a measured efficiency that reflected the mood of his surroundings.

In reality, this idea of Bayern has far earlier origins, back in the late '60s and early '70s when the club made its first moves towards dominating German football. For all the clichés of German organisation, the country didn't even have a professional league until 1963. Before this the champions each year were decided by a sort of grand final, like in Australian Rules football for example, played between winners of the regional leagues. Bayern weren't even included in the first Bundesliga - the more traditional winners in German football had been Schalke and Nuremberg, with Bayern having won just one final, pre-war, back in the 1930s.

They first lifted the Bundesliga in 1969, and for most of the '70s – a golden decade for the German game – they were locked in mortal combat with Borussia Mönchengladbach, as Hesse-Lichtenberger says in 'Tor!' The team was based around the greats – the likes of Beckenbauer, Paul Breitner, Gerd Müller, Sepp Maier – who were also the fulcrum of the German side that beat the Netherlands to lift the 1974 World Cup. The decade represented a genuine struggle between the two clubs, something never more evident than in the fact that Bayern 'only' won the title three times in the '70s, the last of which was in 1974. Nevertheless, this was the period in which Bayern began to establish their dominance of domestic matters, which they have never really let slip. That 1974 title made them the first German club of any era, pre or post-war, to lift three successive championships.

The club's official history refers to the period from 1968 to 1976 as 'The Golden Years.' This is pretty well indisputable. After the famously disciplinarian Branko Zebec took the helm, the club won their first title by a comfortable stretch, along with the DFB Pokal (the German national cup competition). The '70s saw Bayern start to play in the Olympiastadion (built for the 1972 Olympics), an über-stadium befitting the club's soon-to-be-giant status, and the place where they embarked on the record run of consecutive titles.

The official line goes on to relay in talking about this period how 'fondly' Beckenbauer and co are remembered 'all over Germany.' Even most Bayern supporters would have to admit that this claim is stretching it. They were received with little affection at the time, feelings bordering on many an occasion on outright hostility. This was remained the case despite their key players' pivotal role in that World Cup triumph (not to mention Germany's 1972 European Championship triumph), won in their own country, accentuating the nation's footballing feelgood factor. Breitner and Müller even scored the goals in the 2-1 final victory. Hesse-Lictenberger's theory in 'Tor!' is that Bayern just weren't as 'sexy' as Gladbach. They were seen by the German football public outside the club as just a little bit too infallible and assured. They oozed effortless class and didn't care who knew it, in the same way that, say, Manchester United have come to be seen in '90s England.

The smooth dominance of this period was also when Bayern extended their dominance to Europe. Before they reached the 1974 European Cup final, only one German club had done so, when Eintracht Frankfurt (a whole 14 years previously) were beaten by the Real Madrid of Di Stefano and Puskas in Glasgow, in perhaps the most famous final of all. Bayern only escaped defeat against Atlético de Madrid thanks to Hans-Georg Schwarzenbeck's equaliser in the last minute of extra-time, but cleaned up in the replay two days later – both Uli Hoeness and Müller netting twice in a 4-0 win.

As with their initial ascent to domestic power, the moves towards monopoly were sudden and sure. The 1974 win proved to be the first of three successive Champions Cup triumphs, with '75 and '76 bringing victories over first Leeds and then Saint Etienne. This spell of hegemony also started to spread their domestic unpopularity to the continent. While admiring Bayern, much of the talk surrounding the second two finals dwelt on the unlucky losers from England and France. Despite the ultimately emphatic margin of victory in the replay, there was nobody who couldn't already see how lucky they'd been in 1974.

This era was, however, a true dynasty – a core of exceptionally talented, disciplined players delivering a sustained string of successes. As well as the players' individual qualities, continuity was a key element in this domination. Of the 12 players involved in the final against Atlético (only one sub in those days, remember), nine played in Glasgow against Saint Etienne two years later (and had faced Leeds in Paris in between). The influential Breitner may have jumped ship to Real Madrid after the 1974 final, but conversely Karl-Heinz Rummenigge had emerged by the time the European champions turned up in Glasgow. Headline-grabbing signings weren't Bayern's calling card. They may have been less loved than the Ajax side who held the trophy for the three years leading up to Bayern's first win, but they were no less effective a unit.

So associated are they with the professionally ground-out win, that it takes a reality check to recognise that since then (and excepting 2001, of course), Bayern's recent European history is characterised more by agonising failure. The '80s confirmed the passing of Gladbach – themselves losing European Cup finalists in 1977 - as their rivals (as they all do eventually), as Bayern took a firm grip of domestic matters, winning 6 Bundesligas in the decade. However, the 1982 European Cup final, lost to Aston Villa, underlined the passing of the great team of the '70s, even if it did contain an ageing Breitner and even though it was not until 1984 that Rummenigge eventually left for Italy, and Inter Milan. In a way not dissimilar to the parallel struggles of that other giant of the competition, Real Madrid, Bayern went through the '80s consistently failing to grasp the one prize they really lusted after, almost as if rendering their domestic achievements chicken feed.

The tendency always tends to be to dwell on what you missed out on, rather than what you actually have. This is especially true of big clubs and trophies. At the highest level, you are more readily defined by defeats than victories. In Alex Bellos' dissection of the Brazilian game, 'Futebol', he asserts that even after 50 years of passing, not to mention the winning of five World Cups in the interim, it's the defeat in the 1950 final to Uruguay at the Maracaná that 'continues to morbidly fascinate Brazilians like no other event.' The shock of the defeat – in Brazil's case, of the home nation, the overwhelming favourites, in the perfect stadium built especially for the occasion – is what makes it so hard to deal with. Similarly, Bayern were heavy favourites going into the 1987 final, in Vienna, against Porto. Ludwig Kögl gave them a first half lead, and everything seemed hunky-dory. Instead, with twelve minutes left and one Bavarian hand on the trophy, Rabah Madjer and Juary scored twice in as many minutes to send the cup to Portugal. Bayern were crushed. Even the club's official history says it 'destroyed team morale.' Uli Hoeness reputedly refuses to even talk about the game to this day.

Today, however, the Vienna defeat merely defines the '80s. It's Barcelona 1999 that springs to mind when you think of Bayern Munich and the Champions Cup. However bad Vienna was for Bayern, Barcelona was surely ten times worse. Leading from the point six minutes in where Mario Basler curled in a free kick, Bayern were superior throughout. If you watch a recording of the game again today, each near miss – Scholl chipping over Schmeichel onto the post, Jancker's overhead kick crashing back off the crossbar – feels like the precursor to imminent disaster, knowing what we know now. But on the night, they had it. Totally, undoubtedly. It was in the bag. The watching George Best famously left the Camp Nou just before the end, thinking it was done and dusted. Manchester United had been superb throughout the competition, but on the night they were outfought, outthought, outplayed, and utterly toothless in attack. That the goals of substitutes Teddy Sheringham and Ole Gunnar Solskjaer, surely the two most famous injury-time goals in European football history, may have been undeserved on the night but were lost in a frenzy of red ecstasy.

Maybe it's because I'm not a Manchester United supporter, but the images of that night that are the first to come back to me aren't of Schmeichel lifting the cup, Alex Ferguson and his staff running onto the pitch in celebration or of Solskjaer skidding down on his knees after heading in the winner. They're of the distraught Bayern players slumped on their haunches on the turf, of the Ghanaian Samuel Kuffour pounding the turf with his fists and a po-faced Beckenbauer gazing on, incredulously, from the stands. It's hard to imagine that the players involve don't still think about it. If you ever could have genuinely felt the pain of a loser, it was on that night in Barcelona.

These sort of disappointments are the hardest to come back from, but Bayern managed to retain an aura of impregnability, certainly at home anyway, just as they had for decades. Prudent, sussed – critics would say ruthless – management has definitely been part of it. Bayern have rarely shelled out a fortune on glamorous, big-name foreign purchases, a policy endorsed by the fact that on the rare occasions when they have, such as when they bought Jean-Pierre Papin, it's been unsuccessful. Most Bayern stars tend to be German, and successful foreigners like Elber have acclimatised in the Bundesliga with other clubs before joining.

Overseeing this policy, since he became the club's general manager in 1979, has been Uli Hoeness. It could be said that he is Bayern in microcosm – someone who's smart, sure of himself, not especially well-liked, but who couldn't care less. In that same vein of continuity, Beckenbauer and Rummenigge joined the board in the early '90s with Beckenbauer coaching the team in two separate spells before becoming club president in 1994. They already had the Olympiastadion, a grand if slightly impersonal home ground, and now they had the weight of history behind them to make up for the any pizzazz the team itself may have lacked.

Hoeness has constantly sought to reinforce Bayern's position in Germany at the head of a field of one. It's not always been to the liking of public or competitors, but it has been hugely successful. The breaking of the Kirch scandal in early 2003 brought home the extent of Bayern's omnipotence under Hoeness. A German business publication, *Manager*, had uncovered details of a secret deal the club had made with the media group Kirch (owned by Leo Kirch) late in 1999, after Kirch agreed a six-year deal to televise Bundesliga games. To stop the very real possibility of Bayern splitting and marketing the rights to their games individually, Kirch would annually pay the club the €21.5 million difference between what they received as a share of the overall Bundesliga deal (about €14 million per club) and what Bayern estimated they could make by going it alone. Beckenbauer, at least, was initially contrite (though Hoeness was somewhat less so), admitting the club had been 'wrong', but became angry as the DFB (the German FA) refused to retract a statement calling Bayern 'immoral' – perhaps unsurprisingly after the club had paid €3 million in a half-hearted apology. It seemed to strengthen the club's resolve to break away and Beckenbauer even fleetingly talked of Bayern upping sticks to play in Serie A.

Later, in April last year, there were allegations in *Süddeutsche Zeitung* (published in Munich) that Bayern were involved in attempting to bribe smaller countries to vote for Germany's bid for the 2006 World Cup, again in association with Kirch. Bayern would play friendlies in places such as Malta and Trinidad and Tobago, and their associations would clean up via selling TV rights to Kirch. Bayern of course denied that this affected the vote, and nothing was proven. What the Kirch saga did prove, in relation to both this episode and the secret payments deal, is that the DFB needed Bayern more than the club needed it. In the immediate aftermath of the Kirch collapse in April 2002 - which precipitated the whole saga – Hoeness turned his nose up at the government's plans to underwrite the losses that the country's clubs would suffer, saying that 'more businesslike solutions' were the way forward. Bayern, of course, were just about the only club in Germany who could afford to take this point of view.

The Champions League has further strengthened Bayern's position at the top of the German – and European – tree. Much as they may have suffered on a few occasions, and not won the competition as much as they would have liked, they have been ubiquitous (only Manchester United have appeared more in the Champions League), and cashed in during the process. Since the competition became the Champions League in 1992, UEFA figures show that Bayern have earned more than any other club, a total of CHF 237,209,282 (about €153 million). Like Manchester United, the club's combination of careful management and continued high income puts them in a virtually untouchable position.

The fear that their reputation send through the rest of the Bundesliga is what they're hoping can pin back Werder Bremen, the surprise leaders. Bayern are eight points behind Werder at the start of play (and down to third after Stuttgart leapfrogged them by winning yesterday) and with only five matches to go, the leaders are going to have to get pretty freaked out by something if they're to give it up to the champions. Bayern's best shot is to keep Werder in range and ready themselves for their next home game after today. It's against Werder Bremen, in case you wondered, in a real do-or-die clash, a last-ditch attempt to salvage something from the season.

However, there is the matter of today's 199th Munich derby to negotiate first. It's Bayern's 'home' game today – I use the inverted commas as they and both they and 1860 Munich share the Olympiastadion, as they have done since 1996. 1860 president Karl-Heinz Wildmoser (reputedly a Bayern fan himself) was the driving force behind this move, one that was somewhat less than rapturously received by the club's support. The inference is that the move has diluted the identity of 1860 (the year the club was founded), or even merged it with that of Bayern. One of the locals I speak to dismisses the derby aspect of the match with a 'so what?' shrug, and others mutter that it's 'not the same'.

The town centre may be dead or thereabouts, but the Olympiastadion is bristling. Arriving at the station, you walk through the Olympic village to reach the stadium. The entire complex, the Olympic hall, swimming pool etc is covered by the same style of roofing, immediately familiar from pictures of the stadium itself, a series of light, angular waves, giving it a genuinely village feel. Despite being over thirty years old, it still looks good – fresh, almost futuristic in fact. You reach a clearing, which is the area around the stadium, and where all the festivities start. Again, the goodwill and camaraderie amongst fans wearing the opposing teams' shirts (though with, in many cases, lederhosen to complement them) is fantastic.

About 35 minutes before the kick-off, I drink up and leave the beer hall to go and find the press entrance. The place is big enough that I feel it might take a while to find. In the event, I'm sitting comfortably in the press lounge less than five minutes later, but that's ok, because the hospitality is second-to-none. There's free – that's right, I said free – *weissbier* on tap. Straight from the local brewery! It's amongst the best beers I've ever tasted, and it's from a tiny bar for the hacks. And it's free. I look up halfway through my third pint and realise that most others have just taken a couple of sips and left the glass to go up into the stand and prepare. Still, they get this treatment every fortnight, and I don't.

Besides, I'm getting some pre-match research in too. The TV screen in the corner is replaying highlights of the previous home game, a narrow win over Schalke. It's going to be my guide to the apparently enigmatic presence that is Roy Makaay. How anyone can knock a guy with a scoring record like his beggars belief – I remember Uli Hesse-Lichtenberger saying to me with a degree of incredulity that 'people complain that he only scores goals!' – but people do. Anyway, the Schalke game runs the full Makaay gamut, with two contrasting goals. The first is a feeble, half-hit scuff that crawls in, while the second is belted into the corner with no second bidding, almost taking the net off. It's safe to say if either of the two Makaays turn up today, Bayern will be happy enough.

The stands are steep and sloping, giving the stadium an amphitheatre-like quality. It's great for the atmosphere, partially offsetting the distance between the stands and the running track, but the dizzy hike to the top makes me think perhaps I shouldn't have put away four pints in 25 minutes. Still, it's worth it, being tucked under the cover of the trademark roofing, as if sat in an ocean. Being up here makes me think of the first time I saw the Olympiastadion on TV, when I was 11 years old watching the Euro 88 championship at home. I remember the camera panning up to John Motson, sat in the top of this vast arena, with what looked like a giant spider's web behind him, just where I am now. I couldn't have imagined it would still look so grand and worthy 16 years on.

This is an occasion worth savouring. Not only is it the 199th Munich derby, but it might be the last for a while. 1860 are in big trouble, having dropped into the bottom three yesterday courtesy of Hertha Berlin's walloping of Kaiserslautern, at Berlin's own Olympiastadion. They're in poor form too, having won only won of their last seven fixtures. Next season is the last that the two Munich clubs will spend in the Olympiastadion, as in summer 2005 they will move into the Allianz Arena, a jointly-funded new super-stadium which is being prepared specifically for the 2006 World Cup[1]. So the very real possibility exists that this could be the final Munich derby at the Olympiastadion.

If ever 1860 had a chance to put one over their illustrious co-dwellers and do themselves a big favour in the process, though, this is it. Chicken pox has swept the Bayern camp this week, affecting a number of players including Kuffour. Add to this injuries to key players like Lizarazu and Sagnol, and the suspension of Ballack after last week's sending-off at Dortmund, and you're left a little thin on the ground, even given the strength of Bayern's squad.

It shows. Bayern really struggle to string any passes together, and 1860 have four corners before Bayern even manage one. And Makaay, like so many whisper, looks hopeless outside the penalty box. I'd seen him play maybe half a dozen times for Deportivo and never noticed, perhaps because they could always rely on the likes of Valerón to do all the flash stuff and Makaay was just expected to put the chances away, which he did, and did very well. And it's ridiculous that this has even been put into my head – he's scored 30 for Bayern this season, including six in a thoroughly mediocre Champions League campaign by the team. The problem today is that there doesn't seem to be anybody to do the flash stuff for him.

The first half was not great. The Sud Kurve kept singing throughout but the tribunes descended into dissatisfied murmur. My gaze kept drifting to Ottmar Hitzfeld on the touchline. Outwardly, nothing's changed. He stands, as usual. Yet this week Hitzfeld, one of the most successful managers in the European game, announced this week that he would leave when his contract expired in 2005. Presumably, he feels that after Champions League disappointment for the second season in a row, he's reaching a ceiling of achievement here. He is, however, still recognisable as a very 'Bayern' coach, ordered, understated, yet demanding. He openly admitted in the past to being 'authoritarian'. Now is probably a good time for the team to feel some of the old Hitzfeld magic.

When the game restarts, Bayern play like they've taken a bollocking and a half in the break. There's quick passing, urgency and attacking intention. Even Kahn's changed into shorts from the scruffy tracksuit bottoms he was wearing in the first half, now looking more like a footballer and less like someone's dad hunting for the remote control between scratches. Sure enough, 1860 are there for the taking. Five minutes into the half, the Paraguayan, Roque Santa Cruz, sidefoots a left-wing cross high into the net past Michael Hofmann from about six yards out. It's immediately apparent that their opponents don't have it in them to come back.

Bayern should go on to obliterate 1860 from here, but it just doesn't happen. They seem gripped by a hardly-merited anxiety against a toothless foe – maybe it is a proper derby after all – and the home crowd become openly annoyed in the latter stages. Ze Roberto and the otherwise very impressive youngster Bastian Schweinsteiger fluff a breakaway with one return pass too many, before Makaay expertly rounds the last defender only to horrendously miss his kick. This last miss even prompts the 1860 fans, by now having given up on their own side, into a word-perfect English rendition of 'You're shit, and you know you are.' Still, Bayern close the game out.

I came here thinking I might be looking at another Juventus. I would see a team begging for the season's end, desperate to draw a veil over this season's shortcomings. But not here. The culture of the club will not allow them to give in. The Champions League? They'll be back. They have other fish to fry for the moment. Even after today's result (and Werder's draw at Bochum), they are still six points behind the leaders. But when Werder show up in a fortnight, Bayern will be up for a fight. The pretenders know that if they want to take the title home to Bremen, they'll have to truly wrestle it away. With Bayern Munich, it ain't over 'til it's over.

Saint Etienne

Frédéric Mendy picks up the ball on the left wing. Lean and purposeful, like a wild cat, he pulls the full-back one way and then the other, before finally casting him aside to power a shot narrowly over the bar. The crowd exhales as one, and then the chant starts to swell: 'Allez les Verts! Allez les Verts!'

Sorry. It's easy to get carried away here. In fact, this whole chapter could be filed under self-indulgence. Maybe you'll already have picked out this one as the book's black sheep, as Saint Etienne is the only club included not even currently in their nation's top division. But it's not that simple. L'Association Sportive de Saint Etienne (ASSE) isn't just another sleeping giant. The mythology surrounding the club that has captivated France for the last 30 years is still as potent today as it ever was. It's intoxicating, and I can feel myself being at least a little taken in by it.

When I arrive in Saint Etienne by taxi early on a Saturday afternoon in May, the town's magic is only conspicuous by its complete absence. It's a mainly industrial area, and one of my girlfriend's friends who lived here for a year told me recently that the place was 'a complete dump'. Also a French guy from Saint Etienne who I met in London only admitted he was from here under mild duress, having originally claimed for 'geographical clarity' that he was in fact from Lyon. This is pretty much the opposite of Lyon – grey, drab, lifeless and most definitely not bourgeois. It's Saturday, and everything is shut. Everything. The railway station opposite my hotel is the only place to get a newspaper and they don't have *L'Equipe*, so I'm forced to go upmarket and buy *Le Monde*. You would think it was a public holiday but for the fact there is barely a soul on the streets either.

I wasn't expecting Monte Carlo, but the ennui of the town is as about as far from the glamorous image of ASSE is imaginable. Saint Etienne are, and almost always have been, the darlings of French football. Their history is rich, and even now the current team shirts have a single gold star mounted above the team crest, symbolic of their record of being the only club to have won the French league title ten times. Eight of these ten championships were won between 1964 and 1976. This period made up the bulk of the golden era in which *la légende verte* (The Green Legend) still potent today was created. While their domestic dominance earned respect, it was their adventures in the European Cup which built their immortality.

They were led by the charismatic president Roger Rocher – as closely identified with smoking his pipe as Che Guevara was with cigar-smoking – and the coach Robert Herbin, *Le Sphinx Roux*, or The Ginger Sphinx, a former Saint Etienne player and French international. These exploits reached their peak in the mid-'70s. Their epic struggles with the likes of Dynamo Kiev, Liverpool and Borussia Monchengladbach are still the stuff of legend in French sporting circles. Saint Etienne reached the semi-finals of the competition in 1975 before going one better and getting into the 1976 final against Bayern Munich.

In that final, held on May 12th at Hampden Park, Herbin was lacking his major star, Dominique Rocheteau, *L'Ange Verte* (The Green Angel), who was one of a few who came a cropper in the face of some rough treatment in a league game in Nîmes a few days before. This restricted Rocheteau to a brief and futile substitute appearance, with Franz Roth already having scored the Bayern winner. Les Verts were desperately unlucky, none more so that when they hit the crossbar before Roth's goal, with a header from a certain Jacques Santini - incidentally, a squad player who was only in the team due to the raft of injuries. Nicolas Bulostin, who was there as a young Saint Etienne supporter that night, still shakes his head today and mutters about 'those fucking square goalposts.' The French do love a *perdant magnifique* (wonderful loser), and there could be none more so than Saint Etienne on that Glasgow night. The team returned to be given a welcome parade down the Champs-Elysées.

This was the consummation of the French nation's love affair with Les Verts, but it was just in keeping with the heroics that had built the foundations of this relationship between the club and its nation. Saint Etienne built a reputation in the European Cup as the comeback kings, something that is generally acknowledged to have started with the tie against Bayern Munich in October 1969, in the last 32 of the competition. After being beaten 2-0 in Germany, Les Verts mounted a stunning comeback in the return leg. Their 3-0 win was sealed by a late goal by Salif Keita, the Malian who later became the first ever African Footballer of the Year (in 1970), to add to two earlier Hervé Revelli goals. The Stade Geoffroy-Guichard started to become a fortress, and to assume a semi-mythical power. In November 1974, on the way to their first semi-final, they lost the first leg against Hadjuk Split 4-1 in Yugoslavia. Les Verts won the return leg 5-1 to go through. Another breathless recovery took place in 1976 on the way to Hampden, when Rocheteau's extra-time winner took them through a quarter-final against Dynamo Kiev, after they had come back from the first leg in the Soviet Union with a 2-0 loss. 'It became known as *la marée verte* (The Green Tide),' remembers Xavier Rivoire.

The Stade Geoffroy-Guichard was inaugurated on the 13th September 1931. Built on a site purchased the previous year by the supermarket chain Casino, it was logically enough named after the father of then-president Pierre Guichard - Geoffroy Guichard had originally founded the club as his company's sports club. The stadium's undergone several renovations since then – most recently in preparation for the 1998 World Cup – but retains the same atmosphere, one of those rare stadiums where you feel as if you've stumbled across the church of some weird cult. Like so much about the club, the stadium itself is invested with a mythical aura thanks to the glory days of the '60s and '70s. Even now, entering a half or two-thirds empty arena an hour before the start of a game, both scoreboards display the inevitable *Bienvenue dans le chaudron* (Welcome to the cauldron).

Most teams are characterised by their home strip's colour to a greater or lesser extent, but none as much as Saint Etienne. They are so thoroughly defined by their greenness - The Green Legend created by The Green Tide etc – and the streets outside the Geoffroy-Guichard in the hours before kick-off on match day can't really be described as anything else but, well, a sea of green. With it being a pretty uncommon colour (I can only think of Sedan also sporting it in French football) it's another thing that sets them apart from all the mere mortals of the French game. The club shop's window carries a great example of this iconography. There are large signs advertising the re-release of replicas of the classic cotton 1976 team shirt, perhaps prompted by the revival in fortunes which has seen the team climb to the top of the Ligue 2 table and within touching distance of promotion. Quite a few of the regulars have taken advantage of this offer already (10,000 have been sold in the month they've been available), quite unwisely in some cases where the owners' nostalgia has got the better of any reservations they might have had about trying to fit into a slim-fit number in late-30s or early 40s.

Before I encounter the town's almost hidden hub of life, I'm hungry, so I find a bar that's open near the station to get some food. There's an unmistakable air of the small town in there – neither the guy behind the bar or the sole patron are in any way rude or unwelcoming, but curious eyes run over me and try to work me out. Eventually the barman asks me where I'm from, and the answer lends his face an even more inquisitive look. Being slightly off guard and frankly incapable of making up anything believable, I tell him that I'm writing something about Les Verts. Both he and his catatonic customer nod and furrow their brows conspiratorially, as if I've just asked for the best bottle of wine from the cellar that only the regulars know about. It turns out they

207

couldn't get tickets for tonight's game against Angers, as it's been sold out for 'a few weeks', they tell me. This is the first signal of excitement I've received regarding the team, but they are in a good position at the moment. Getting promotion is one thing, but staying up is another. How do they think Saint Etienne will fare in the top flight next season? The barman answers with as much courtesy is possible for a question he clearly thinks to be daft. 'They'll do very well, of course. They're one of the biggest teams in France, you know.'

More recent stats prove otherwise. Saint Etienne have won nothing since they lifted the last of their ten titles in 1981, when Michel Platini, the heartbeat of the team, was still yet to recognise his own greatest achievements – lifting the 1984 European Championship with France, and winning domestic and European titles with Juventus. The occasions since in which they have come closest to silverware were a losing French Cup semi-final to Nantes in 1993 and an exit at the same stage of the League Cup, to Ligue 1 Sochaux, this season. Relegated in 1984 and promoted to the top flight in 1986, they spent ten years back in Ligue 1 before 1996's demotion (they had been lucky not to go down the previous year, spared only when Marseille were refused promotion on the say-so of the DNCG, the body responsible for overseeing the financial management of French clubs). Saint Etienne have been the quintessential yo-yo club since this point. In their first season down, they were almost relegated again, to the National League, and it took them until 1999 to come back up. The current spell in Ligue 2 began in 2001.

Even apart from the decline in fortunes on the pitch, the post-1981 period has been inglorious for Saint Etienne. In April 1982, Roger Rocher's empire began to implode, when an investigation began into allegations that one of the most recognisable faces in the French game had been operating a slush fund – *la caisse noire*. The investigation dragged on excrutiatingly throughout the remainder of the decade, mainly due, as Jean-Philippe Leclaire wrote in *Le Foot*, to various authorities – including the Ministry of Finance, which declined to instigate any proceedings – passing the buck to avoid trashing such a shining beacon of national sporting pride. 'In France, there are certain people you can't say bad things about,' explains Xavier Rivoire. When a conclusion was finally reached in summer 1990 ten players, including international stars like Patrick Battiston, Didier Lacombe and Platini, along with coach Herbin and Rocher, were found guilty of involvement. The chairman took the brunt of it, being sentenced to four years in prison (30 months suspended) and a fine of FF 200,000. It's estimated that he had skimmed off more than FF17million to pay players their tax back - Platini himself is thought to have accepted around a million francs in under-the-table payments – as well as to subsidise his struggling business. This wasn't the end of the affair for Rocher, as in May the following year the Court of Appeal in Lyon commuted the sentence to three years in prison (still 30 months suspended) and an FF 800,000 fine. In a farcical but somehow fitting final twist to the saga, Rocher actually received a partial presidential pardon in October 1991 from François Mitterand.

With Rocher gone, you would assume that such financial tangles were something of the past. Before the the 1976 final the club had been proud of home-growing its stars, but after Rocher had fired a culture of supplementing the ranks with big name players, befitting of a big name club, Platini having been the first. While it would be false to say this culture continued unabated, the club's self-image had been indelibly altered by years of success and by the 1990s, the club found itself in a spiral of increasing debt. There was brief respite when SAEMS (a financial company 'with sporting interests') bought into the club in the summer of 1996 and pumped in FF 10million, but by the 1998-99 season, the club's liabilties had grown to FF 40 million as it struggled to return to the upper echelon. Promotion at the end of that season should have helped to sort the club out, but the next scandal was just around the corner.

When Saint Etienne took on Toulouse in a Ligue 1 match in December 2000, a Toulouse official questioned the nationality given next to the name of Brazilian striker Alex on the team sheet, which had listed him as Portuguese. In the subsequent LFP enquiry, Alex's fellow Brazilian Aloisio and Russian goalkeeper Maxim Levytsky were implicated with him, and in mid-January Alex and Levytsky were both found guilty of holding fake passports (a Greek one, in the goalkeeper's case). They were each banned for four months, with two suspended. Worse, Les Verts were docked seven points by the league, which saw them drop into the bottom three. President Alain Bompard, appointed when SAEMS bought in, took the club's case to a French administrative court, but the team had had the stuffing knocked out of them. Alex was the club's top scorer and had hit 12 goals by Christmas, but he scored only two after. Bompard failed to get the points back and Saint Etienne were relegated again.

Yet despite financial scandals being the most notable elements of the Saint Etienne story over the last twenty years, they're aspects seldom discussed in France. The myth still prevails. Xavier Rivoire explains this as being a product of Saint Etienne's success in the golden age of the European Cup. 'When you look at things, Saint Etienne hasn't won anything since 1981, but still people think it's a great side, and they're kidding themselves. One has to remember that football that was played in Europe back in the '60s, '70s and '80s, people had this romantic view of the European Cup of that time, and I don't think it will ever be the same. Most of the teams (from that era) have virtually disappeared, like the eastern European teams. You had east versus west, and it was a true cup, with knockout stages all the way and great ties.' Not only this, but Les Verts were trailblazers in the '60s and particularly the '70s, as the first French team – club or national – to really 'awaken the passion for football' in France, as *France Football* put it in a recent retrospective of the 1976 final. 'This is the moment where football became the most popular sport in France,' says writer Paul Yonnet.

Les Verts' feats in Europe will, for a lot of French men in their mid-30s now, always summon nostalgia of their childhoods. The author of *Jouer juste*, Francois Bégaudeau, said to *Le Monde* that 'the public tells itself that something has changed in today's football, that a touch of amateurism has been lost.' *Le Monde* also points out that on the sports channel ESPN Classic, by far the largest viewing figures in France are recorded when a Saint Etienne match from their European Cup vintage is broadcast. Like people often remember Elvis clad in the black leather suit for the '68 comeback special, the mention of Les Verts conjures up images of Rocheteau, Herbin, Revelli, Curcovic and Glasgow '76.

On the fifteen-minute stroll to the ground from the station, the streets gradually start to become populated. When the Stade Geoffroy-Guichard begins to come into sight, it's immediately apparent where the town's life is. Tonight's is the penultimate home game of the season and the ground is full to its 35,000 capacity, just as it is likely to be for the remaining two home matches after tonight. Having hit the summit for the first time this season less than a month ago, Saint Etienne need just one more win to guarantee the end of their three-year exile from Ligue 1. The opponents, Angers, are placed in lower mid-table at the moment, needing a few more points to make certain of safety from the drop but are assumed to be incidental to the occasion.

It's a terrific ground. It has a reputation as being *typique anglais* and is compact, closely hemming in the pitch. The atmosphere is thick with anticipation and it's almost full even though there's more than twenty minutes to go before kick-off. Then a song starts being played over the public address. It's familiar, like a '60s-style guitar-led builder, tuneful and anthemic. All the fans in the Kop (as even the club's official literature knows it, in another nod towards past European Cup battles) behind the goal know the words. I realise where I recognise it from; it's the holding music that plays when you're on the line ringing the club's offices. Having been kept waiting on the line for the press office a few times in recent weeks, I know it fairly well already.

Later, I find out that the song is called 'Allez Les Verts'. It was actually written in 1976 by a man called Jacques Monty, a musician, writer - he's written for Petula Clark amongst others - and die-hard *stéphanois,* and released under the name 'Monty et Les Supporters'. It is pretty much alone in the murky world of football records in that a) it isn't a total laughing stock (in fact it's pretty damn fine), and b) was a genuine hit. In fact, when released it was at number one in the French singles charts for over ten months. Since then it has been adopted as the club's official anthem.

The first time Nicolas Bulostin heard the song that has gone on to become a huge part of his life was when he was 10 years old. He and his father were on the way to Glasgow, to see Saint Etienne play in the 1976 European Cup final. 'It was a real…challenge,' remembers Nicolas from behind raised eyebrows. 'My father only told me we were going two days before, and I had lost my passport. So we managed to get it (a replacement) at the last minute, and then we got to the airport and had missed the 'plane.' They were waiting in the departure lounge at Paris Orly when Nicolas' father brought out a tape recorder.

'He said he'd written this song for the team, and wanted to know what I thought. I wrote my first song when I was seven, so he thought I had good ears.' Nicolas taps his temple with his index finger. 'It went straight in.' But it was after the pair had landed in Glasgow, and were taking the train to Hampden Park, that the young Nicolas realised this was more than just a catchy tune. 'We were on the train, full of Saint Etienne fans, and my father brought out his cassette recorder again, and played the song. The whole of the carriage sang along. They all knew every word (already).'

Though neither Nicolas or his father could have known then that 'Allez Les Verts' would go on to sell more than three million copies in France, this is the point where the legend of the song was born. It's the fans, and their singing of the song, that has kept it alive, and fresh. 'It's now the fourth generation of people singing it (today),' says Nicolas. 'When we sing it together, it's like a swap of love. For the club, for the fans and for the song.1'

'Allez Les Verts', Monty et les supporters

Dans le vestiaire avant de rentrer
Pour commencer a nous echauffer
Tous en choeur nous chantons
On est les rois du Ballon
Quand on arrive sur le terrain
On les entend frapper dans leurs mains
Avec eux nous chantons
St. Etienne sera champion

Refrain:
Allez: qui c'est les plus forts? Evidemment c'est les verts
On a un bon public, et les meilleurs supporters
On va gagner! ca c'est jure, allez
Allez: qui c'est les plus forts? Evidemment c'est les verts
Nous on joue au football et on n'a pas de frontiere
Main dans la main on va plus loin, plus loin
ALLEZ, ALLEZ les VERTS

Les supporters sont venus de loin
Ils sont fideles, ils nous aiment bien
Ils font sauter les bouchons
Quand St. Etienne est champion

Refrain:
Allez: qui c'est les plus forts? Evidemment c'est les verts
On a un bon public, et les meilleurs supporters
On va gagner! ca c'est jure, allez
Allez: qui c'est les plus forts? Evidemment c'est les vents
Nous on joue au football et on n'a pas de frontiere
Main dans la main on va plus loin, plus loin
ALLEZ, ALLEZ LES VERTS

(With kind permission of Nicolas Bulostin.

(c) Gatemanor Ltd

Website : www.allezlesverts.com)

As Les Verts 2004 take to the pitch, just before 8, 'Allez Les Verts' gets another airing on the PA. Sure enough, everyone in the ground seems to be singing, word for word, and the sound is so loud I start to feel it in my jawbone. I can feel the hairs on the back of my neck standing up.

All around there are signs of somewhere trying to preserve the characteristics of a bygone, more pure era. I'm drawn to some of the banners which line the perimeter fences- 'Pour le football populaire – stop business', 'Non aux matchs le lundi' (no to Monday matches). There's also a banner saying 'Lyon nous voilá' to remind their near-neighbours of the natural order of things. A few rows in front of me, there's a boy of about 11 or 12 wearing a green t-shirt with the club crest and the phrase 'La legende continue' printed on it; something I saw earlier in the club shop and will see on a fair few more chests before the night is out. ASSE seems almost more like a museum piece than a living club. Then again, as the players prepare to kick off, the Kop Sud is a blur of green fabric, with almost everyone swinging their scarves around their heads. I've never seen anything quite like it.

The current team cope admirably with the expectation cast by the shadow of the past. Even by French standards, this is a young team, something forced upon the club by years of hardship, both in terms of finances and trophies. The current coach Fréderic Antonetti has done a great job, although as he acknowledged earlier in the season; 'Most of our players have never played in Le Championnat (ie Ligue 1) and most of them are just beginning their careers.' The captain Patrice Carteron, still the club's record signing at £2 million from Lyon in 2000, is the exception to this, now approaching 35 years old. Still, young players like Nicolas Marin and Fréderic Mendy have had their confidence buoyed by the run to the semi-finals of the League Cup this season, in which they beat Ligue 1 teams Lille and Nice, and this has arguably been the catalyst for the promotion push.

Angers are well organised and Les Verts, to their credit, stay patient in their approach, despite the density of crowd noise willing them forward. Then, with twenty-five minutes to go, the visitors hit the crossbar following a set-piece. Saint Etienne's cool melts, they push forward, winning a few corners and force the Angers 'keeper into a few smart saves. The crowd sense something, a climax maybe, and renew their own efforts. Carteron bounds forward for one of these corners, waving his arms in exhortation to the stands. For once the home team's inexperience shows, as they get over-excited and Angers miss a pair of highly-presentable chances on the break. Finally, with virtually the last kick of the game, a cross from the left finds the head of Les Verts' top scorer Lilian Compan. Compan's header drifts towards the corner of the goal, but drops just outside it. Goalless, and Saint Etienne will have to try again to seal promotion next week, away to Niort.

On the walk back to the centre, all the people in green disappear as suddenly as they arrived, into some Rhône Valley black hole. When I get to the station, it's all gone quiet again. The passion in the Geoffroy-Guichard is beyond question, but it's so firmly rooted in the past that it almost carries an element of pantomime. 'The last great Saint Etienne team was probably at the beginning of the '80s. Curcovic was still there, Platini was there, and then it all fell to pieces,' says Xavier Rivoire. 'The core of supporters is pretty small. It's a myth to think the whole city and the whole Loire *département* is behind Les Verts. As a matter of fact, more and more people in the whole of this south-east, Rhône-Alpes area are going to Gerland to see good European football. I've got friends who are Saint Etienne fans who are quite happy to go to Gerland. It's quite paradoxical.'

Nevertheless, it's hard not to feel something for the passion of a night like this one at the Stade Geoffroy-Guichard. It shows the European Cup's unique power to create lasting legends. It's because not just the fans, but all of French football needs to believe in Les Verts.

France Football put it best in that recent retrospective; '…in the hearts of the French, Les Verts remain Les Verts. Forever.'

Manchester United

Virtually everybody else seems to have retired to the press room, but there's a morbid fascination that demands I stay in my seat and keep watching. Having just played their final home game of the season, Manchester United are proceeding to take a lap of honour around the Old Trafford pitch. I use the expression 'lap of honour' in the loosest possible sense, however. The team plods around, most of them not even breaking into a jog, managing the odd royal wave to the stands. The seats themselves are half, maybe two-thirds empty. It's difficult to say if this is more painful for the players or the fans. This is one lame, embarrassing exercise in formality.

Old Trafford's corporately inspired 'Theatre of Dreams' nickname is frequently – and not unreasonably – mocked, but the imperiousness it alluded to at least had some basis in fact. They had the trophies and the team, a genuine dynasty of success spawned in the '90s. Though writing United off would be a nonsense, it feels like the Premiership's hierarchy has undergone a genuine sea change. This is the first time since the Premier League's foundation in 1992 that the club have finished outside the top two. This may seem a minor inconvenience - bringing with it the obligation to go through a Champions League qualifier in the first few weeks of next season – as, you may say, what is the difference between second and third, apart from ceding a little prize money and a little pride?

The answer lies in all those empty seats left at the end of the game. The season doesn't end here, with the FA Cup final (where United will be overwhelming favourites against Division One Millwall) still to come after next week's final league game at Aston Villa. Yet that final, in what we've come to assume as the greatest domestic cup competition in the world, will feel like going through the motions. United have only occasionally been bettered during the Premier League years, not often, which makes defeat all the more bristling. But this season, they have been completely upstaged, trumped, humbled by Arsenal. The newly crowned champions, presumed to be in some sort of psychological thrall to United having gifted them the title last season, have shown not just more style, in being the most aesthetically perfect champions in living memory, but significantly more substance than their rivals.

Arsenal even stand on the threshold of being officially the greatest English side of the modern era, unbeaten in their 36 games to date and at arm's length from becoming the first side to complete an entire unbeaten top-flight season since Preston in 1889. This is something that scarcely seemed possible in the modern era of English football, and is something United never came close to even at the peak of their domination – which lest we forget, included league and FA Cup doubles in 1994 and 1996 as well as the treble of 1999. United haven't even been able to push Arsenal to the limit this season. Before the start of today's play, with two games remaining, a chasm of 13 points lay between United and the top of the pile.

This season has been a disappointment, but perhaps not really a shock. When Arsene Wenger lamented that his side were 'still the best team in the country' after losing last season's title, the sentiment may well have smelt of the sourest of grapes. Still, he had a point. Last season's title fell into United's lap – though a testament to their persistence - whether they can bring themselves to recognise it or not. Despite United's impeccable post-Christmas form – unbeaten after Boxing Day and dropping a mere six points – Arsenal would still have retained their crown had they not inexplicably ceded a two-goal lead in the latter stages at Bolton in late April, before suffering a similarly baffling defeat at home to lowly Leeds the next week which sealed United's triumph.

Though United's robust approach in taking a point from Highbury in April's 2-2 draw marked the seriousness of their intent, the moment when the pendulum definitively swung towards them was when Arsenal dropped those points at Bolton. Wenger's famous *sang froid* disappeared, and he stood helpless on the touchline, furrowed brow telling of his desperation, having jettisoned his tie and unbuttoned his top button. The run-in reinforced the stereotypes. Arsenal had the moves, United the mental toughness.

Yet United's celebrations during their trophy presentation at Everton (after the final league game) told of near-incredulity at their win. They say that brashness often masks deeper insecurity, and I certainly had that feeling from watching grinning faces atop red shirts jumping up and down on the makeshift podium, singing 'We've got our trophy back.' Sir Alex Ferguson scoffed at Wenger for maintaining his team's superiority in the face of defeat, but his players' response was more telling, as their post-Everton demeanour mocked not Arsenal's ability, but their perceived weakness. This was relief, and a backhanded compliment to Arsenal, acknowledging them as a genuine long-term rival to United, as had the London team held their nerve, the Premiership trophy would have spent more than a year away from Old Trafford for the first time since its launch.

So the signs of a loosening of United's iron grip on the league were there before this season. Yet placed against the backdrop of Arsenal's achievements this season, the sight of United's fallibility laid bare has been simply jaw dropping. They have been as faltering between Christmas and now as they were formidable in the corresponding period last season. They've lost six league games since the turn of the year, including away defeats to the likes of Wolves, Portsmouth and Blackburn, as well as dropping home points to Leeds and Middlesbrough. As indicative of United's wan showings of late is the fact that the deadly Ruud van Nistelrooy has scored only twice since mid-February, both coming in the FA Cup quarter final win against Fulham.

Then there's Europe. Oh, Europe. A large factor – ok, the main factor – in United's New Year tail-off has been their exit from the Champions League. With all due respect to United's outstanding FA Cup commitments, their season all but ended on that Tuesday night in March at Old Trafford, when they were flattened by Porto's late, late equaliser at Old Trafford. Costinha's goal, neatly gobbled up after Benni McCarthy's free-kick had been inadequately parried by Tim Howard, had the problems of United's season writ large all over it. It was just so fallible, such a common mistake. The shock reverberated not just around this corner of M16, but through a watching nation. This was the sort of thing that United had done to other teams in Europe, but this time they were the mugged, having lost their characteristic ruthless streak. This just wasn't supposed to happen to them. 'There was a sense of injustice, particularly over the second Scholes goal (wrongly ruled out for offside with the score at 1-0),' remembers Tony Moylan, an Old Trafford season ticket holder of many years standing. 'But there had also been a far greater attacking impetus in previous years.'

The first stage had been negotiated, smoothly, with total United-ness. This really is the only way to describe it – as the years have gone by in the Champions League, United have turned breezing through the first group stage with the minimum of fuss into a minor art form. This season was no different, aided by the top seeding afforded them by years of continuous success in the competition. There was even the false alarm of the now-standard minor stumble, as they suffered a narrow away defeat against the emerging youngsters of VfB Stuttgart in their second game. The Germans did - of course - receive a comprehensive lesson from their elders and betters at Old Trafford when the home side needed a win to top the group. The second round draw pitting them against Porto seemed to be a kind one, making their sudden and dramatic failure even more of a jolt.

Safely negotiating the group stages like old pros and putting down the killer performances at the tournament's business end are, however, two entirely different things. If we're honest, Manchester United have never quite been the same in the Champions League since the 1999 final. It wouldn't be right to say they've never looked like winning the competition since, but they've never again come close to building up the irresistible momentum that powered them in '99. They were well beaten in quarter-finals by Real Madrid in both 2000 and 2003, and by Bayern Munich in 2001. Even when they came closest in the period since, in losing the 2002 semi-final on away goals to Bayer Leverkusen, the manner of their defeat was relatively tame and deflating.

Looking back at the victorious 1998/9 campaign, it's easy to see how everything since has reeked of anticlimax. Though they may have sneaked victory in the final, United won Europe over with their swashbuckling brand of football during that season. They went to places like Bayern Munich and Barcelona, played with an attacking mindset and not only lived to tell the tale, but almost swept their hosts away, racking up an astonishing 20 goals in the group stage alone (still a Champions League record). There were frequent reminders of how far they'd progressed, like when playing out a thrilling 3-3 draw in the Camp Nou, where they'd been humiliated by Barca four years before, or in clinically dispatching Inter in the quarters, and especially in breaking Juventus' hold over them with that mesmerising comeback in the Delle Alpi. Even the underwhelming final performance against Bayern was thoroughly redeemed by the last ditch heroics of Sheringham and Solskjaer. It was a simply breathless campaign from beginning to end (perhaps also because it was the last season before this one with only one group stage, as well as for the undoubted quality of United's game).

The final's climax in Barcelona was the most tumultuous imaginable to a football match, let alone to a Champions Cup final. Those few minutes of injury time also conjured the most incredible end to an entire campaign, transforming a great season into the ultimate season. Maybe that's the whole point. It was such a timeless *climactic* moment, that it felt as if some definitive peak had been reached. It's as if United's ruthless streak, at least in Europe, began to wane after this point.

In the Champions League, as with any high level competition, every defeat is more closely magnified when you're the champions, as was the case with the group stage defeats to Marseille and Fiorentina in 99/00, red herrings in a generally seamless passage. 'We'd had our fair share of luck in '99,' Tony concedes, 'but we really were the best team in Europe the season after.' Yet, as mentioned before, it's the latter stage knockout games that are the real indicators of a team's power, when the margins are finer and every inch may as well be a mile. The nerve they showed to tip the balance in the games against Inter, Juve and Bayern was exactly what they seemed to lack by the time it came to defend their trophy. United thought they had already done the hard yards in the quarter-final with Real Madrid, bringing a goalless draw back from the Bernabéu. But the Spanish (admittedly, the eventual winners) picked them off expertly at Old Trafford, sailing into a three-goal lead in a little over 50 minutes with an masterclass in slick passing, economical movement and clinical finishing, masterminded by Fernando Redondo and Raúl at the very crest of their powers. The late goals of David Beckham and Paul Scholes were mere gloss on an unflattering scoreline. This was the start of a series of narrow exits in the competition's latter stages. 'We lost to the winners twice - Real Madrid, then Bayern Munich – then the finalists (Bayer Leverkusen) the year after,' argues Tony, 'so there was the feeling that if we'd have overcome them, what would've happened?'

El Real, of course, made a return journey down Sir Matt Busby Way to lord it again three years on, this time having firstly given United a hiding in Madrid. Ronaldo's sublime hat-trick saw the home side off, before two late Beckham goals gave them a consoling 4-3 win on the night. The reaction in the British press was self-delusional, trumpeting one of the greatest European ties of modern times and a struggle between two great sides. Arsene Wenger may not have been the most neutral observer, but when he said that after the first 15 minutes of the tie's first leg, 'at no point' did United look like winning it, he was a lone voice of reason. The then-holders were a class apart, and the only reason

United got so much as a sniff was that El Real, by now completely in the grip of Florentino Pérez' *galácticos* policy, completely took their collective foot of the gas with the game won – an act typical of their burgeoning devil-may-care attitude. Despite the addition of the ultra-prolific van Nistelrooy United, it seemed, could no longer mix it with Europe's biggest players.

All this begs the question of why United have been unable to translate their total domination of the domestic scene through the '90s into the continental arena. There's no doubt that they had the will to move on towards world domination, something which they seemed to show immediately after Barcelona. In the summer of 1999, before the season where they were to defend the Champions League (and, of course, the league and cup), United announced that they were declining the opportunity to defend their FA Cup too, and instead going to compete in the World Club Championship of January 2000 in Brazil. The heckles were immediate – United though they were too important to be bothered with trifling domestic matters, and were prepared to sacrifice the world's domestic cup highlight to go global. Ferguson, for his part, always insisted that United had come under governmental pressure to go to Brazil in order to strengthen England's bid to host the 2006 World Cup, and that they'd had no choice. Meanwhile, FIFA president Sepp Blatter always denied this would be a consideration, a view endorsed by Germany's eventual winning of the World Cup race, despite the non-participation of Bayern Munich (who would have replaced United had they turned down the invite) in Brazil.

Whatever you believed amongst the mixed messages coming from Old Trafford – Ferguson apparently taking the competition seriously, plc chairman Martin Edwards saying they'd rather be playing in the FA Cup – the football side was unsuccessful. They were humbled by Vasco da Gama, and Beckham was sent off for a wild challenge in the draw with the Mexican side Necaxa, as the team failed to reach the latter stages. They had neither made a good impression nor strengthened their global standing, while undertaking a potentially draining long-distance trip in mid-season.

United looked like they had the Premier League licked in much the same way they did with the group stage of the Champions League (winning it by a huge 18 points in 99/00), but it eventually became apparent that they were not equipped to boss Europe's latter stages. The different demands are obvious – think of Real Madrid, who won 3 Champions Leagues in five years between 1998 and 2002. They lifted their own national championship just four times in the period that United racked up their eight titles of the modern era. Everything United did in the second half of the '90s was leading towards what happened that night in Barcelona. The club's report on their financial performance in the year up to July 1998 even told us that United's spending on players like Jaap Stam, as they covered the extra mile to become successful in Europe, had halved the club's profits. Maybe their striving for their grail, their second Champions Cup, was so single-minded that they lacked a clear direction of where they would go afterwards.

Maybe Barcelona was just a moment, the culmination of one great season - of ten glorious days - swept along by the fluency of Dwight Yorke and Andy Cole, the dash of Beckham and Ryan Giggs, and the saves of Peter Schmeichel, all in their pomp. In this way, it could be said this team resembled the club's other Champions Cup winners, the side of Bobby Charlton, George Best, Nobby Stiles and Alex Stepney that beat a Benfica side containing the great Eusebio, 31 years before. The 1968 winners' defence, where they narrowly lost out to eventual winners Milan in the semi-final, was the closest United came until 1999. A barren spell followed – having won the league in 1967 and the European Cup the following year, United of course went without either trophy up until winning the inaugural Premier League in 1993.

A similar fate was never going to befall the '99 version. But five years on, there's little doubt that the extraordinary fire in the bellies of that side has left United, whether it be temporarily or permanently. The question is, taking the anomaly that is post-Abramovich Chelsea out of the picture, how have the financially strongest club in the world fallen from their perch of domestic monopoly? They have cemented their position at the top of English football in the domestic game's most lucrative years ever – ie post-Premier League. However much Arsenal's name is part of English football's historical tapestry, it is little short of a financial miracle that they have been able to mount a sustained challenge to United. For all general assumptions that clubs' success is cyclical, Manchester United have gone way beyond that, being the first to aggressively and firmly establish themselves as a true global brand, rather than simply a footballing dynasty trading on the goodwill of past achievements, like Liverpool, for example. They have become unassailable in the minds of the public and, up to this point, largely in fact.

Yet this season, a clearly developing malaise at Old Trafford has come into view, suggestive of a changing of the guard at the top of the tree, rather than a mere hiccup. The reasons are multiple, and well documented – Rio Ferdinand's drug test ban and Ferguson's row with Coolmore stud (run by the Irishmen John Magnier and JP McManus, owners of nearly a third of the club's shares) being the two most obvious, with controversy also lingering from the summer sale of Beckham. The first of these - Ferdinand forgetting to attend a random drug test – was simply careless. The harsh punishment made it significant too, as United had the Premiership's best defence when he started his eight-month ban in January, but had fallen 12 points behind Arsenal and exited the Champions League by the time his appeal was thrown out by an independently chaired panel in March. 'It had a direct impact,' says Tony, 'but everyone was behind him. Even though he hadn't convinced (on the pitch), we thought the incident had been blown out of proportion because it was United.' The Stretford End had good reason to feel like this. Months before, Christian Negouai (a Manchester City player) had committed a near-identical offence, but was fined £2,000 (£148,000 less than Ferdinand had to shell out, in addition to his suspension) and let off with a warning. Ferdinand paid heavily for his profile. The issue may have been costly and infuriating to United – and far more than it should have been - but these things happen. Players make mistakes and get into scrapes at every club.

Ferguson's troubles were a different kettle of fish entirely. Magnier had earlier given him the chance to buy a stake in the racehorse Rock of Gibraltar, which Ferguson accepted, presumably as an acknowledgement of the manager's peerless and continuous achievements. In August last year it became apparent that the two parties were disputing the ownership of the potentially highly-lucrative stud rights after the horse retired from racing. Ferguson threatened legal action and Magnier launched a counter-writ for defamation. In February, Magnier also issued through his and McManus' company, Cubic Expression, a list of 99 questions to the club's board, alleging that United were failing to implement 'best practice'. This was where the issue started to impact directly on the club. The suspicion was that the Irish were deliberately making difficulties for the board because of the Coolmore dispute.

The two parties eventually concurred on a settlement and dropped their respective actions, though just a day before the Old Trafford return against Porto. Ferguson's conduct was hard to fathom. Quite apart from the fact that most who know their racing could tell you that assuming stud rights of a horse you have racing rights to is far from a given, you can't help but wonder what this already-wealthy man was doing, starting on the equivalent of picking a fight with his boss. He's made his reputation on digging his heels in, but on this occasion Ferguson showed little concern for the harmony of the club in recklessly, and publicly, coming out of his corner of the ring with his arms swinging[1]. His talent for discretion and keeping problems in-house, always one of United's strengths over the years, had gone missing.

The Beckham issue was a little less cut and dried. It hadn't seemed so at the season's start. So much was made of his commercial value - rather than his football talent - when he was allowed to join Real Madrid that I, along with a lot of others, thought it was a good call. This was simply on the basis that there's surely got to be a limit to the amount of United replica shirts with 'Beckham 7' printed on the back that you can sell. The man was all marketed out. There had been tension too, most notably when Beckham had left Old Trafford after the FA Cup defeat by Arsenal sporting stitches in a cut above his eye. This had been caused, it emerged, from being struck by a flying football boot kicked across the dressing room by the manager in a blind rage. This was the culmination of increasingly distant relations between the pair, with Ferguson said to resent how Beckham's fame had propelled him from his manager's protective clutches that had held Ryan Giggs, for example, so tightly.

'Everyone felt it was inevitable, really,' says Tony. 'United fans are great for getting behind players. With the likes of Cantona, Ince and Kanchelskis in the past, when it looked as if they could be on the way out, there was a great swell of support behind each player. You know, everyone would make a big point of singing the player's name again and again. Especially in 1994, with Ince (before he was sold to Inter). But that never happened with Beckham.' It wasn't only Ferguson who felt that the shadow of Beckham the superstar was looming over Beckham the footballer. 'Most people thought that his celebrity had overtaken his football.'

These theories on the advantages of life minus Beckham were virtually all floated, however, before we'd seen United play without him. 'Opinions definitely changed as the season went on,' admits Tony. The team's shape had been indubitable, but was now hazier. Juan Sebastian Verón, after two largely disappointing seasons since arriving in a club-record deal from Lazio, was supposed to benefit from this new lack of rigidity and finally come into his own, in a more freeform United side. He looked the part pre-season, but Ferguson was obviously not convinced and the Argentine was packed off to Chelsea. And after? How they missed Beckham's sumptuous crossfield passes. A main supply line - a get out of jail free card, even – had been cut. None of the various replacements, including Kleberson, Darren Fletcher or Eric Djemba-Djemba (or the developing teenager Cristiano Ronaldo, handed the burden of Beckham's old number 7 shirt) had Beckham's very specific qualities. The goals have hardly dried up, but you can only imagine how the directness of the England captain's passing might have swung a few tight games – including one particular one in Europe.

And Europe is where it all comes back to, isn't it, because when Costinha's tap-in hit the net, it was the beginning of the end of United's season. The trouncing they received in the Manchester derby on the following weekend (4-1, their worst result in the fixture for 15 years) merely confirmed it. The earliest point from which they'd exited the competition in nearly 10 years left a hole that the team – and probably Ferguson – had no idea how to fill. Hence, perhaps, Chelsea being able to creep up on the blindside and steal a march for second place.

It's Chelsea who are today's visitors to Old Trafford, for the Saturday lunchtime kick-off. In the morning I get a lift to near the ground from a friend, but the traffic is static for a good few miles around the stadium, so I stroll the rest of the way. The weather's good for Manchester – it's only lightly drizzling rather than pissing it down, so you can tell that summer's on the way. Despite the increasingly corporate sheen of the club's public face in the last 10 years, the ground and the area around retains a real traditional working-class football bustle. As soon as you cross on to Chester Road on the approach to the stadium, there are people huddled on both sides of the street, with a bigger swell outside the famous Lou Macari chip shop - talking, debating, supping from cans of lager, in full public forum. It's heartening that the fans continue to express themselves in an ever-more sanitised climate. It also goes some way to explaining how much more likeable United are when you're actually in Manchester. I can understand rival fans' hatred of the club in other parts of the country (ok, in London), faced with a hoard of satellite television-worshipping glory hunters as United's representatives. But here, where it counts, they're mainly vocal, intelligent and passionate.

Inside, it's a little different. The stands are packed to their 67,500 as usual, but there's something missing. I guess it's the lack of something real to play for. When the match starts, United themselves seem to feel the same, lacking vim and vigour. There's a definite feeling that we're watching two teams passing each other, heading in opposite directions. A quick, crude comparison between the rival centre-backs plays out the situation in microcosm. Chelsea's John Terry is poised and alert, near-faultless. It's hard to see how he isn't an automatic pick for the England side. On the other side, Wes Brown (claimed as the 'best centre-half in England' by Ferguson not so long ago, lest we forget) is stilted and hesitant, and looks off the pace. Later, when Paul Scholes is replaced by Louis Saha as a cautionary measure towards the end of the first half (shortly after fortuitously avoiding a second booking for a poor challenge on Frank Lampard), the Chelsea fans sing a pointed rendition of 'Super Frankie Lampard'. Just a year ago, to so much as question Scholes' automatic right to an England place would have been unthinkable. Where Terry and Brown have already swapped trajectories, these two England midfielders are liable to soon.

Brown is not, however, the only culpable United defender. They give the ball away far too much while trying to play it out of defence, and their uncertainty soon costs them. Before we reach the 20-minute mark, United fail to properly clear a corner. The Danish winger Jesper Grønkjaer has an age to bring the ball down on the edge of the box, pull it onto his favoured right foot and blast a superb angled shot into the top left-hand corner of Tim Howard's goal. Far, far too easy. This just adds to the party mood that the travelling fans from London are in, and a chorus of 'where were you when you were good?' starts up, in barbed response to the home fans' earlier 'where were you when you were shit?' dig at the social climbers. If you're a United fan at this moment, it will hurt. Losing the title is bad enough, but to have these 'nouveau riche cockney twats' (as thousands of Mancs are no doubt muttering under their breath) coming up here and taking the piss out of you is something else. Old Trafford can only sigh in resignation.

Relief seems to present itself just before half-time, when Robert Huth drags Saha to the floor in the penalty box, and the referee points to the spot. Van Nistelrooy steps up, but with little conviction, and

Carlo Cudicini parries the shot to his right in relative comfort. Ferguson doesn't flinch, stood in his trademark pose in the cusp of the stand, chewing furiously as normal. It's shortly after this point that I spot the currently helpless Ferdinand about 10 seats to my left. He is grudgingly but politely signing a few autographs to pass the half-time interval. He looks thoroughly miserable.

You expect United to come out for the second half with a bit of zip, given that they need to win to have any chance of avoiding the bother of a Champions League qualifier, which they presumably would love to. But Chelsea look comfortable, poised. Even bearing in mind that Liverpool won the last league game here, it's hard to imagine the last time that an away team was less tested here. After their Champions League semi-final exertions in midweek, it's ideal for Chelsea. The United fans refer to that defeat, with a taunt of 'you're gonna win fuck all' at their rivals. When was the last time that you heard United fans singing that to someone rather than opposition fans singing it at them, or even need to? Is it significant of a genuine power shift in the Premiership?

United do eventually manage to salvage something from the game. The impetuous Huth (no pun intended, really) drags down van Nistelrooy as the Dutchman runs clear, and Chelsea are left to face the last 17 minutes with only 10 men. Chelsea gift United their equaliser shortly afterwards, when the otherwise-admirable Cudicini spills an innocuous Mikael Silvestre cross for van Nistelrooy to do the necessary from point blank. The visitors never look like relinquishing their hold on a point, though, and finish the match guaranteed second place in the Premiership.

Ferguson tackles the obligatory lap of honour with a great deal of dignity and grace, which is very admirable in the circumstances. He makes a short speech through a microphone thanking the supporters for their loyalty, and ends with an almost cheery 'Enjoy yourselves in Cardiff.' Such is the feeling of flatness that I'd completely forgotten that the cup final is still to come.

While I gaze at the supporters who've stayed in the ground for this, I talk on the phone with one of the many who didn't hang around. Tony sums it up perfectly. 'They weren't exactly bursting blood vessels to get the winner at the end. It was a bit of an anti-climax. Just like the whole season really.' And that's it in a nutshell. The '90s golden age reached a ecstatic peak with the treble. Every great party, though, is followed by a big old hangover. There have been enough cans left in the fridge at Old Trafford to put it off so far. But they're running out, and I think they might just be reaching for the last half of the bottle of scotch on the sideboard.

Chelsea

Even in the precarious business of football management, there's surely never been anyone looking as much a 'dead man walking' as Claudio Ranieri (phrase copyright of the manager himself). Having endured a season not so much of interminable speculation but more an agonisingly slow demise, a death by a thousand cuts, Ranieri's lowest point followed his team's Champions League semi-final first leg defeat in Monaco. Uncharacteristically grey-faced and despondent, he admitted: 'We lost the plot.' If there was to be anything resembling a dénouement of this painful saga, this was it. The Italian's season of defiant crawl up the muddy hill of his club's expectation had always been destined to end in disappointment. Chelsea aren't Real Madrid just yet, but given that winning the Champions League couldn't save Jupp Heynckes - seeing that he delivered the coveted *séptima* – then what chance Ranieri? Exactly.

That's not to say, of course, that Chelsea don't want to be Real Madrid. Even discounting new owner Roman Abramovich's determined lurch towards world domination, Chelsea have been striving to inhabit the same sort of territory as the Spaniards for some time now. As befits a club situated in such a painfully fashionable part of south-west London, Chelsea have been the Premiership's most cosmopolitan club since its inception. Whether the majority of English football fans would like to admit it or not, it was Glenn Hoddle - his horizons broadened by a spell at Monaco under Arsene Wenger in the twilight of his career - who began to sculpt 'New Chelsea' while manager back in the mid-'90s.

'Chelsea have always been very European (since the start of the FA Premier League).' Tim Danaher has been a regular visitor to Stamford Bridge since childhood in the early '80s. The present would have been unimaginable back then, when the team yo-yoed between divisions and played in a crumbling, ramshackle excuse for a stadium. Stamford Bridge was most definitely Falling Down. 'Hoddle started it all, signing Ruud Gullit and (Mark) Hughes (in the summer of 1995).' The signing of Gullit was particularly crucial. Sure, Hughes was a star, but Gullit was a world football legend, and moreover the first major foreign star to come to the Premier League. He set a new high watermark for the League in terms of status, and also brought with him a new professionalism. Barely a season later Hoddle left to take the national team job, and the Dutchman was left to mould the team in this image in his place as the club's new manager.

Gullit was a clear catalyst for change. Chelsea were a club who'd enjoyed sporadic success, winning the league once in 1955, as well as an FA Cup and the European Cup Winners' Cup in the '70s. By the '80s the club was more famous for their fans' reputation and their rucks with rival cliques at the likes of Leeds and West Ham, and for having an especially abrasive chairman in Ken Bates rather than any great feats on the pitch. Chelsea represented an old-school, pitbull-like, very 'British' image of a football club. Although broadly established as Premier League perennials by the mid-'90s, it was the charismatic Dutchman that made the Blues headline material rather than mere column filler. 'He changed the culture of the club from top to bottom,' remembers Danaher, 'which was pretty insular before, maybe even tending towards nationalistic.' When Gullit arrived at Stamford Bridge he was approaching his 33rd birthday and there was the suspicion he was gradually winding down his career, having been a central figure of the legendary AC Milan side of the late-'80s/early-'90s. Such was the relative poverty (quality-wise) of the Premier League compared to the likes of Serie A that it was assumed that overseas stars would only consider England as an option for one last payday as they watched their peak years fade into the distance. You always had the feeling that Gullit was more important for what he represented than simply what he offered on the pitch.

So Hoddle's departure in May 1996 actually presented Bates with a handy opportunity to move the club on. While the appointment of someone with no managerial experience was theoretically a gamble, Gullit was as close as you will ever get to a sure thing in football. Not only did he have the intelligence and background for the job, but he never seemed remotely bothered about his dressing room popularity, as shown by a number of spectacular fall-outs with colleagues and coaches at Milan and with the Holland team in particular. Gullit would not have the problems others would in defining a new boss-to-player relationship with his charges, and he knew his own mind. Crucially, he had the connections that would make Chelsea be taken seriously in the higher echelons of European football. He was able to bring in Gianluca Vialli from Juventus, who was followed by Roberto Di Matteo, Frank Leboeuf and Gianfranco Zola.

Gullit made Chelsea think in widescreen – Bates even took to flying European flags over The Shed – and his vision quickly paid off as Chelsea won the FA Cup in 1997, the first major trophy the club had bagged in 26 years. That he is still highly regarded by many Chelsea fans speaks volumes for the giant steps that the team – and the club – took in a short period. He was sacked in February 1998, officially after a 'contract dispute', with the team second in the league table and still in all cup competitions. Bates accused Gullit of greed and arrogance, though the chairman seemed to take umbrage to his protégé's burgeoning popularity. It wouldn't be the first, or last time that Bates felt the need to forcibly wrestle back the spotlight from someone he felt in danger of being overshadowed by – remember, this cultural improvement in the club was made possible by the investment of insurance millionaire Matthew Harding, who died tragically in a helicopter crash on the way back from a game in October 1996. Harding was a real fan, loved by the hardcore for his common touch and thoroughly resented by Bates for his popularity.

What had started under Gullit was no passing phase. Chelsea were committed to the pan-Euro vision, and settled on another foreigner, and another current player, to replace him – Gianluca Vialli. Vialli got lucky, inadvertently benefiting from boardroom machinations to walk into a dream job in a highly enviable situation. How many managers get the sack when their team's second in the league? All of three months later the Italian was ending his first season in charge polishing two more trophies on the sideboard, the League Cup and the European Cup Winners' Cup – largely, it must be said, on the back of his predecessor's hard work and innovation.

Nevertheless Vialli did a decent job in his two and a half years in charge, not only winning that European trophy but taking the next big step, qualifying for the Champions League, and expertly overseeing their first forays in the competition. Gullit's reign had changed European football's perception of Chelsea, and though Vialli was not quite on Gullit's plateau image-wise, he was still a highly-respected figure, and a Champions League winner with Juventus to boot. He attracted names such as Marcel Desailly and Didier Deschamps, not just names, but players with stacks of top level experience to help the team adapt to the highest tier of European competition. Vialli's reign was the natural progression of Gullit's time in charge. He completed Chelsea's transformation from the tough '80s image to a cosmopolitan, metrosexual incarnation, gradually ditching the Stamford Bridge old guard of players like Frank Sinclair, Eddie Newton, Steve Clarke and Michael Duberry. Of the 22 signings Vialli made while manager, only one – Chris Sutton – was British. Chelsea also became the first team in English league history to go into a game with a starting eleven composed entirely of non-British players, at Southampton in December 1999.

Chelsea's Europeanisation proved to be highly successful in the sense that when they did enter the Champions League (in 1999-00), they played like they'd been there for years. Eventually they found themselves seven minutes shy of reaching the semi-finals at the Camp

Nou before eventually succumbing to an extra-time defeat against Barcelona. It was easy to think, looking at both the team's largely continental composition and their sussed European performances, that Chelsea were more comfortable breathing in the more rarefied air of the Champions League than in the Premier League's diesel fumes. Vialli's Chelsea were caught cold in the cut-and-thrust of domestic competition often enough to keep them short of Manchester United and Arsenal while prompting plenty of murmurings about 'bottle' and 'desire'.

Maybe this now-established image is what attracted Roman Abramovich to invest in Chelsea, rather than another debt-ridden Premiership big boy (Leeds, Newcastle perhaps). It's impossible to know for sure as Abramovich is unfailingly mysterious. He would attract suspicion anyway as, well, a 37-year-old multi-billionaire who appeared from nowhere to pluck Chelsea from the roundabout at the bottom of Skid Row to Saville Row with an unlimited tab. Though the thinking man's pub wisdom has him down as a morally bereft, post-*perestroika* carpet bagger, Abramovich has not felt the need to make any public defence or vindication of himself. Or, indeed, any public statements at all. Even his presence at virtually every game since his purchase of the club has told us nothing about him. If anything, the sight of him applauding politely, looking detached, unmoved, even distracted, confuses even more. What's he thinking? Is he aware of what's going on? Does he really care? We will ever find out the answers to any of these questions?

I would imagine not. Which is fairly irrelevant – all that counts is that this takeover changed the face of football like none before or probably ever again. The deal was reportedly worth £140 million, around £80 million of which was used to wipe out the club's potentially crippling debts. Many were racked up by parent company Chelsea Village, though the role of football-related management happy to indulge the expensive tastes of successive managers until the cupboard was not so much bare as without any doors and teetering on two legs were highly significant too. City rumours strongly suggested Chelsea were on the brink of financial collapse when Abramovich showed up in the nick of time in July. Certainly no-one had been in any doubt of the importance of the Sunday afternoon in mid-May 2003 when Chelsea had faced Liverpool at Stamford Bridge, in what was effectively a play-off for the Premiership's final Champions League place. That the home side managed to win was not solely crucial for the team's progress, and the brightest moment of Claudio Ranieri's tenure to that point, but a financial lifeline for the club. The Champions League booty was desperately needed to keep the wolves from the door, and as such defeat against Liverpool would have been disastrous.

Abramovich's arrival turned Chelsea from rag-wearing party gatecrashers to sitting at the top table enjoying the host's finest cognac at a stroke. The club had been transformed previously by Harding's millions, but this was just a different ballpark. Top football clubs are not cheap, and takeovers therefore tend to be painstakingly pieced together between syndicates, financial advisers and clubs over months of careful negotiation. The Russian didn't need to borrow to buy Chelsea, with the full cost barely a graze on his personal finances. Having bought the club and taken up residence in the UK, spending most of his time at his vast estate in Sussex, he is now Britain's richest man – according to the Sunday Times Rich List, he is worth half as much again as the next richest man in Britain, the Duke of Westminster. He is also the sixth richest man in Europe and the 22nd richest man in the world.

Barely before the entrance doors at Stamford Bridge had swung shut behind him, Abramovich started to make a seismic impact on the transfer market the like of which had never been seen or even seriously imagined before. In a world where too many clubs were counting the cost of keeping up with the Joneses and even the game's biggest names were tightening their belts, he was a man who could afford to spend money as if Armageddon was just around the corner. Although the suggestion that this had no real effect on the market was nonsense – the club's willingness to splash huge sums on players gave the selling clubs unexpected windfalls to reinvest, and therefore stimulate the market

– the truth was Chelsea had started to live in a bubble. From now on, they would have no limits.

It's hard to imagine Claudio Ranieri being anything but bemused by the developments of summer 2003. Ranieri had a difficult introduction to the Premiership back in September 2000, as the furore over the popular Vialli's sacking hung around (more rumours of a fall-out with Bates) and the new coach struggled to express himself, speaking no English. Meanwhile you would have struggled to find a Chelsea fan who had even heard of their team's new boss. A series of bizarre television interviews in his first season conducted through an interpreter who seemed a touch lost himself hardly helped to raise his popularity, and the media parodied him as 'The Tinkerman', forever switching personnel and formations – something which Ranieri himself always insisted was just the Italian way. Bates - whose appointment of the man from Rome was a conscious decision to maintain the club's European approach - has to be credited for sticking with his coach through some tougher times outside the Champions League, realising that Ranieri was at least partially suffering from his predecessors' easy come, easy go attitude with the transfer kitty.

Last summer Ranieri found himself able to look proudly back at his most successful season at the Bridge, an achievement particularly notable for the fact that he had been unable to spend a single penny to strengthen his squad before or during that season. His one signing had been a squad player, Quique de Lucas, on a year's loan. It would have been surreal enough for Ranieri had the new owner handed him a blank chequebook from which to build the squad of his dreams. Yet though the club spent around £110 million on players in the summer, it's questionable how much input the manager himself had in choosing the signings. 'Buying players for a top Premiership team isn't like buying a Fantasy League team,' says Tim Danaher. 'The way Chelsea bought players (last summer) was like watching a kid let loose in a sweetshop.' He's right. It was hard to make out any coherent sporting strategy behind the signings, beyond an exercise in raising profile, collecting big-name trophy players, to show the world how big Chelsea had become. One could even argue that the biggest signing of the Abramovich era so far was that of chief executive Peter Kenyon from Manchester United. It was a statement of intent, showing that the Russian was determined to get the very biggest and best of everything for Chelsea, and that no-one, not even United, could stop them. It even started people in the media muttering about 'power shifts'. Ranieri, meanwhile, got some players he wanted, whereas he was probably just given others.

Bates' public line on the sale of his shares to Abramovich – bear in mind that his pride would never allow him to explicitly admit that he was helped out of a hole created by the realisation of his Chelsea Village dream – was that the club needed someone 'with deeper pockets' to take it 'to the next level'. He seemed confident that Chelsea would continue to follow the direction that he had vigorously pursued for the past eight or so years. *The London Evening Standard* of 3rd July 2003 quoted the chairman as saying that '..we are recognised as one of England's elite clubs and this extra financial power will help to make us one of Europe's elite clubs. The immediate benefit is that we will have a fund to purchase players.' While Ranieri had tended towards buying British – Frank Lampard being his most successful signing – the signings of players of the pedigree of Verón, Crespo and Makelélé spoke volumes of a club looking towards the wider European picture rather than just domestically. From the start Abramovich's Chelsea had its eyes on the Champions League.

It was the day before a Champions League game that I first came face to face with Claudio Ranieri, at a press conference at Chelsea's Harlington training ground, a surprisingly spartan facility near Heathrow airport. His team were due to face Sparta Prague at Stamford Bridge - their fifth Champions League game of the group stage - knowing a win would see them through to the knockout stages, having already won three of the first four. Still, the manager had a tangible aura of the underdog about him, talking in defensive, finite terms. 'We have showed good performances and good football, but it's finished.' If you hadn't known you certainly wouldn't have guessed that Chelsea had taken 32 out of a potential 39 Premiership points up to then, to accompany their progress in Europe. His manner was especially noticeable, as overall the atmosphere was less wired than that which would surround a league game, with his captain Marcel Desailly impassive at Ranieri's side, reflecting the greater degree of comfort that the team exude in the Champions League. I was tip-toeing through the usual minefield of questions about who's fit and who's not, would the game be difficult, and have you had a row with such-and-such player Claudio (in this case supposedly Desailly, though unsurprisingly no-one has the balls to ask the imposing Frenchman outright). What I was really trying to do was get at the divide between the Premiership Chelsea and Champions League Chelsea. While I've never thought for a minute that either coach or club would (at least outwardly) prioritise one over the other, there must be a different sort of approach for either type of game, maybe as much via personnel as application?

'No. It is no different. It is eleven players against eleven players and we try, we fight,' says Ranieri, thumping right fist against left palm in that endearingly passionate way that has become so familiar, even caricatured, while his captain gazes out of the window, biting his lip to stifle a titter. 'We are fighters.' Thinking back to the successful days under Gullit and Vialli, Chelsea were always sneered at as Fancy Dans, bottlers. Not so now. 'Ranieri's greatest achievement, without a doubt, has been making the team more resilient,' emphasises Danaher. Ranieri talks a lot about his 'young lions' and has made a conscious effort to toughen the team by giving it a British spine, making John Terry and Frank Lampard his mainstays, along with Wayne Bridge, an Abramovich-era purchase that looked to be a sure Ranieri choice. 'The best performance of the season, in the league at least, was beating Leicester at the Walkers' Stadium (4-0, in January),' remembers Danaher. 'The team that started the game had nine players in it that were there the previous season, which says a lot.' Transfer funds can be a huge advantage (just ask mid-'90s period Blackburn Rovers) but

Ranieri used a lack of them to foster a spirit of unity that had often been lacking previously. He did his best work for Chelsea in 2002/3, moulding a solid, coherent and durable group when he had no choice but to work with what he had.

We may never know the complete truth of why Chelsea splashed such substantial sums on Verón and Crespo. Dark rumours persisted throughout the season that Abramovich sanctioned the purchase of the two on the advice of Sven-Goran Eriksson – the press discovery of whom visiting Abramovich's home in October so brutally exposed the transience of Ranieri's position – who counted them as mainstays at Lazio. In flashes both players showed their potential worth to the Chelsea grand plan, particularly in the 4-0 win at Lazio, and Crespo in particular was bought for those moments, having scored nine Champions League goals for Inter in the previous season. In the Premiership though, with Crespo's constant injury niggles and Verón showing little sign of negotiating the pace of league games any better than he had at Manchester United before succumbing to injury, their influence was largely peripheral.

Ranieri is a proud man with a considerable loyalty to his players, but he still deserves to be applauded for carrying on so effectively under such widespread public knowledge of his imminent departure. The quarter-final win at Arsenal was his ultimate vindication, as well as the season's defining moment. Don't let anyone kid you that it was that collapse in the semi-final first leg in Monte Carlo – the Italian's fate was already sealed, as rumours swept the Principality that April day of Roman Abramovich and his right-hand man Kenyon entertaining Porto boss José Mourinho's representatives on his private yacht on the harbour. It was Wayne Bridge's late winner at Highbury that was Ranieri's special moment in a season of toil. It meant many things – Chelsea reaching their first Champions League semi, beating Arsenal for the first time since 1995, and trashing the inferiority complex they suffered against their highly-gifted neighbours. But it also gave Ranieri a respect that he had never before enjoyed in England, from media and fans alike. Sure, people had grown to love him, a sincere man who made comedic light of his awkward grapple with the English language, but nice guys never succeed in the British game, right? Chelsea trumped what is unquestionably England's best side for many a year in front of a watching continent, with one of his key young English 'lions' applying the stylish and dramatic *coup de grace*. It was such a beautifully eloquent defence of his tenure that it's little wonder the Italian was on the brink of tears at the final whistle.

So here we are, at Stamford Bridge on the season's last day for a dead rubber, with the hosts guaranteed second place and visitors Leeds United having been relegated almost a fortnight ago. The walk up Fulham Broadway to the stadium is quite different to how it was in the '80s. Even though the crowds are (more often than not) twice the size nowadays, it's far less intimidating. The whole atmosphere seems somehow lighter. Not quite a queue for the opera, as some would have you believe, but certainly muted in comparison to its past incarnations.

The crowd are in fairly celebratory mood for what's the manager's wake in all but name, with questions about Mourinho's imminent arrival being simply ignored now by the club as opposed to being politely denied or stonewalled. Leeds are getting into the carnival spirit of the occasion by employing the offside trap in the game's early stages, though it becomes clear why when they're opened up embarrassingly easily for the first goal, nodded in by Jesper Grønkjaer (another who might reasonably expect this to be his Chelsea swansong). Leeds are feeble, and Chelsea are toying with them, though only at training pace, as rightfully befits such a pleasant sunny day.

Joe Cole tells us it's really party time at the beginning of the second-half, almost setting Lampard up with the sort of outrageous back-heeled flick that players generally don't attempt in proper games. Then it starts. A huge rendition of 'Ranieri's Blue And White Army' fills the stands, and the manager rises from the bench to applaud the fans, at which the chorus intensifies further. The whole of Stamford

Bridge then give him a standing ovation, with even the Leeds fans joining in – with one or two from those down from Yorkshire taking a break from their curious habit of turning round to the press box and angrily shouting 'you killed this club!' at bemused hacks. This then gives way to a heartfelt chant of 'There's Only One Ranieri'. It's pure theatre. After being substituted, Glen Johnson is hugged proudly like a lost son greeted by his father. Significantly, Lampard and Terry receive similar grateful thanks later when they come off, as Ranieri grants his favourites end-of-season ovations. The most telling touch is when he prepares to bring on Robert Huth for Terry. There are barely six minutes left in the season, running down the clock in a meaningless game, but Ranieri takes out a tactical plan scribbled on a side of A4 from his blazer pocket and starts carefully pointing out to Huth his on-pitch brief. You can't fault the man's commitment and dignity.

Ranieri is philosophical afterwards – 'I had a good chance to show what I can do' – though he was clearly retained simply for his availability, and never truly trusted with Abramovich's cash. It's ironic, when he will soon be removed largely due to his lack of profile, that of the trophies they went for this season, Claudio Ranieri came closest to bringing the Champions League trophy to Stamford Bridge – the one trophy that would announce to the world, not just England, that Chelsea are one of football's dominant forces. To again recall the example of Blackburn's 1995 Premiership win, it's inconceivable that the Russian riches will fail to land Chelsea a trophy at some stage in the near future. As the Champions League has shown so clearly this season, success is about so much more than big names though, and the extent and duration of the club's success will require wisdom as well as a wallet. It's hard to believe that Mourinho is being courted – despite his excellent pedigree – as anything other than another headline grabber, a flavour-of-the-month, but if Porto's nous in the competition is anything to go by, then Chelsea may be about to get lucky. A Chelsea fan I spoke to in a pub after the game said that '..the Premiership is what we want more than anything.' 'We' means the fans, I think. Chelsea are looking further afield, as they have been for some time.

The Final

It's been quite a journey to get here, and no, I'm not talking about the last nine months. It is an impressive, vast, state-of-the-art and indeed spanking new stadium, but God only knows why UEFA picked the Arena Auf Schalke to host the 2005 Champions League final. Like many new stadiums of the last ten years or so, it 'enjoys' a distinctly out-of-town location, being a good twenty minutes' tram journey from the centre of Gelsenkirchen. This description, though, doesn't quite do it justice. It really is in the middle of nowhere, set back from the autobahn with not so much as a trading estate for company. This wouldn't be so bad were it not for the fact that even Gelsenkirchen proper is the most featureless of northern German industrial towns. When I told the German girl in my French class from nearby Cologne last week that I was off to her homeland, she smiled and raised her eyebrows excitedly. When I elaborated that I would be coming here, her look changed to somewhere between faintly-concealed horror and 'do you know what you're doing?' incredulity. Imagine holding the Champions League final in Coventry. But without the pubs or the passers-by.

Just to address the other journey for a moment, the very act of being here shows me just how far this has all pushed me to the brink of obsession. This is a busy old week, with me squeezing this into the middle of a week full of exams – jetting in at lunchtime before retiring back to the airport for a snooze and catching a flight back at the crack of dawn, before heading in for a Spanish paper. So you've never heard about preparation being 90% of the battle in exams? Well, me neither, obviously. This is though the culmination of nine months' worth of travel, tension and tight finishes, for me as much as it is for Monaco and Porto.

One underdog in the final is the feeling of a refreshing breeze, but two represents the sound of every jaw in European football dropping and hitting the floor. Yet there's no suggestion that the successes of either of these two sides in this season's competition are anywhere approaching a fluke. Monaco's humiliation of Deportivo back in November may have been a freak, but overall they've got here the hard way. After squeezing past Lokomotiv on away goals, they shocked Real Madrid in the quarters, in what was arguably the tie of the tournament so far. Fernando Morientes' late goal at the Bernabéu against the holders of his registration was supposed to be just a minor inconvenience to El Real. But it proved decisive when the Spaniards 'melted' – in the now famous words of Zinedine Zidane – in the second half at the Louis II, as the hosts came back from one down to win on away goals, thanks to two on the night from Ludovic Giuly and a trademark towering header from – you've guessed it – Morientes again. Fresh from burying the hopes of the club that still pays 65% of his wages (something that Florentino Pérez is no doubt still finding highly embarrassing), 'El Moro' was instrumental in his team again springing a surprise, seeing off the favourites in the semi-final, and perhaps the whole competition, Chelsea. After building a handsome first leg lead, it was the Monégasques that let an advantage slip this time, going two down at Stamford Bridge, and heading out at that point on away goals. The visitors were undeterred though, and after Hugo Ibarra pulled one back on the night, it was Morientes again who sewed it up with a firm right-footer. The goal that sealed Monaco's place at the Auf Schalke also made the Spaniard the Champions League's top scorer this season.

Porto's path here has been less dramatic – well, give or take the odd game at Old Trafford - but no less impressive. In the second leg of their quarter-final with Lyon, they expertly picked off the French champions on their own patch, with Maniche's two goals meaning they were home and hosed long before Giovane Elber's last-minute goal struck the most hollow of blows for the hosts. The semi-final victory was, again, Perfectly Poised Porto. There was only one goal over the two legs, a Derlei penalty in the Riazor following a turgid stalemate at the Dragão. That Porto's run to the final has incorporated considerably less fireworks than Monaco's probably make them slight favourites, to the logically-minded (or cold-hearted) among us.

So what of our other clubs? The losing semi-finalists will be feeling a fair few pangs of regret today. Chelsea, though, will get over it. Of all the last four, they are the club mostly likely to become a regular fixture at that stage. Money isn't everything, but the only unlimited war chest in the game's history means that Chelsea's ascension to the European elite falls more under the heading of probability than possibility. They will have plenty more chances in the future, particularly when, as seems inevitable, the worst kept secret in football becomes hard fact and Claudio Ranieri is replaced by José Mourinho as coach. Chelsea may be merely running with the zeitgeist, but Mourinho is close to being the best, as well as the currently hippest coach in Europe.

Depor, meanwhile, will never have a better shot at glory than this. They may have finished third in the league again, but they're stagnating. That they reached the semis despite this is a reminder of the beauty of this competition. It's incredible to think that but for the odd goal in their semi, they would have again been facing the same team that handed them the mother of all defeats just a few months ago, in the Champions League final. Maybe they peaked too soon. After a very impressive second phase win over Juventus, in which they beat the Italian champions home and away, there came their quarter-final win over AC Milan, which has already become the stuff of legend. After losing 4-1 in the San Siro, Depor humbled the holders 4-0 in the Riazor to complete the unlikeliest comeback in Champions League history. It was too tough to follow, and maybe will remain Depor's Champions League pinnacle.

Milan must be still struggling to comprehend what happened to them in Galicia. There can't be many worse circumstances in which to lose the title of European champions. Of all the teams you could imagine being the victim of this sort of comeback, Milan would have to be near the bottom of the list. They did at least have the consolation of regaining their domestic title (for the first time in five years), as did Celtic. The Scots' progress in the Champions League down the years will probably be viewed now as more crawling than steady. Only Juninho's 86th minute penalty in Lyon prevented them going through to the second round for the first time since the Champions League began, but though this was a painfully cruel way to fall, it doesn't tell the whole story. That defeat at the Gerland kept up Celtic's extraordinary record of never having taken a single point from a Champions League away match. They went to great lengths to keep up that record this season – relinquishing the lead before losing to a freak goal in Munich, and then losing to an Anderlecht side who played an hour against them with just 10 men in Brussels, before that night in France. Yet this closest of near misses could be more a case of one last hurrah for Celtic than the start of something new. They were put out of the UEFA Cup in the quarter-finals by an industrious Villarreal side who clinically exposed their limitations. Stalwarts like Lambert, Lennon and McNamara are into their thirties, and the frankly irreplaceable Henrik Larsson is leaving. Martin O'Neill's team is getting old, and requires plenty of new blood just to maintain, let alone flourish, in Europe.

Lyon themselves at least managed an honourable exit, going out to the eventual finalists. They also showed in the earlier rounds that they were no lightweights, coming out on top of a tough group with the highlight being the away win at Bayern Munich – Elber's winner, followed by him then breaking down with emotion, being one of this season's more wry twists. They also dispatched Real Sociedad in the second phase with little bother. They have quality, although they probably lack the dead-eyed striker who would bring the team closer to Europe's best, with a midfielder, Juninho, being their top scorer. Having just won their third league title in a row, they'll be back to have another go with a year's more experience to boot.

Marseille's season, meanwhile, was just typically...Marseillaise. Their Champions League campaign proper began with Didier Drogba giving them an improbable lead in the Bernabéu. However, they went on to be spanked that night, with Real Madrid and Porto eventually both qualifying comfortably from the group. Naturally, there was managerial change. By the time the UEFA Cup campaign started, Alain Perrin had departed and José Anigo was in charge. Amid rumours of dressing room in-fighting, the team managed a miserable 7th place in the league, though the Velodrome did enjoy some great nights in Europe, with exciting matches against Porto and Real Madrid (even if both did end in defeat), and Drogba's hat-trick against Partizan Belgrade which gave them their only Champions League win of the season. The Ivory Coast striker's 11 European goals made him the star of their shambolic campaign, which ended bizarrely last week with a UEFA Cup final appearance against Spanish champions Valencia. Characteristically, this also ended in catastrophe, when goalkeeper Fabien Barthez (who returned to Provence in the January transfer window) was sent off before Rafael Benítez' side swatted aside the French challenge.

The three who will really be gnashing their teeth, watching tonight's game on the television at home, are Bayern Munich, Juventus and Manchester United. Not only did they all receive second round defeats – which Juve and United especially will also feel were rather avoidable – but they all rather meekly surrendered their domestic crowns. The latter two couldn't even muster a second place between them. Juve finished behind Roma, and 13 points adrift of Milan's champions, while United ended a whopping 15 points short of Arsenal, and Chelsea beat them to second. Meanwhile, Bayern succumbed to the inevitable a fortnight after the Munich derby, when they suffered the ultimate indignity of Werder Bremen clinching the title by hammering them in their own backyard at the Olympiastadion. The final six-point gap between Bayern and the new champions would have been even greater had Werder not eased off considerably with the league safely in the bag. They did at least qualify automatically for the Champions League next season, but Ottmar Hitzfeld has since drawn the curtain on his career in Bavaria, deciding to leave now rather than in 12 months' time. Stuttgart's Felix Magath, himself the scorer of the goal that won the 1983 Champions Cup for Hamburg, has been confirmed as Hitzfeld's replacement and a new era looks set to start. All these three clubs will feel it's imperative that they put on a far stronger Champions League showing next season.

Real Madrid stand alone, probably in the deepest shock right now, looking back on how their season imploded. The calamitous Monaco defeat precipitated the unthinkable, starting a domino effect as El Real blew La Liga even more comprehensively than they had managed to do in the King's Cup and the Champions League before it. They finished the season horribly, with a club-record five consecutive defeats, and finished a miserable fourth in the table, meaning they, like Juve and United, will face a Champions League qualifier in August. The real unthinkable, of course, is the very real possibility this raises of the Champions League 2004/5 not even having El Real in it.

Those just in the Champions League for the ride got their money's worth, though. Lokomotiv Moscow and Real Sociedad will both have been chuffed just to reach the second phase. Lokomotiv, though, may feel a little wistful too, knowing they let slip a fantastic chance to put out tonight's finalists. Not only could they have easily finished the job in the first leg in Moscow, but they will kick themselves in the knowledge that their narrow defeat in the return was at least partially self-inflicted, having played 70 minutes with 10 mean after captain Loskov's red card. In contrast, the Basques rarely looked to be in their tie against Lyon. In a season of real struggle in the league – it took them until May to ensure safety - they're probably just relieved to finish the season relatively unscathed, and will reflect with fondness on the European campaign's better moments, like the win in Istanbul. After all, it will probably be a long time until they enjoy an experience like that again.

Those who lived the dream a bit too hard are still suffering. The malaise surrounding Borussia Dortmund's season completely enveloped the club. The omens weren't great before that UEFA Cup second round return at Sochaux, and the fears proved well founded. Salvatore Gambino was sent off for a professional foul in the first five minutes, and it all went downhill from there. BVB were eventually roasted 4-0 by their hosts. Being humiliated on the pitch was the least of their worries. The financial news got worse. By Christmas, the club were in negotiations over a €100 million loan with the Anglo-German investment bank Stephen Schechter, similar to the one for €75 million taken out a few months earlier by local rivals Schalke with the same bank. The difference was that after their loan, Schalke were able to spend on players like Elton John going flower shopping. Borussia would be mortgaging the club to the hilt merely to stay afloat. They didn't go ahead with this plan in the end, but still ended the campaign over €120 million in debt. After being involved in Champions League qualifiers last year, they must get through the Intertoto Cup if they are even to make it into next season's UEFA Cup.

Still, they could at least thank goodness they weren't Leeds. The slow-motion car crash of their season reached its climax at Bolton, where Viduka was sent off (again) after giving his team the lead, after which the team crashed to a 4-1 loss that sealed their relegation. The lasting image of that day was the TV footage, and the pictures in the following day's newspapers, of Alan Smith weeping uncontrollably. It was like he was mourning a death. He may well be soon. With Leeds' income about to be drastically reduced and Smith one of few remaining saleable assets, the future looks bleak. Leeds' Champions League exploits seem destined to become just an anomaly in the competition's history.

Conversely, Saint Etienne are on the way back. They did win that game at Niort the following week to seal the return to Ligue 1, thanks to Frédéric Mendy's goal. They went on to lift the Ligue 2 title and at last get the curator at the Geoffroy-Guichard's trophy room back to work. Europe may still be just a speck on the horizon, but they're back to take on Marseille and Lyon. The French sports media will barely be able to contain their excitement.

But for tonight all of France, as the headline on today's *L'Equipe* said, will be Monégasque. Looking at those around the stadium sporting Monaco colours, you get a sense of how this is quite literally the case. It's a club with a tiny average crowd, but they're not short of numbers in Germany. Walking around the supporters' parks outside the Auf Schalke (there's one for each team), chatting with a few people, there seem to be a lot of people here from France just for the ride, fans of French football rather than Monaco in particular. So, just like any big game involving Monaco then.

There's a different vibe in the Porto park, a stronger celebratory feeling. I stand around with a beer watching a Portuguese band (in team colours, naturally) play on a small stage. Somehow, there's more bustle amongst the Portuguese. There's the banter, the songs and the camaraderie that tells of people who've been going to watch their team for years. Most of the Monaco fans seem curiously polite, like tourists on a day out. UEFA have tried to make a day of it for the supporters, with parties, mini football and shooting competitions in which to take part. They are obviously taking the idea of a carnival of football very seriously. It makes the most of such an unfortunate location for the final. Then again, maybe this is the whole idea safety wise. You can't really imagine it kicking off out here in this cultural and social vortex.

Activity here is limited enough that I end up taking a stroll around the grounds, which include some very plush training facilities, and the Schalke museum, a mildly diverting journey through the domestic and European achievements of Germany's pre-Bayern giants. Reading about the trips to play Wolverhampton Wanderers and Honved in the early '50s (pre-European Cup) does at least start to whet the appetite for the big match. When I walk back towards the stadium, early evening dusk is almost upon us and people are arriving in droves. Again, the Porto fans are the ones that you hear all around.

The inside of the stadium – which I reach after the obligatory scrum at the gates – may give away nothing of the club's rich history but speaks volumes of an exciting future. Aside from its technical merits, it's actually a surprisingly suitable venue for a final. It's large enough to fit the fans in, but the relative steepness of the stands and their closeness to the pitch undoubtedly add to the atmosphere. I got my ticket off Ebay in the end (the shame) after my accreditation fell through, and though I have a few neutrals around me, the area is basically Porto, in the corner next to the goal behind which most of their fans are. The swell of blue and white, and at the other end, red and white, is a beautiful sight.

If there's one area in which Champions League matches fail though, it's in UEFA's insistence in defining them all so clumsily as showpieces. Especially before a game such as the final, it should all be about the fans trying to outsing each other, rather than trapeze artists accompanied by a bombastic, near-deafening PA soundtrack. It's as inappropriate here as it always is, a ham-fisted attempt to shout from the rooftops that the competition is the real deal, equivalent to the World Cup or the Olympics. The football says all that needs to be said itself, and far more eloquently. Just look at this year's tournament. The great matches and occasions speak to the fans, not this nonsense.

Being completely non-plussed by this makes me reflect on the final, in a calm-before-the-storm moment. It promises to be a bittersweet moment for either or both clubs, and unusually, it's difficult to judge whether the two will look to the future with optimism or trepidation after tonight's game. That they both started the competition as outsiders shapes their future just as much as the final itself. Win or lose, it's quite possible that both these teams face being dismantled. Even if both clubs have enjoyed periods of domestic dominance, they have not and will not build the same sort of hegemony in Europe. It's all about the natural order of things in European football. Their stocks may go up and down, but the leagues of Spain, Italy and England will always have a hold in Europe. Add to the cream of these three big leagues Bayern Munich and you have all of Europe's biggest football clubs. France and

Portugal will always lag behind. These are countries that produce great talent, but even football's current recession can't completely close the wealth gap between them and the biggest European leagues.

Moreover, it's a matter of perception. The players, having won a European Cup at a French or Portuguese club, often feel they have reached a peak there and search out a new challenge. That goes for managers too, of course. Mourinho's imminent replacement of the much-maligned Ranieri would appear to be a *fait accompli*, and Didier Deschamps has attracted admiring glances too, being linked with his other old club Juventus as well as Chelsea, and even the French national coach's job. On Mourinho's staff, Deco is rapidly moving into the category of the 'crack', as they say on the continent, though Porto may avoid a mass exodus as their success is perceived to be thanks more to teamwork than any particular individual. Monaco are unlikely to be so lucky. They need not worry about 'doing a Leeds' – they won't have a chance. They will recognise the need to pay close attention to their continued financial recovery rather than embark on a wildly ambitious expansion plan. Dado Prso has already decided to move on, with his contract expiring next month, and you don't have to look far to clock the other saleable assets who have attracted plaudits for the performances in the Champions League this season – besides Giuly, there's Rothen, Evra and Roma, to name but three. There's also little prospect of them being able to afford to hang on to star loanees Morientes and Ibarra (borrowed from Porto, funnily enough).

When the teams come out, it looks unlikely that Prso will be able to perform any farewell heroics. He's left on the bench, as is his counterpart Benni McCarthy for Porto. Deschamps has – not unreasonably – reverted to his first choice European line-up, opting to flesh out midfield with the muscle and industry of Zikos, Cissé and Bernardi, while using Giuly to support the lone Morientes up front. Porto have their own midfield workhorses in Pedro Mendes, Costinha and Maniche, with the only slight surprise being the selection of the 19-year-old Brazilian Carlos Alberto in place of McCarthy. That said, the youngster has started all the Champions League knockout games thus far, and Mourinho clearly has a lot of faith in him.

If Monaco are going to win this, they really need to get at Porto. The Portuguese are a strong unit and have so many players who are good at dictating a game's pace (Deco, Costinha, Maniche) that Monaco can't let them settle. They at a sprightly enough tempo – in a way very typical of an underdog in a cup tie, actually – but hit a problem just past the 20 minute mark, when Giuly pulls up holding his thigh. He won't be able to carry on. Prso replaces him, but this is a huge blow to them. Giuly is not only an inspirational captain, but their most versatile and threatening attacking outlet.

The match begins to drift a little. Perhaps we shouldn't be surprised. Both are unfancied teams in the biggest final in club football, and will be feeling that this is a lifetime's opportunity. Both seem terrified of fluffing their lines, and don't want to give anything away. It's going to take something special to open the game up, and that's what we get. Out of nothing, the ball breaks to Carlos Alberto, just inside the area. He controls on the thigh, and blasts a sumptuous volley past Roma's left hand into the top corner from 15 yards. The blanket of blue and white around me erupts. When you dream of your team taking the lead in a cup final, the goal is always this good. It's rarely the case in reality though, and for it to be in the Champions League final too is incredible. It could only be the work of a Brazilian.

Porto are a difficult side to beat at the best of times, and in truth, I can't see them relinquishing a lead. If any team, though, can manage a comeback, it must be Monaco. Lacking Giuly is unfortunate, but they still have Rothen, Prso, and of course Morientes. If ever there was a time for the Spaniard to seal his place as a Principality legend, this is it. The French apply the pressure from the off, and Deschamps signals his intentions by bringing on Shabani Nonda for Cissé. Nonda is still feeling his way back from a knee ligament injury, but his vital goal against Chelsea in the semi shows that even while not 100%, he can be a great pinch-hitter for the side. He has the pace and strength to get at

Porto and the quality to finish off anything that comes his way.

Twenty minutes remain and Monaco are banging on the door. Porto look like they must crack. Morientes, meanwhile, looks as if he has been fouled, 25 yards from the Porto goal. Referee Kim Milton Nielsen waves play on and Porto break at speed. Russian midfielder Dimitri Alenitchev – brought on for Carlos Alberto on the hour, as Mourinho sought to shore things up and consolidate – transfers the ball inside to Deco, who composes himself, and slots in the second from 10 yards. The Portuguese fans don't so much explode as exhale. They know that this goal must clinch it and if so, there could be no more fitting goalscorer than the Brazilian-born midfielder. Monaco are flattened. Just four minutes later, Alenitchev finds himself free to stroll through unchallenged and gleefully thump in the third. Now the Porto fans do erupt. The party has officially started. Game, set and match.

When the whistle goes, all the focus is on the players' emotions - after all, the celebrations in the stand have been in full swing for the best part of twenty minutes by the time Nielsen calls proceedings to a halt. Porto are jubilant, while Monaco's players, of course, either sink to the turf or wander listlessly around the pitch, lost. The achievement of a season in which they've lit up European football might be a source of pride when perspective sinks in in a few months' time, but it means nothing now. The cruellest moment for the losing finalists is when they go up first to the podium to collect their runners-up medals, walking past the trophy decked in ribbons of the victors' colours. Every single one of the Monaco players gives the trophy at least a brief mournful glance on the solemn procession past the silverware, as does Deschamps. He may be the most decorated French footballer of all time, but he's no stranger to this empty feeling either, having lost successive Champions League finals in 1997 and 1998 as well as lifting the pot twice in the same decade.

Porto are genuinely worthy winners, and looking back, logical winners as well. They may not have touched the peaks of Monaco, Chelsea, Deportivo, Real Madrid or even Arsenal (in their 5-1 win at

Inter Milan), but theirs has been a real team effort, and a triumph of consistency. In fact, they only lost one game in the whole campaign, a home defeat to Real Madrid back in the group stages. When I get back to London and watch my recording of the game, the footage of the presentation reveals the real star of the show. Even as Jorge Costa is lifting the famous trophy through a collective Portuguese roar and a hail of blue and white tickertape, he and his team-mates' moment of glory is fleeting. The camera pulls away to focus on Mourinho, pulling his winners medal from his neck like a child tearing off his school tie at the day's end, and disappearing down the tunnel. The coach later explains that he was upset and didn't feel like celebrating, after death threats to him and his family from some idiot annoyed at his impending departure. Mourinho's words are lost, though, in the stark imagery of that moment. The press and public have already decided what it meant. Winning the Champions League may be the pinnacle of most coaches' careers, but not this one. Normal day at the office. Job done. On to the next one.

Even granting Porto and their coach their deserved due, there are questions. This is the Champions League, a format supposedly tailored for the biggest clubs to joust exclusively amongst themselves. We've had outsiders in the final before – Borussia Dortmund in 1997, Valencia in 2000 and 2001, Bayer Leverkusen in 2002. But the only winners in the list are BVB, and the winners since the millennium read as follows: Real Madrid, Bayern Munich, Real Madrid, AC Milan. So what happened this year, with the final that (the cynical would say) nobody wanted?

The importance of the return to having just one group stage, for the first time since 1999, cannot be overstated. This cut five matches per team for those qualifying for the first group stage, with group stage two being replaced by a knockout round to qualify for the quarter-finals. It's not rocket science. More emphasis on the knockout part of the competition gives the lesser lights with smaller squads a bigger chance of springing a shock. It also makes the competition more intense (just look at this year's quarters) and improves the quality of viewing, leaving less dead rubbers at the end of group stages. And, of course, the players will presumably perform better for playing less games, something that high-profile club and country managers have campaigned for over the last few years.

This didn't stop our old chums in the G-14 (now bolstered to 18 with the addition of Valencia, Bayer Leverkusen, Arsenal and Lyon) kicking up a fuss about these plans when they were introduced in August 2002. The biggest clubs weren't just looking at the retention of a format that could be said to favour their chances, but at maximising revenue from the extra games, whatever the cost to the quality of the football. Peter Kenyon, still chief executive of Manchester United at the time, said he felt 'disappointment, because in the UK audiences are increasing and attendances at European games are still going up.'

Kenyon was perhaps being a little optimistic in thinking this was a trend that would continue. It's hard to believe that UEFA's motives in 'improving' the competition were completely altruistic. In fact, the change in format for the 2003/4 season is perhaps the closest that a football committee or governing body has come to admitting that football, internationally, is reaching saturation coverage. The level of interest, and therefore the level of television income, is simply unsustainable. Whatever the motivation may have been, the fact remains that this year's competition has been the most exciting for years.

This is a (small) start to European club competition regaining a sense of balance. The Champions League, as it has grown, has concentrated all the biggest clubs in one competition, to the detriment of the UEFA Cup, which is now perceived as distinctly second-rate (this could also be said to have precipitated the death of the Cup Winners' Cup, 'merged' into the UEFA Cup after the 1998/99 season). The attempts to bridge this gap, by ferrying Champions League group stage losers into the UEFA Cup third round, and the creation of group stage in the UEFA Cup itself from next season, merely enforce the view of the competition as a 'Champions League Second Division.' Even UEFA's chief executive Gerhard Aigner admitted earlier this season that '...by concentrating the top clubs in one competition, it diminished somewhat the appeal of the other UEFA competitions.'

Besides this, the financial gap the Champions League is creating means the game has become, and is becoming more, segregated like never before. Porto and Monaco may be underdogs, but neither club is exactly amateur. They both have a history of trophies, and line-ups stacked with quality international players. It would still take a mightily optimistic person to suggest that the likes of Hamburg, Nottingham Forest, Red Star or Steaua Bucharest could get anywhere near lifting the trophy again.

I remember something that Paul Lambert said to me, when I met him in Glasgow. He said that when he was in the dressing room before BVB's final against Juventus, he had been flicking through the match programme, and had read than you made the least out of winning the Champions League that any of the European trophies. This was because teams spent huge amounts trying to win it. Seven years on, this pattern shows no sign of abating. Forget the weekend millionaires of Leeds and Dortmund. Bayern reacted to last season's failure by spending heavily on Roy Makaay. Similarly, Manchester United splashed over £12 million on the teenage potential of Cristiano Ronaldo. And it's a fair bet that the bankers of Munich, Manchester, Madrid and Turin will be writing a fair few cheques this summer as the big boys go all out to make up for a season where they fell – for them – unacceptably short. Sometimes, the more things change, the more they stay the same…

Appendix I

Champions League results, season 2003/4

Third qualifying phase

First leg – 12/13 August 2003

FK Vardar 2 Sparta Prague 3
MTK Hungaria 0 Celtic 4
Rangers 1 FC Copenhagen 1
Austria Vienna 0 Marseille 1
Club Brugge 2 Borussia Dortmund 1
Shakhtar Donetsk 1 Lokomotiv Moscow 0
Lazio 3 Benfica 1
Dynamo Kiev 3 Dinamo Zagreb 1
Rosenborg 0 Deportivo La Coruña 0
Grasshopper Zurich 1 AEK Athens 0
MSK Zilina 0 Chelsea 2
Celta Vigo 3 Slavia Prague 0
Partizan Belgrade 0 Newcastle 1
Galatasaray 3 CSKA Sofia 0
Anderlecht 3 Wisla Krakow 1

Grazer AK 1 Ajax 1

Second leg – 26/27 August

Sparta Prague 2 FK Vardar 2 (aggregate 5-4)
Celtic 1 MTK Hungaria 0 (agg 5-0)
FC Copenhagen 1 Rangers 2 (agg 2-3)
Marseille 0 Austria Vienna 0 (agg 1-0)
Borussia Dortmund 2 Club Brugge 1 (agg 3-3, Brugge win 4-2 on pens)
Lokomotiv Moscow 3 Shakhtar Donetsk 1 (agg 3-2)
Benfica 0 Lazio 1 (agg 1-4)
Dinamo Zagreb 0 Dynamo Kiev 2 (agg 1-5)
Deportivo La Coruña 1 Rosenborg 0 (agg 1-0)
AEK Athens 3 Grasshopper Zurich 1 (agg 3-2)
Chelsea 3 MSK Zilina 0 (agg 5-0)
Slavia Prague 2 Celta Vigo 0 (agg 2-3)
Newcastle 0 Partizan Belgrade 1 (agg 1-1, Partizan win 4-3 on pens)
CSKA Sofia 0 Galatasaray 3 (agg 0-6)
Wisla Krakow 0 Anderlecht 1 (agg 1-4)
Ajax 2 Grazer AK 1 (agg 3-2)

Group stage

Group A

Results

17 September
Lyon 1 Anderlecht 0
Bayern Munich 2 Celtic 1
30 September
Celtic 2 Lyon 0
Anderlecht 1 Bayern Munich 1
21 October
Anderlecht 1 Celtic 0

Lyon 1 Bayern Munich 1
5 November
Celtic 3 Anderlecht 1
Bayern Munich 1 Lyon 2
25 November
Anderlecht 1 Lyon 0
Celtic 0 Bayern Munich 0
10 December
Lyon 3 Celtic 2
Bayern Munich 1 Anderlecht 0

Final table

	P	W	D	L	F	A	Pts
Lyon	6	3	1	2	7	7	10
Bayern	6	2	3	1	6	5	9
Celtic	6	2	1	3	8	7	7
Anderlecht	6	2	1	3	4	6	7

Group B

Results

17 September
Dynamo Kiev 2 Lokomotiv Moscow 0
Arsenal 0 Inter Milan 3
30 September
Inter Milan 2 Dynamo Kiev 1
Lokomotiv Moscow 0 Arsenal 0
21 October
Lokomotiv Moscow 3 Inter Milan 0
Dynamo Kiev 2 Arsenal 1
5 November

Inter Milan 1 Lokomotiv Moscow 1

Arsenal 1 Dynamo Kiev 0

25 November

Lokomotiv Moscow 3 Dynamo Kiev 2

Inter Milan 1 Arsenal 5

10 December

Dynamo Kiev 1 Inter Milan 1

Arsenal 2 Lokomotiv Moscow 0

Final table

	P	W	D	L	F	A	Pts
Arsenal	6	3	1	2	9	6	10
Lokomotiv	6	2	2	2	7	7	8
Inter	6	2	2	2	8	11	8
Dynamo Kiev	6	2	1	3	8	8	7

Group C

17 September

AEK Athens 1 Deportivo La Coruña 1

PSV Eindhoven 1 Monaco 2

30 September

Monaco 4 AEK Athens 0

Deportivo La Coruña 2 PSV Eindhoven 0

21 October

Deportivo La Coruña 1 Monaco 0

AEK Athens 0 PSV Eindhoven 1

5 November

Monaco 8 Deportivo La Coruña 3

PSV Eindhoven 2 AEK Athens 0

25 November

Deportivo La Coruña 3 AEK Athens 0

Monaco 1 PSV Eindhoven 1
10 December
AEK Athens 0 Monaco 0
PSV Eindhoven 3 Deportivo La Coruña 2

Final table

	P	W	D	L	F	A	Pts
Monaco	6	3	2	1	15	6	11
Deportivo	6	3	1	2	12	12	10
PSV	6	3	1	2	8	7	10
AEK	6	0	2	4	1	11	2

Group D

Results

17 September
Juventus 2 Galatasaray 1
Real Sociedad 1 Olympiakos 0
30 September
Olympiakos 1 Juventus 2
Galatasaray 1 Real Sociedad 2
21 October
Galatasaray 1 Olympiakos 0
Juventus 4 Real Sociedad 2
5 November
Olympiakos 3 Galatasaray 0
Real Sociedad 0 Juventus 0
25 November
Olympiakos 2 Real Sociedad 2
2 December
Galatasaray 2 Juventus 0

10 December

Juventus 7 Olympiakos 0

Real Sociedad 1 Galatasaray 1

Final table

	P	W	D	L	F	A	Pts
Juventus	6	4	1	1	15	6	13
R Sociedad	6	2	3	1	8	8	9
Galatasaray	6	2	1	3	6	8	7
Olympiakos	6	1	1	4	6	13	4

Group E

Results

16 September

Rangers 2 Stuttgart 1

Manchester United 5 Panathinaikos 0

1 October

Panathinaikos 1 Rangers 1

Stuttgart 2 Manchester United 1

22 October

Stuttgart 2 Panathinaikos 0

Rangers 0 Manchester United 1

4 November

Panathinaikos 1 Stuttgart 3

Manchester United 3 Rangers 0

26 November

Stuttgart 1 Rangers 0

Panathinaikos 0 Manchester United 1

9 December

Rangers 1 Panathinaikos 3
Manchester United 2 Stuttgart 0

Final table

	P	W	D	L	F	A	Pts
Man Utd	6	5	0	1	13	2	15
Stuttgart	6	4	0	2	9	6	12
Panathinaikos	6	1	1	4	5	13	4
Rangers	6	1	1	4	4	10	4

Group F

Results

16 September
Real Madrid 4 Marseille 2
Partizan Belgrade 1 Porto 1
1 October
Porto 1 Real Madrid 3
Marseille 3 Partizan Belgrade 0
22 October
Marseille 2 Porto 3
Real Madrid 1 Partizan Belgrade 0
4 November
Porto 1 Marseille 0
Partizan Belgrade 0 Real Madrid 0
26 November
Marseille 1 Real Madrid 2
Porto 2 Partizan Belgrade 1
9 December
Real Madrid 1 Porto 1

Partizan Belgrade 1 Marseille 1

Final table

	P	W	D	L	F	A	Pts
R Madrid	6	4	2	0	11	5	14
Porto	6	3	2	1	9	8	11
Marseille	6	1	1	4	9	11	4
Partizan	6	0	3	3	3	8	3

Group G

Results

16 September

Sparta Prague 0 Chelsea 1

Besiktas 0 Lazio 2

1 October

Lazio 2 Sparta Prague 2

Chelsea 0 Besiktas 2

22 October

Chelsea 2 Lazio 1

Sparta Prague 2 Besiktas 1

4 November

Lazio 0 Chelsea 4

Besiktas 1 Sparta Prague 0

26 November

Chelsea 0 Sparta Prague 0

Lazio 1 Besiktas 1

9 December

Sparta Prague 1 Lazio 0

Besiktas 0 Chelsea 2

Final table

	P	W	D	L	F	A	Pts
Chelsea	6	4	1	1	9	3	13
Sparta	6	2	2	2	5	5	8
Besiktas	6	2	1	3	5	7	7
Lazio	6	1	2	3	6	10	5

Group H

Results

16 September
AC Milan 1 Ajax 0
Club Brugge 1 Celta Vigo 1
1 October
Celta Vigo 0 AC Milan 0
Ajax 2 Club Brugge 0
22 October
Ajax 1 Celta Vigo 0
AC Milan 0 Club Brugge 1
4 November
Celta Vigo 3 Ajax 2
Club Brugge 0 AC Milan 1
26 November
Ajax 0   AC Milan 1
Celta Vigo 1 Club Brugge 1
9 December
AC Milan 1 Celta Vigo 2
Club Brugge 2 Ajax 1

Final table

	P	W	D	L	F	A	Pts
Milan	6	3	1	2	4	3	10
Celta	6	2	3	1	7	6	9
Brugge	6	2	2	2	5	6	8
Ajax	6	2	0	4	6	7	6

Second round

First leg – 24/25 February

Sparta Prague 0 AC Milan 0
Celta Vigo 2 Arsenal 3
Lokomotiv Moscow 2 Monaco 1
Bayern Munich 1 Real Madrid 1
Deportivo La Coruña 1 Juventus 0
Porto 2 Manchester United 1
Stuttgart 0 Chelsea 1
Real Sociedad 0 Lyon 1

Second leg – 9/10 March

Juventus 0 Deportivo La Coruña 1 (agg 0-2)
Manchester United 1 Porto 1 (agg 2-3)
Chelsea 0 Stuttgart 0 (agg 1-0)
Lyon 1 Real Sociedad 0 (agg 2-0)
AC Milan 4 Sparta Prague 1 (agg 4-1)
Arsenal 2 Celta Vigo 0 (agg 5-2)
Monaco 1 Lokomotiv Moscow 0 (agg 2-2, Monaco win on away goals)
Real Madrid 1 Bayern Munich 0 (agg 2-1)

Quarter-finals

First leg – 23/24 March

AC Milan 4 Deportivo La Coruña 1
Porto 2 Lyon 0
Chelsea 1 Arsenal 1
Real Madrid 4 Monaco 2

Second leg – 6/7 April

Arsenal 1 Chelsea 2 (agg 2-3)
Monaco 3 Real Madrid 1 (agg 5-5, Monaco win on away goals)
Deportivo La Coruña 4 AC Milan 0 (agg 5-4)
Lyon 2 Porto 2 (agg 2-4)

Semi-finals

First leg – 20/21 April

Monaco 3 Chelsea 1
Porto 0 Deportivo La Coruña 0

Second leg – 4/5 May

Deportivo La Coruña 0 Porto 1 (agg 0-1)
Chelsea 2 Monaco 2 (agg 3-5)

Final – 26 May

Monaco 0 Porto 3
(Arena AufSchalke, Gelsenkirchen)

Appendix II

Footnotes

Lyon

[1]Of the main objectives that the G-14 states on its website, the most striking is its will to 'promote cooperation and good relations between G-14 and FIFA, UEFA and any other sporting institutions and/or professional football clubs, *paying special attention to negotiating the format, administration and operation of the club competitions in which the member clubs are involved* (my italics)'.

Celtic

[1]The Inter-Cities Fairs' Cup was the UEFA Cup's previous incarnation. It became the trophy as we know it in 1971.

[2]This was the start of a spell of Dutch dominance in the competition. Ajax won the trophy in each of the three following years.

[3]After winning the first leg 2-1 at Parkhead, a 1-1 draw in Kiev a fortnight later on October 4 gave Dynamo a 3-2 aggregate win in the tie, meaning Celtic lost the European Cup just 19 weeks after winning it Lisbon.

Borussia Dortmund

[1]It was a big year for the region as a whole, with Schalke winning the

Lokomotiv Moscow

[1]The FAW (Football Association of Wales) lodged a protest in January after Russia's Spartak defender Yegor Titov was banned for 12 months following a positive drugs test after the first leg of Russian and Wales' Euro 2004 play-off in November. The Welsh appeal for Russia to forfeit their Euro 2004 place in Wales' favour has since been rejected, with the appeal set for next month.

[2]CSKA eventually signed an estimated $54 million sponsorship deal over three years with Sibneft, the company of Chelsea owner Roman Abramovich, in March 2004. This is the biggest shirt sponsorship deal in world football, outstripping Manchester United's £36 million, four-year agreement with Vodafone.

[3]Semin also doubled up as Russian national team coach for two spells, between 1992 and 1994 and then again from 1996 to 1997.

Leeds

[1] Raúl came clean after the game, and UEFA fined him $5,000, also banning him for one match. UEFA later overturned the decision on appeal.

[2]Under PFA rules, players can be fined a maximum two weeks' wages, unless they consent to a higher figure, which Woodgate did. Bowyer initially refused, and was accordingly put on the transfer list, before eventually relenting.

[3]Part of this sum was reached by the first-team squad's agreement to defer 30% of their wages, something they were originally reluctant to do and a source of tension between the team and its fans. They got it all back under Krasner anyway.

Juventus

[1]1935 proved to be an unfortunate watershed for the club – shortly after the title was clinched, Edoardo died in a plane crash. It was 15 years

before Juve won the championship again.

[2]Giampiero Boniperti, the Juve president in 1985, had famously said in the initial aftermath of Heysel that the club could not count the trophy until the European Cup was won again, and that it would not be displayed. In fact, the Champions Cup took pride of place in the trophy cabinet as soon as it got back to Turin.

Bayern Munich

[1]1860 president Wildmoser was released on bail last month by state prosecutors, who are investigating him on suspicion of taking a multi-million euro bribe from the contractors building the new stadium

Saint Etienne

[1]Later, Nicolas tells me how he and Jacques went onto the pitch after the final home game of the season, against Châteauroux, and how Jacques led the near-40,000 crowd in a rendition of 'Allez Les Verts'. 'I was shaking, virtually in tears,' Nicolas admitted, 'and I'm 39 years old.' The fans themselves spontaneously sang it time upon time at the end, over and above the music playing on the PA. 'It was something I'd never felt in my life.'

Manchester United

[1]He showed little concern for his own position either. Magnier refused to allow Ferguson to be offered a new contract while the dispute remained unresolved.

ISBN 141208073-8